John Owen is professor of international journalism at City University in London and has played a leading role in international journalism for the past 30 years. He spent 20 years with the Canadian Broadcasting Corporation (CBC) and held all of its senior television news positions, including five years as its chief news editor. He left the CBC to become the founding director of the European Centre of the Freedom Forum in London, and is also the founding executive producer of News Xchange, the largest international broadcast conference group underwritten by the European Broadcasting Union. John is the founding chairman of the Frontline Club Forum in London, is a newly appointed trustee of the Open Society Foundation and a trustee of the Crimes of War Project, and is a founding editorial board member of the International News Safety Institute. He is co-author with Chris Cramer of *Dying To Tell the Story*.

Heather Purdey is a senior lecturer in the Department of Journalism and Publishing at City University in London, director of the MA International Journalism course and internationalization coordinator for the School of Arts. She has been a journalist since 1976 and has worked in newspapers, radio and television. She was the director of training for GWR, one of the largest commercial radio companies in the UK, and set up the first vocational undergraduate programme in broadcast journalism in the UK. Heather has worked as a consultant in Eastern Europe, designed training programmes for Slovakia and Kenya, and published about journalism education and training in journals and books. Her Master of Philosophy looked at the training needs of journalists and she is the vice-chair of the Broadcast Journalism Training Council, the industry body which accredits broadcast journalism courses in the UK.

D1169597

The Kurt Schork Memorial Fund

All royalty earnings generated by the sale of this book will be donated to the Kurt Schork Memorial Fund (http://www.ksmfund.org), which was created in honour of Kurt Schork, a highly admired and respected international journalist, killed while on assignment in Sierra Leone in May 2000. The picture below shows Schork in Sarajevo coming to the rescue of a civilian who'd become a casualty. Photo courtesy of Associated Press/ photographer Javier Bauluz.

The fund underwrites annual awards to outstanding freelance and local journalists. Applications can be made through the IWPR website: http:// www.iwpr.net/index.php?apc_state=henh&s=o&o=top_ksa.html.

International News Reporting

Frontlines and Deadlines

Edited by
John Owen and Heather Purdey

WILEY-BLACKWELL

A John Wiley & Sons, Ltd., Publication

This edition first published 2009
© 2009 Blackwell Publishing Ltd except for chapters 1 (© 2009 Janine di Giovanni), 9 (© 2009 Anthony Borden), and 11 (© 2009 Mark Brayne)

Blackwell Publishing was acquired by John Wiley & Sons in February 2007. Blackwell's publishing program has been merged with Wiley's global Scientific, Technical, and Medical business to form Wiley-Blackwell.

Registered Office
John Wiley & Sons Ltd, The Atrium, Southern Gate, Chichester, West Sussex, PO19 8SQ, United Kingdom

Editorial Offices
350 Main Street, Malden, MA 02148-5020, USA
9600 Garsington Road, Oxford, OX4 2DQ, UK
The Atrium, Southern Gate, Chichester, West Sussex, PO19 8SQ, UK

For details of our global editorial offices, for customer services, and for information about how to apply for permission to reuse the copyright material in this book please see our website at www.wiley.com/wiley-blackwell.

The right of John Owen and Heather Purdey to be identified as the authors of the editorial material in this work has been asserted in accordance with the Copyright, Designs and Patents Act 1988.

Library of Congress Cataloging-in-Publication Data

International news reporting: frontlines and deadlines / edited by John Owen and Heather Purdey.
    P.   cm.
Includes bibliographical references and index.
ISBN 978-1-4051-6038-4 (hardcover: alk. paper) — ISBN 978-1-4051-6039-1 (pbk.: alk. paper)
1. Foreign news. 2. Reporters and reporting. I. Owen, John, 1942–. II. Purdey, Heather.
PN4784.F61587 2009
070.4'332—dc22

2008040260

A catalogue record for this book is available from the British Library.

Set in 11/13.5pt Dante by SPi Publisher Services, Pondicherry, India

Contents

Contents

Notes on Contributors

Peter Apps joined Reuters in 2003 and has worked throughout Southern Africa and Sri Lanka. After breaking his neck in a minibus crash while on assignment in Sri Lanka in 2006, he returned to work at Reuters nine months later, assigned to the Reuters Foundation website AlertNet. He is currently working on Reuters main news wire desk in London covering emerging markets and economics.

Nigel Baker is executive director of television news at Associated Press. Prior to helping set up the agency's video wing in 1994, he held senior editorial positions at British broadcasters ITN and Sky News and at Reuters. Field assignments have included the first Gulf War in Iraq, the fall of communism in the Soviet Union, and the break-up of Yugoslavia. In his current role, he negotiated with the North Korean government for the opening in 2006 of the first bureau for a Western news organization in the reclusive communist state.

Anthony Borden is executive director of the Institute for War & Peace Reporting (IWPR), which supports training, reporting and institution-building programmes for local journalists in areas of crisis and conflict around the world. IWPR has established the Sahar Journalists' Assistance Fund, to provide support in cases of exile, disability or death of local journalists it works with in crisis areas; for information on how to contribute, see www.iwpr.net.

Mark Brayne is a psychotherapist and trainer specializing in trauma and journalism, having served for 30 years as foreign correspondent and senior editor for Reuters and the BBC World Service. He developed and implemented for the BBC a programme of trauma awareness and support training in which he has also trained journalists, editors and managers at news organizations around the world. From 2002 to 2007, he served as director Europe of the US-based Dart Center for Journalism and Trauma, working with journalists, mental health professionals and educators towards improving media coverage of violence and trauma, and mitigating the emotional consequences of such coverage on those who report the stories.

Tony Burman has been the managing director of Al Jazeera English since May 2008. At the time of writing his chapter, he was the editor-in-chief and executive director of CBC News. While head of CBC's news and current affairs operations, he implemented the successful integration of its radio, TV and online operations. He is an award-winning news and documentary producer with field experience in more than 30 countries and several continents.

Chris Cramer was formerly the president and managing director of CNN International and is now a global media consultant. He is the honorary president of the International News Safety Institute. He is also co-author (with John Owen) of *Dying To Tell the Story*.

Ben Hammersley is a print and broadcast journalist who has been one of the leading proponents of new media journalism. He is associate editor of the UK edition of *Wired* magazine. His freelance work includes regular contributions to the BBC and MSN/UK.

Janine di Giovanni is an award-winning war correspondent who has been covering global conflicts since the 1980s. She is a contributing editor to *Vanity Fair* and a columnist and essayist for many publications, including the *Guardian*, the *Evening Standard* and the *New York Times*. She is also the author of four books, the last a book of essays, *The Place at the End of the World*. Her book on the Balkans War, *Madness Visible*, has been optioned for a feature film by Julia Roberts.

Bridget Kendall has been the BBC's diplomatic correspondent since 1998 and a winner of the James Cameron award for distinguished journalism. She was based for a number of years in Moscow and is a Russian-language speaker.

Gary Knight is an award-winning photojournalist, primarily concerned with human rights and issues of crimes and justice. He has written widely on photography and journalism. Knight is a founding member of the VII photojournalism agency. He is also the co-editor of a new quarterly publication, *Dispatches*.

Nick Pollard has been a journalist for almost 40 years, working in print, radio and television news. For 10 years until 2006 he was head of Sky News at BSkyB. Under his leadership, Sky News became the most watched 24-hour news channel in Britain and won numerous awards for its coverage of major stories. He is a fellow of the Royal Television Society and was awarded the RTS's Lifetime Achievement Award in 2007.

Richard Sambrook is director of the BBC's Global News division, responsible for leading the BBC's international news services across radio, television and new media.

David Schlesinger has been editor-in-chief of Reuters since January 2007. He was previously the global managing editor of Reuters. He has been a correspondent and run editorial operations for Reuters in China, Hong Kong and Taiwan.

Vaughan Smith is an award-winning freelance cameraman and video news journalist who has covered conflicts in Iraq, Afghanistan, Bosnia, Chechnya and Kosovo. He helped found the Frontline News Television agency, which he ran for many years, and is the owner and founder of the London-based Frontline Club and Restaurant. He was a joint winner of the MediaGuardian Innovation Award in 2008 for his independent blog while on assignment in Afghanistan. He is the co-producer of a new film, *Blood Trail*, that will be screened at the Toronto Film Festival.

Preface

John Owen

For the past six years, I have had the privilege of teaching a course in international journalism to postgraduate and undergraduate students at City University in London. It is a course created by the former Reuters correspondent Colin Bickler, who kindly asked if I was interested in taking over his class, as he had decided to cut back on his teaching load. I said yes without fully understanding or appreciating the challenge that I was facing.

It meant trying to devise a course that could prove both interesting and relevant to upwards of 70 students who came from more than 30 countries in all of the continents. Thanks to Colin and Heather Purdey and other highly dedicated professors, City had established an excellent international reputation for attracting outstanding young developing journalists who were already working for leading newspapers and broadcasters in their home countries. Many chose City and London because it is the world's global media headquarters, and they dreamt of working someday for the BBC World Service or one of the top British newspapers. They realized that City and London would help them master English, a key to future employment. Others simply hoped to get the academic credentials that they needed to return home to their own news organizations and the prospect of more senior positions.

Throughout my years of teaching at City, I have found it humbling to be in the company of so many wonderful young journalists, many of whom had already demonstrated courage and resourcefulness working in countries without a truly free and independent press or a culture of free expression. One of my students, Sandra Nyaira, had been the political editor of the *Zimbabwe Daily News* and had won the 2004 International Women's Media Foundation award for courage in journalism. Her newspaper had been firebombed, and she and many of her fellow journalists had narrowly escaped being killed. Another student, Iraqi Shadha Muheissn, had been the BBC's reporter in Baghdad, and this year received the Knight International Journalism Award for service to international journalism.

In the 2007–8 class, one of our students is Salam Abdulmunem, a one-time architecture student in Baghdad who in the war in Iraq became known throughout the world as Salam Pax, the Baghdad Blogger. (Richard Sambrook writes about him in his chapter on citizen journalism.)

I had decided that my international journalism class would be of most value to this highly diverse and ambitious group if I could succeed in doing the following.

- Make the class relentlessly relevant to understanding and working in a global world of journalism and media that was undergoing dramatic change.
- Introduce the students to the best and most respected professional journalists, who were also self-critical and humble about their work, and could serve as role models for them.
- Provoke reflection on ethical journalistic issues that would confront them in their journalistic lives. I've always told my students that if in their journalistic moments of crisis, they remembered a conversation or insight about what was the right thing that they should do, then I'd consider that my course had proven valuable to them.
- Gain insights from analysing the coverage of major international news stories that took place while they were studying at City, hearing from British-based editors who assigned them and the reporters who covered them, and reviewing their own media's comparative coverage.
- Make certain that they understand fully what technological and new media challenges face them – from multi-skilling to blogging to user-generated content.
- Ensure that these young journalists understood all aspects of safety in journalism and what they needed to know in order to take the right risks in pursuing stories that were potentially dangerous, whether covering

conflicts or natural disasters, or pursuing local investigative stories where they were at the greatest risk.

• Provide them with awareness of the new body of journalistic literature about trauma and journalism; how their own impartiality and detachment can be influenced by their exposure to troubling and disturbing stories; how in understanding better those they're covering, they might find new skills in how to gain information and the trust of their sources.

In deciding what chapters should be included in *International News Reporting* and then approaching outstanding journalists to write about them, we had to try and identify those issues and subjects that are fundamental to journalism around the world and essential to grasp in order to be better practitioners, whether in daily journalism or some other media-related career.

It was difficult to narrow the choice to these 14 subjects because there are so many other issues that lend themselves to greater scrutiny. We've had to leave out of this first edition the stories and reflections of journalists who've contributed to our classes, sharing their experiences and exposing themselves to hard questions about how they handled certain assignments.

We are indeed fortunate that so many illustrious journalists who are heading or have headed the most influential broadcast news organizations in the world have agreed to contribute to this book. They did so knowing that they would receive no money for their efforts and be forced to give up what little free time they have to organize their thoughts and write 6,000 words. Many are old friends and colleagues and could easily have told me that there was no way that they could take on any additional commitments. But they did take it on and proved once again that it is those with the biggest and most demanding jobs that somehow find the energy to tackle projects like this one. I am deeply grateful to each of them: Chris Cramer (formerly with CNN), Richard Sambrook (BBC Global News), Nick Pollard (formerly with Sky News), David Schlesinger (Reuters) and Anthony Borden (IWPR).

Also, *International News Reporting* changed emphasis along the way, and we decided later to add additional chapters. Again, we were so impressed by how exceptionally busy news executives like Nigel Baker (APTN), Tony Burman (formerly CBC) and – very close to the deadline – Peter Apps (Reuters) accepted the last-minute challenge and crafted excellent chapters.

We are equally indebted to our 'field journalists' and other experts for their generous support of this book. Not only did Janine di Giovanni (*Vanity Fair*), Gary Knight (VII), Vaughan Smith (freelance and Frontline), Bridget Kendall (BBC), Ben Hammersley (BBC) and Mark Brayne (ex-Reuters and Dart Center for Journalism and Trauma) waive any fee for their contributions, they found time beyond their deadlines and assignments to discuss their craft and share their experiences. They have in effect given the student readers of this book a master class in journalism.

It is our hope that tomorrow's journalists, whether they work inside newsrooms or in the field, or aspire to become news executives, will find this book both insightful and provocative; that they will put into practice what they've absorbed from these outstanding journalists.

As we neared our deadline for this book, I stumbled onto a profound little book, *Liberty and the News*, by the great American journalist and man of letters Walter Lippmann. Writing in 1920 when he was only 31 years old, Lippmann despaired at the poor quality of American journalism. He urged the creation of journalism schools that helped turn journalism from a 'haphazard trade into a disciplined profession'.

Lippmann said what was needed was:

> to send out into reporting a generation of men who will by their sheer superiority, drive the incompetents out of business. It means two things. It means a public recognition of the dignity of such a career so that it will cease to be the refuge of the vaguely talented. With this increase of prestige must go a professional training in journalism in which the ideal of objective testimony is cardinal. The cynicism of the trade needs to be abandoned, for the true patterns of the journalistic apprentice are not the slick persons who scoop the news, but the patient and fearless men of science who have laboured to see what the world really is. (Lippmann 2008: 48)

In that spirit, we hope that *International News Reporting: Frontlines and Deadlines* helps to inspire a new generation of young journalists to bear witness to the world as it really is. In doing so, they will keep faith with brave journalists everywhere who believe what they do does matter to a free and democratic society.

City University's MA in International Journalism

Heather Purdey

City University's Master's course in international journalism has been educating and training journalists from all over the world for more than 25 years.

Up to 80 students from 30 different countries attend each year for a practical course which not only teaches them the skills they need to have to work as reporters in print, radio, television and online, but also gives them the opportunity to reflect on some of the issues which are affecting the practice of international journalism today. City's multi-national, multi-cultural, multi-religious, multi-ethnic student mix reflects the complex, globalized society in which we all now live and encourages an exchange of views and perspectives which broadens their and our minds, and widens horizons.

We want to turn out journalists who are not only highly skilled but thoughtful and critically aware of the major issues faced in international reporting today.

This book complements our teaching. Each chapter, all of which have been written by prominent and experienced journalists, looks at a specific aspect of journalism, from 'bearing witness' to reporting diplomacy; from breaking news stories to the effect of new technology on the work of the international news agencies. Introductions set the context, and at the end of each chapter there are suggested questions for students to work through, either by themselves or under the guidance of their professors. The topics addressed by the contributors, the questions they raise, the practical problems they pose, all affect journalists covering international stories, and newsmen and women today need to consider them if they are to succeed and survive.

We hope lecturers and students alike will find this book a useful tool. It is dedicated to those brave freelance journalists who risk their lives to report the world so that we can understand it better.

Reference

Lippmann, W. (2008) *Liberty and the News*. Princeton University Press.

Acknowledgements

The editors would like to thank the following for their help in compiling this book: all the contributors (in order of chapters): Janine di Giovanni, David Schlesinger, Nigel Baker, Vaughan Smith, Gary Knight, Bridget Kendall, Nick Pollard, Tony Burman, Anthony Borden, Chris Cramer, Mark Brayne, Richard Sambrook, Ben Hammersley and Peter Apps; Susan Moeller, whose thoughts and publications have been invaluable to the editors; the Pew Research Center, AP and PQ Media for permission to use their graphs; Baywood Publishing Company for permission to reproduce part of the chapter on risk and safety; photo editor Kavita Sharma, for her help in tracking down and getting permissions for the photographs; City University, particularly the head of journalism and publishing Adrian Monck and the tutors on the international journalism programme, and all the students on the international journalism course who have inspired this book.

This book is dedicated to David Purdey, who has been an indispensable source of support, and the memory of Richard D. Yoakam, professor of journalism at Indiana University.

The authors and publisher wish to thank the following for permission to use photographs and video stills:

p. ii: Photo courtesy of Associated Press/Photographer Javier Bauluz
p. 3: Photo courtesy of Associated Press/Photographer Gemunu Amarasinge
p. 4: Photo courtesy of Magnum Photos/Photographer Alex Majoli
p. 18: Photo courtesy of Associated Press/Photographer Santiago Lyon
pp. 27–8: Photos courtesy of Thomson Reuters
p. 42: Photo courtesy of Associated Press/Photographer Lauren Rebours
pp. 50–1: Photos courtesy of Associated Press
pp. 57 and 67: Photos and video still courtesy of Vaughan Smith
p. 73: Photo courtesy of Associated Press/Photographer Nick Ut
p. 74: Photo courtesy of Associated Press/Photographer Richard Drew
p. 76: Photo courtesy of Sean Smith
pp. 79–80: Photos courtesy of Gary Knight
p. 97: Photo courtesy of Associated Press
p. 119: Photo courtesy of Sky News
p. 129: Photo courtesy of CBC News
pp. 154–5 and 159: Photos courtesy of IWPR
p. 164: Photo courtesy of Associated Press/Photographer Khalid Mohammed
p. 165: Photo courtesy of Thomson Reuters/Photographer Sergei Karpukhin
p. 168: Photo courtesy of CBC News
p. 205: Video stills courtesy of BBC News
p. 228: Photo courtesy of Michael Hughes
p. 245: Photo courtesy of Ben Hammersley
pp. 255 and 257: Photos courtesy of Thomson Reuters

The publisher apologizes for any errors or omissions in the above list and would be grateful if notified of any corrections that should be incorporated in future reprints or editions of this book.

1

Bearing Witness

Janine di Giovanni

Introduction

JOHN OWEN

At the core of this book is the belief that first-person reporting is fundamental to international journalism.

The late David Halberstam, who established his journalistic reputation in Vietnam in the early 1960s with his tough-minded reporting for the *New York Times*, wrote in the Associated Press's tribute to its journalists, *Breaking News: How the Associated Press has Covered War, Peace, and Everything Else* (2007: 16):

> [To me] that is what journalism is all about, sending good reporters to difficult and dangerous places that are about to become important but are not yet household words, covering stories when coverage means something, not, as all too often happens these days, too late in the story, when it doesn't really matter any more .... They [journalists] come to a story a little late and then leave a little too early.

We live in a global media world that can, when it chooses, have the capacity to link us all with dazzling technology – the Al Gore Live Earth global rock concert in July 2007 springs to mind – and has the capacity to influence us to care about developments anywhere on the planet.

Yet all that technology is seldom used to enlighten us about what is happening around the world, especially in Africa (Darfur is our most recent shameful example). The more than 100 networks that own and operate 24-hour news channels don't make international news a high priority with the exception of huge breaking news stories like 9/11, the London bombings, the death of Diana, the invasion of Iraq and the tsunami.

There are notable exceptions, and internationally minded networks such as BBC, CNN (I refer to the English-language channels that I can see and understand), Sky News and the new Al Jazeera English-language channel do often commit huge resources to support dedicated news teams to take substantial risks to get to conflict zones and areas where natural disasters are occurring.

Yet few working in mainstream media today are proud of the international news output of their own newspapers or networks. It often falls to NGOs (the non-governmental organizations such as Human Rights Watch, the International Crisis Group and the World Food Programme) to chronicle stories and issues that are not on the radar of the mainstream news media.

But no website, however worthy and informative, or no packaged report, slickly produced in London or New York, will ever be able to surpass the impact of original journalism, the discoveries of a single reporter or documentary maker or photojournalist on assignment somewhere in the world.

For those of us who have worked alongside brilliant correspondents and camera crews and witnessed for ourselves the reality of dramatic stories and major news events, there remains a reverence for those who take the risks to cover the world. Their contributions – their 'rough drafts of history' – are valued by leading historians, are digested by our most insightful policy makers, and do provide a reality check for politicians and office holders who understand that men and women with cameras and notebooks are an indispensable part of democratic societies; that what they write, record and broadcast cannot be ignored even when the reading and viewing is at odds with the official line.

Pontificating so-called experts on 24-hour news channels cannot ever replace or should never replace the reporting that is only possible if men and women continue to be assigned or, in the case of freelancers, independently pursue the stories that give us – in renowned investigative reporter Bob Woodward's definition – 'the best obtainable version of the truth'.

There is a terrible price paid by those who are prepared to 'take the torch to the back of the cave and show what is there in the darkness' (that magnificent and moving phrase of American journalist and writer Pete Hamill from his wise little book *News is a Verb* (1998)).

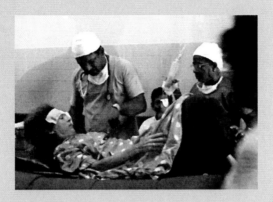

Sunday Times correspondent Marie Colvin, blinded in one eye and badly wounded, reporting on the Sri Lankan civil war in April 2001
PHOTO COURTESY OF ASSOCIATED PRESS/PHOTOGRAPHER GEMUNU AMARASINGE

A thousand journalists lost their lives covering the news between 1996 and 2006 according to the International News Safety Institute's 2007 study *Killing the Messenger*. The overwhelming numbers of journalists who die are local journalists who are murdered for trying to pursue stories that governments and authorities do not want published or broadcast. The killers of journalists are seldom, almost never, arrested and prosecuted.

This book begins with one outstanding reporter's tale of her own life of reporting and 'bearing witness'. Before we consider the major trends and issues facing journalism and media today and tomorrow, we first want to examine the role and responsibility of the reporter herself.

Janine di Giovanni is an expatriate American correspondent who filed dispatches from the frontlines of wars and conflicts that took place after the Berlin Wall came down in 1989. She and many other outstanding reporters of her generation chronicled the wars fought in the Balkans, first in Bosnia and then in Kosovo; the Intifada in Palestine; the Russian battle against the breakaway Chechens; and the civil wars in Africa. She also covered Afghanistan, East Timor and Iraq.

Janine di Giovanni's many highly dangerous assignments – she was one of the few correspondents to watch the Russians pulverize Grozny, the capital of Chechnya – resulted in award-winning reports for the *Times* of London and *Vanity Fair Magazine*.

References

Associated Press (2007) *Breaking News: How the Associated Press has Covered War, Peace, and Everything Else.* Princeton Architectural Press.

Hamill, P. (1998) *News is a Verb: Journalism at the End of the Twentieth Century.* Ballantine.

International News Safety Institute (2007) *Killing the Messenger: Report of the Global Inquiry by the International News Safety Institute into the Protection of Journalists.* INSI.

Bearing witness: Janine di Giovanni with a KLA soldier, reporting during the Kosovo war in 1999

PHOTO COURTESY OF MAGNUM PHOTOS/PHOTOGRAPHER ALEX MAJOLI

On the morning of September 19, 2002, in a deserted cattle market in Abidjan, the capital of the Ivory Coast, at a time I should have been drinking my first cup of tea, a government soldier stood a foot away from me with an automatic weapon pointed at my heart.

There had been a coup d'etat but neither the soldier nor I knew that yet. All I knew was that I had gone to bed in a calm city – known as a beacon of stability in an otherwise violent West Africa – and woken up to gunfire; in other words, exactly what I had moved to Abidjan to escape: a war.

The confrontation in the cattle market was the aftermath of a short, sporadic battle between the government forces and some mysterious rebels no one had yet seen. Like me, the soldier was confused. He didn't know who was launching the coup, or why. He had probably been dragged out of bed at dawn by a superior. He was probably scared and a little drunk from drinking bad gin the night before. He stood, soaked in sweat, boots too tight, pointing an AK-47 at me and looking as if he had every intention of using it.

I wasn't alone. There was a man near my foot, groaning in pain. There were smears of blood on his clothes and the bullet wounds in his legs were small and neat. A moment before I'd squatted on the dirt and tried to drag him into my taxi. I wanted to get him to a hospital.

Hence, a government soldier threatening to shoot me.

'He's a rebel, he no good', he said in thick Ivorian French.

'He's hurt, I'm taking him to the hospital', I said.

He raised his gun, which had the safety catch off.

'Leave him', he said. 'He's ours.'

By the time this incident occurred, I had been reporting from war zones for nearly 15 years. I should have known that you don't argue with a man with a gun – particularly one who has just shot someone. The sensible thing would be to realize I had wandered into the wrong place at the wrong time – before an execution was about to take place – back up, apologize, and run. But the same 15 years had also given me the over-confidence of the survivor. I knew what would happen if I left. The injured man, who was grabbing my ankle, pleading, 'Sister, help me!', would be shot and tossed into a grave or left with the dead cows to rot, which in tropical Africa can happen quickly. I had never seen this man before, but I knew what his body would look like by lunchtime.

So I argued badly – telling this soldier, who probably could not read and write, about the Geneva Convention, the rights of man, and Christian compassion. His impatience was turning to rage when another journalist pulled me back into our taxi and said: 'This is Africa, what the hell were you thinking?' Then we drove off. I don't know how long it was before they killed that man, but I do know it was my luck or what the Arabs call *Maktoub* – 'it is written' – that got me out of bed at 4 a.m. and to the cattle market. It was also luck that someone was there – someone who later became my husband, as it happens – to save me from my dangerous compassion. Bad luck followed by good luck. I was lucky not to be shot. Several colleagues and friends had been killed taking much lower risks.

Two years earlier, in another part of West Africa, I ate my last meal with one of them, Kurt Schork. We went to the best restaurant in Freetown, Sierra Leone, and had grilled prawns. Schork was a 52-year-old Reuters correspondent who had been a Rhodes Scholar at Oxford with Bill Clinton. He was legendary for his bravado and his scalding humour. During our Christmas season in Sarajevo, then besieged by the Serbs, we'd attended a midnight mass and then drunk a bottle of black-market champagne as we listened to mortars falling on the snowy city.

Now, drinking beer in the Freetown restaurant, I told him about a group of stoned teenage soldiers called the West Side Boys that I'd encountered earlier in the day. They'd surrounded my car, punched the hood, aimed their RPGs in my face, and demanded money, cigarettes, marijuana and sex. While my driver cried with fear, a colleague in the same car shouted at him to drive through the crowd. 'Just run them down!'

'Total amateurs', Schork said of the West Side Boys. 'They sound like a pick-up basketball team.'

The next morning, I sat eating breakfast with another journalist I'd known in Bosnia, Miguel Gil Moreno, by the slime-green pool of our decrepit hotel. It was the end of the rainy season in West Africa, and as we ate we could see dozens of frogs procreating by the edge of the water.

Like Schork, Miguel had a reputation. He was devoutly religious as well as courageous. In 1999, we had shared a frontline base camp with rebel Kosovar soldiers when it was being aerially bombarded and we hid in trenches for days. He was the first person I phoned for advice before I went to Chechnya. 'Remember to try to leave at least a week before the shelling drives you insane', he said.

Over breakfast, Miguel asked me about a homemade video I'd been given which showed men who might have been UN soldiers being tortured by rebels in Sierra Leone. It should have been a warning to both of us – look; this is the madness that happens here. But instead we said goodbye and Miguel followed Kurt and his crew up the road towards Rogbury Junction, to find out if the video was real. By lunchtime both men were dead, ambushed and killed by teenagers. War, as Thucydides remarked when reporting on the Peloponnesian wars in the fifth century BC, is a violent teacher. As a reporter covering wars, you can learn a few lessons in staying alive from the mistakes of others, but no amount of judgement and caution can save you from bad luck.

What does it do to you? I once, on a rainy London afternoon, sat on the couch of a well-known psychiatrist who was evaluating the impact on journalists of post-traumatic stress disorder. It was to be a three-year study, and I was one of his early subjects. He asked me about my sleep habits, whether I drank or took drugs, whether I was sexually promiscuous. Then he asked:

'How many dead bodies have you seen?'

I thought hard, trying to remember events and places; fields of bodies, mass graves, wells with blue corpses stuffed down them, the man in East Timor who washed up in the sewer, the slabs of dead flesh on my daily trips to the morgue in Sarajevo, the soldier in the snow in Chechnya, the miles and miles of dead Rwandans on a road near Goma.

'I don't know; hundreds?' I thought again. 'I have no idea.'

The psychiatrist was silent as he wrote in his notebook. After a while, he looked up.

'Don't you find that odd?' he said, not unkindly. 'Most people only see their grandparents, or their parents, at their funerals.'

Other than my grandmother's, my first dead body was in Bosnia. I arrived in the early autumn of 1992. It was still warm enough to get stung by a wasp, the last balmy days before a brutal winter. The war that would ruin the country was still young and enthusiastic, rather like me. I wasn't a complete ingénue about conflict – I'd been tear gassed in the crowd during Israeli–Palestinian clashes – but Bosnia was my first war zone.

Before that, I had been a rather haphazard academic trying to discover whether or not Katherine Mansfield had plagiarized Chekhov in her early short stories. But I grew claustrophobic in libraries, I was impatient with Mansfield's lukewarm feminism, and I did not have the real drive to see it through. I threw away my PhD thesis in the late 1980s after I met an Israeli human rights lawyer who defended Palestinians. She led me throughout the West Bank and Gaza, introduced me to politicians and activists, and advised me to dedicate my life to writing about people who would otherwise be voiceless.

By then, I was working for the *Sunday Times*, and I fought to be sent to Bosnia – my editors kept trying to get me to write about style – but I eventually won the battle, and once in Bosnia, simply refused to leave. I stayed, on and off, for nearly three years.

That first trip, I travelled with a nervous Australian photographer and a young Croatian interpreter down small roads that had been commandeered by various rag-tag militias. Vesna, the interpreter, gave a potted history of the former Yugoslavia and smoked all my cigarettes. We passed empty villages with shuttered houses and fields of dead animals. There were no people on the road. Through the car window came the smell of distant explosives and petrol and fire. Near Vitez, we passed empty munitions factories which Vesna said had been part of a major industry during the Tito years.

A ghostly bus full of young soldiers, faces pressed against the windows, drove past with a sign hung on the side: VOLUNTEERS FOR JAJCE. Jajce, the ancient Bosnian capital, was now the scene of a bloody battle raging in the north that would soon be lost by Bosnian forces with many casualties. Vesna waved to one soldier; he waved back. She said: 'He will never come back from Jajce.'

There was another photographer in the car behind us. He was French and silent. Sometimes, I drove with him. He was known to be fearless and somewhat strange, almost mystical. Once, on a particularly spooky road, we came to a Bosnian checkpoint and I lowered my window to hand the soldier our passports. The soldier reached out, but instead of taking the passports, he stared hard at the photographer's pale face.

'What strange eyes you have, my friend', he said flatly.

The photographer frowned. 'Strange?' he asked. 'What do you mean, strange?'

The soldier laughed, enjoying his discomfort. 'You have death in your eyes', he said matter-of-factly. He handed back our passports, lit a cigarette and lifted the frayed rope that was the checkpoint. He motioned us through, not talking, not smiling, not waving.

The photographer was silent for the rest of the trip until we reached the car wreck. Then we saw the real dead, two of them, a couple who had been trying to flee something – fighting, a village being burnt, none of us would know. Vesna had studied some medicine and she said they could only have been dead a few hours. Long enough, I remember thinking, for their souls to fly away.

They had driven into a tree at what must have been full speed, and they had flown through the windscreen so that their bodies lay half in, half out of the car. Their necks were broken and hung down like chicken gizzards. Their eyes were still open. Their bodies fascinated me. I walked closer and stared, trying to memorize their surprised expression, caught in the exact moment of death.

Why and to what private or public benefit? I don't know, but in more than 10 years – and the 1990s was a decade of wars – I followed armed conflicts like a homing pigeon: the former Yugoslavia, then Chechnya, Somalia, Liberia, Sierra Leone, Algeria, Palestine, East Timor, Kosovo, Ivory Coast, and later Iraq and Afghanistan. I got good at reporting a war the way that you get a good serve at tennis if you practise long and hard enough. When I would watch television and see a conflict gathering in some remote part of the world, I found it impossible to stay still, not to pick up the phone and ask to be sent there, and as a result, I honed great skills: intuition, bravery, I guess, or perhaps it was foolhardiness, the ability to talk or push my way into any situation, but more importantly, to deal with tremendous pressure without cracking.

Then there are the stories. It is always a cliché to write about women and children during war time, but the fact is that those are the images that stick with you, and I felt in some way that when I wrote them these people would not suffer in vain. Perhaps that is very grandiose. And it was often painful. The first time I saw the agony of a child writhing on a dirty cot in a field hospital with his guts ripped open and no painkillers, I went outside, leaned against a wall and cried and vomited. But I did that only once. The rest of the time, I observed and wrote, and then got back into my car and left.

I tried to behave safely, but the thing is, you never think about your mortality when you are actually so close to it being cut short. A famous war photographer, a woman who had hidden behind a bush in Africa to photograph an execution, once said to me, 'I never thought I would get killed because my mother loved me too much.' My equally irrational assumption was that, as a woman in her very early thirties, I wouldn't die because I hadn't really lived enough yet. All the statistics made no impression on me.

Out of the most shocking recent figures on Iraq[1] comes the theory that journalists are targeted, and by both sides in the conflict. In 2004, Eason Jordan, the former chief news executive of CNN, resigned from his job after insinuating that journalists were being targeted by the American military (Kurtz 2005). But if journalists are being specially selected for expunction in Iraq, this is nothing new. No British journalists died in the Falklands War of 1982, but a popular story returned from the fleet carrying British forces to the South Atlantic. A marine officer is instructing his marines. Question: 'What do we do if we capture some Argentinian troops?' Answer: 'Shoot them.' Question: 'What do we do if we capture some Argentinian troops and we're with a television crew?' Answer: 'Shoot the television crew.' During the battle of Mostar in the spring of 1993, it was rumoured the Bosnian Croat militias put a price tag of 50 Deutschmarks on the head of every journalist. Fifty DM, even then, couldn't buy a good lobster dinner with wine in Split. If nothing else, the price proved that William Howard Russell, who reported the Crimean war for *The Times*, was right when he described his fellow members of this new profession, war reporting, as a 'luckless tribe'.

The practice of war reporting has changed a lot since the 1990s, when it could still be conducted alone or among groups of like-minded journalists, travelling together for company, cheapness (three to a hire car, two to a hotel room), and at least the notion of greater safety. Now reporters go to war with their own militias. There are always exceptions, but most reporters covering Iraq and Afghanistan – particularly the television networks – employ small armies of security guards, with high-tech tracking equipment, weaponry, and chase cars in the event the journalists are kidnapped.

The guards are usually former Special Forces soldiers who are employed by private British or American companies which promise 'physical security and protection'. In January 2003, I went to one of these companies, Centurion, based near the Special Air Services (SAS) headquarters in Hereford, to learn some 'hostile environment' training. According to the Centurion website, 'Knowledge dispels fear. In an ever more volatile and hazardous world, the reward of accurately assessing risk is the confidence of being alert to potential danger and knowing instinctively how to deal with it. This is the difference between managing threats to safety and security and merely surviving them' (Centurion 2007).

It is true one feels safer in their company. In December 2001, during a bombing in Tora Bora, Afghanistan, I cowered on a ridge while a security guard working for CNN shouted instructions – which way the rocket was coming in and where I should throw myself on the ground. I found his authority comforting, but I also wondered if it didn't dull my own instincts for danger, and if the habit of travelling with armed men merely attracted the trouble the armed men were meant to repel. At the start of the Iraq War, the militia accompanying an American TV crew to Tikrit opened up on a group of insurgents and were soon involved in a gun battle.

The course I took in Hereford taught me how to treat a bullet wound and which way to run during a firefight. I learned how to be a good hostage when my tutors tied a hood over my head, kicked me in the ribs, and made me lie on frozen earth for 45 minutes with my hands and legs spread wide while the sound of shots came from some nearby woods. Other advice, such as how to get out of a minefield using a long steel instrument (would that be in my luggage?), was not so useful.

'What do you do when you approach a checkpoint?' asked our instructor, choosing a rather humourless American reporter for the answer.

'Look into their eyes', she answered in a monotone drawl. 'Always make eye contact.' I said nothing, but I knew this was dumb advice. Had I made eye contact when I was briefly taken captive by a band of Serb paramilitaries in a remote mountainous region on the Kosovo–Montenegro border in 1999, I would probably be either dead or gang raped. I was with two French journalists and we had been on a mountain ridge interviewing the refugees who were fleeing the fighting. It was bad luck I was caught and bad luck I was with Frenchmen. French Mirage planes had just bombed Belgrade, injuring relatives and friends of the soldiers who were holding us captive.

My captors were drunk and maddened with violence. Looking them in the eye, it seemed to me, would have been mistaken for insolence – an insolent foreign woman among strong, drunk men. My eyes never left the ground and I spoke the Hail Mary again and again as they fired over our heads and marched us through the woods, beating my companions with rifle butts. They joked about how and where they would kill us, who would go first.

What saved us in the end was luck. The soldiers had a call on their radio. Their commander had captured a far bigger prize than us – an American airman. Their interest in us suddenly vanished and we were abandoned at the side of a snow-covered logging road. As we limped down the mountain to the nearest town, one of the Frenchmen broke our silence to say, 'I was sure they were going to rape you.' He paused for a few moments and then added, 'And I am not sure we could have stopped it.'

The truth is that for many years I did not have a real life. I felt I lived in a parallel universe filled almost exclusively with violent conflict. Of course, people wondered why I did it. When my father was dying of cancer, I sat by his bed and we talked about many things, including faith, death and war. My father came to the USA from Naples. As a college student at the time of Pearl Harbor he enlisted in the US Air Force. 'It was the right thing to do', he said, 'but I was afraid. I was chicken. I didn't like war. I didn't like being away from my family.' All that was normal, he said. 'But what you do, that's not normal, it really isn't.'

War attracts certain types. There are those who want to witness, describe and communicate the important and often tragic facts: a noble motive, because the world should know these things, and among most of us a noble posture (we are 'bearing witness'). There are also those who just love it, who have a perverse attraction to suffering and danger and the euphoria that follows exposure to them: war as a higher form of bungee-jumping. I'd like to think that most of me belongs to the first camp, but I know some of me must belong to the second. Why else would I have stared into the faces of the dead couple in their crashed car in Bosnia all those years ago? Or, in Kosovo, felt the thrill, hand shaking round a cigarette, of crawling undamaged from a field where a sniper had fired at me again and again?

I went to Iraq during the invasion in 2003 for nearly five months, but even as I was packing my bag to go, I thought it would be one of my last wars. I was getting married, and I wanted a child. I knew I couldn't sustain the pace or the loneliness. My son was born nine months after I came home from Iraq. When I first saw him, seven weeks premature and vulnerable, it seemed impossible that I'd ever want to report a war again. And yet when he was six months old I was back in Baghdad, leaving him with his father in Paris. My motive was partly curiosity – would I be a different being now that I had given birth? – and partly the fear that if I did not go back to war, I would lose my standing, my reputation and, most importantly, my nerve. In a sense, it was also a test. Would I be able to continue the life I lived before now that I was a mother? While I was pregnant,

I lived in a state of denial, even going to Gaza eight weeks before my son was born. But now that he was here, I was not sure I could stomach being separated from him.

One afternoon, I got stuck in an elevator at the Al Hamra Hotel with a new crowd of young reporters I'd never seen before. They were male, this was their first conflict, and they were acting like macho asses. Some had shaved their heads to look like Bruce Willis. For years I'd insisted that war reporting was an asexual activity, that there was no difference of perception between male and female war correspondents, or at least none caused by their gender. In the lift, this seemed wrong. I had a baby. Giving birth to him had opened receptacles of fear that had been clamped shut years ago, perhaps on that first trip to Bosnia.

I would be lying if I said I did not miss the excitement of reporting a war. When the conflict in Lebanon began, I was in America teaching my son to swim. Which was more important? Logically, I knew the answer, but yearning is not logical. Reporting war had been most of my life for many years and suddenly to be pulled from it was like a junkie having their stash of drugs stolen.

The reporting I have done since Luca arrived is more tame. The responsibility I feel for his life, for keeping his mother alive long enough to see him grow up, is vast. I go to Gaza, I go to Africa, I will soon go to Afghanistan. But when I now hear gunfire, I run away and cower in a building like a normal human being. I am not sure I would drive up the nasty road to Rogbury Junction where my friends were murdered. If I found myself in a Grozny suburb while the city was falling, as I did in February 2000, I would get out as quickly as possible. And as painful as it is to admit to myself, if I found myself back in that cattle market in Abidjan with a bleeding man clinging to my leg begging me to save him, and an armed man about to kill me for my misplaced compassion – I would disentangle myself and quietly walk away.

Note

1 Editor's note: 235 journalists and media workers were killed in Iraq between the beginning of the conflict in 2003 and November 2007. Figures from the International News Safety Institute (INSI), 28 November 2007, http://www.newssafety.com/stories/insi/insideaths281107.htm.

References

Centurion (2007) http://www.centurionsafety.net.

Committee to Protect Journalists (2006) *Journalists killed in 2006*. CPJ, http://www.cpj.org/killed/killed06.html.

International News Safety Institute (2007) News deaths hit all-time high. INSI, 28 November 2007, http://www.newssafety.com/stories/insi/insideaths281107.htm.

Kurtz, H. (2005) CNN's Jordan resigns over Iraq remarks. *Washington Post*, February 12, http://www.washingtonpost.com/wp-dyn/articles/A17462-2005Feb11.html.

Questions for students

1 Journalists can pay a heavy personal and psychological price for 'bearing witness' to conflicts and human suffering around the globe. What are the arguments for and against such sacrifices?
2 Janine di Giovanni notes that war reporting has changed dramatically since she started doing it in the early 1990s. What are those changes and how do they affect the quality of newsgathering?
3 Is the world now too unsafe to send 'Western' correspondents to cover conflicts such as Iraq, Somalia and Afghanistan? What are the arguments for and against using foreign reporters as opposed to local reporters?

2

The Future of News Services and International Reporting

David Schlesinger

Introduction

JOHN OWEN

The next time you unfold your hometown newspaper (assuming it's not the *New York Times* or *The Times* of London) and read the international stories that are published there – assuming again there are some – look carefully at the bylines. It's virtually certain that you'll be reading a dispatch from a correspondent from Reuters or the Associated Press (AP) with a dateline of Kabul or Baghdad. Next look for any international photographs and once again note the credit. The chances are that the photograph will have been taken by a Reuters or AP photojournalist somewhere in the world.

Or if you've never started the newspaper-reading habit or have forsaken newspapers for a variety of reasons and get your news from websites, read more carefully where they're getting their international news. Again you'll find, if the stories are sourced as they ought to be, a Reuters, AP or Agence France-Presse (AFP) byline or credit.

Wire-service or agency journalists are the world's unsung journalistic heroes. Rarely do we know their names or take note of their bylines, yet without their coverage our newspapers, broadcasts or websites would be starved of first-person information gathered from around the world. Long-time AP correspondent Mort Rosenblum called agency reporters the 'packhorses of the profession' who are expected to work around the clock and beat the competition:

'When major news breaks, agencies rush off a first despatch and then follow each development, writing new leads with every turn of events. Somewhere, always, a newspaper is on deadline' (Rosenblum 1993: 57).

What today's journalists who read all of the news agency material on their computers will never experience is the excitement of being in a newsroom when the wire services, transmitted on a separate tele-type machine, set off alarms that alerted you to a big story. Rosenblum captured the excitement this way:

> In an earlier time, humpbacked Model 15 printers spewed snakes of paper at the elbow of every editor. The steady clack at sixty words a minute was every newsroom's Muzak. Periodic alarm bells cut short conversations, and editors waited for what followed the terse slug: 'BULLETIN.' Then they dashed off cables to their correspondents, each beginning, 'AP says ...' and ending, 'proceed soonest.' (ibid.)

And once there, or first there as most often the agencies are with their worldwide staffs and stringers, the wire-service reporters have to translate what they've seen and experienced and gathered by talking to credible sources into a coherent story beyond a jumble of information. More often than not, according to the late columnist and writer Lars Erik Nelson, it was the 'hard-nosed wire-service reporter' who could first answer the question that made and still makes grown men and women journalists perspire and reduces them to a bundle of anxieties on deadline: 'What's the lead?' (quoted in Moisy 1996: 2).

It is the news agencies that have historically made the deadline judgements about the lead and what the news was in the event or story they'd covered on behalf of their clients – newspapers, radio stations and TV networks around the world.

And if today the news agencies are taken for granted, their journalism not fully understood or appreciated by the general public, there is a rich and dramatic history for each of them. The AP grew out of one New York newspaper owner's determination to be the first to get coverage of the Mexican War that broke out in 1846, using pony express relays, stagecoaches and then the telegraph to scoop the competition.

But then Moses Yale Beach of the *New York Sun,* whose brainchild this was, decided to share his exclusive with other papers in exchange for recouping the costs of this daring but expensive assignment and transmission. In his brief history of AP, Walter Mears, himself one of AP's outstanding political reporters, writes how this first sharing of coverage and costs led to the creation of the AP in the United States (AP 2007b).

How a German refugee in Britain, Paul Julius Reuter, seized on the idea of exploiting the newly laid Dover-to-Calais sub-English-Channel cable in 1851 is a tale of enterprise and journalistic risk taking.

As it's recounted by journalist-historian John Hohenberg, Reuter stole a march on everyone else trying to supply London's financial community with the latest information about the European markets. Instead of using the precarious cross-Channel steamers, Reuter cabled the stock market results. Shortly thereafter, according to Hohenberg, the major papers, led by *The Times*, were signing up to Reuters for the fastest and most accurate information about the markets (Hohenberg 1995: 8–11).

But then Reuter began also reporting on world events that would naturally affect the performance of the markets, and again, exploiting this faster delivery system, moved ahead of his competitors.

What both Beach (AP) and Reuters (with the s added to his name) understood was that the journalism of being first mattered and the logistics of gathering information had to be mastered as well as figuring out the story.

Indeed, this journalistic reality has never changed. CNN made its international reputation in the first Gulf War by taking the highly risky decision to keep its news team in Baghdad when most networks and news organizations had decided to pull out, fearing a lethal American air attack on Baghdad and any and all targets that appeared to be used by Saddam Hussein for military purposes. While it was impossible for the news agencies or the established networks to transmit live pictures from Baghdad, CNN had its own secret weapon – an old-fashioned '4-wire' direct audio link between Baghdad and Amman in Jordan and a satellite link to the world. It was CNN's Bernard Shaw, John Holliman and Peter Arnett who gave the world an eyewitness, real-time, exclusive account of the American air attack from their ninth-floor suite in the Al Rashid Hotel.

If the journalists and photojournalists who have worked for the news agencies weren't household names and big media stars, they were revered by their fellow journalists. Two of the most admired journalists during the Vietnam War worked for the AP – correspondent Peter Arnett and Horst Faas. Both won Pulitzer Prizes.

And it was two agency journalists, one a cameraman for Associated Press Television News (APTN), and the other a correspondent for Reuters, who gained international reputations for their work in the Balkans wars. Both came late to journalism after working in other fields. Both were killed while covering the same story, the civil war in Sierra Leone, on 24 May 2000.

Miguel Gil Moreno (right) in Sierra Leone, 2000
PHOTO COURTESY OF ASSOCIATED PRESS/PHOTOGRAPHER SANTIAGO LYON

Miguel Gil Moreno de Mora was a young corporate lawyer in Barcelona who was troubled by the television pictures he was seeing of the suffering in Bosnia. He plunged into journalism by riding his motorbike to one of the battlefronts, Mostar, and began filing stories for a Barcelona newspaper. But his intelligence and quick grasp of working in war zones brought him to the attention of the news agencies, first with Worldwide Television News (WTN) and then with AP's new television news service, APTV. Within five years he had won British television's most coveted award for cameramen for his courageous work in Kosovo, where he was the only Western cameraman who remained in the capital, Pristina, when NATO launched its air attack.

Kurt Schork had been an investment banker and held a senior post with the New York transit system before he gave it all up to become a journalist. Already in his forties, Schork began his career as a freelance journalist based in Singapore. After reporting wars in Sri Lanka and Afghanistan, covering the Kurds in Northern Iraq, he began reporting the Balkans wars for Reuters.

It was in Sarajevo, covering the beleaguered Bosnian Muslim community under fire from Serb snipers, that Schork did some of his most outstanding reporting. British journalist Anthony Loyd, who became one of Schork's closest friends, wrote, 'His work was succinct, sincere, and consistently credible, its power singly lifting the level of reportage throughout the Bosnian and Kosovo conflicts. Innumerable journalists can crank out professional reports, observe, and criticise. Kurt was different because of his vision and profound, Solomon-like sense of justice' (Loyd 2007: 27).[1]

Agency journalists have paid a high price for their work around the world. But it is the Iraq War that has become the most dangerous of all conflicts in recent memory and made it next to impossible for Western journalists to work independently outside of the Green Zone. Only journalists who are embedded (attached to military units and given full military protection) have any real opportunity to assess whether 'coalition forces' are winning the war against Iraqi insurgents. But their movement is greatly restricted. That has meant local Iraqis and Arab-language media have been the only journalists able to move freely. Yet they too have been at great risk. Many Arab-language journalists have been targeted, as have those Iraqis working for the news agencies.

What is the future of the news agencies? What's in a name?

After 156 years as Reuters, on 15 May 2007, the company founded by Paul Julius Reuter became Thomson Reuters. Thomson (founded in Canada) is the world's largest financial news and data company, and by combining with Reuters ensures that it has a larger market share of the sales of financial information than its nearest rival, Bloomberg. But Bloomberg has also expanded its newsgathering operation.

Reuters, however, remains the name of the news and financial information operation in the new Thomson Reuters Company.

Charting the editorial course of Reuters, in chapter 2 below, is its editor-in-chief David Schlesinger. The American-born and -raised Schlesinger has made a steady climb up the corporate Reuters news ladder. But his route into journalism was an indirect one. He began his professional life as an academic and a Mandarin-speaking Asian studies expert. In 1987 Schlesinger jumped into journalism as the Hong Kong-based correspondent for Reuter. He worked throughout Asia before moving to New York as financial editor for the Americas. Then he was promoted to the post of global managing editor before being elevated to editor-in-chief.

In chapter 3, the second chapter about the role of news agencies in international newsgathering, Nigel Baker, the executive director of APTN, explains how the Web 2.0 has created a boom in markets for news video and photographic images. And while the agencies no longer have a monopoly on material, due to the rise of citizen journalism and an abundance of user-generated content, it is the news agencies themselves that have used the latest developments in new digital technology to record and distribute stories from all over the globe.

Baker played a leading role in helping create Associated Press Television (APTV) in 1994. APTV surprised the news industry by establishing itself so quickly as a rival to Reuters and the other major video news agency, WTN. APTV purchased WTN four years later and formed APTN.

The creation of APTV and its meteoric rise to prominence is a fascinating story in itself about the news industry. Much of the credit has to go to its first managing director, Stephen Claypole, who recognized that APTV could only succeed if its coverage of world events was produced in a superior fashion to those of the rival agencies. To achieve that objective, Claypole turned to leading broadcasters, led by ITN, and recruited several of its senior producers, including Nigel Baker, to inject vastly improved scripting and storytelling techniques into its service.

Now it is in the area of cutting-edge technical prowess that APTN under Nigel Baker is increasingly making its mark in the highly competitive news agency business.

Note

1   The editors of this book are donating all their royalties to the Kurt Schork Memorial Fund, a foundation established in his name to honour outstanding freelance print journalists who have done distinguished work in their countries.

References

AP (2007) *Breaking News: How the Associated Press has Covered War, Peace, and Everything Else*. Princeton Architectural Press.

Hohenberg, J. (1995) *Foreign Correspondence: The Great Reporters and their Times*. Syracuse University Press.

Loyd, A. (2007) *Another Bloody Love Letter*. Headline Review.

Moisy, C. (1996) *The Foreign News Flow in the Information Age*. Joan Shorenstein Center, Harvard University, http://www.hks.harvard.edu/presspol/research_publications/papers/discussion_papers/D23.pdf.

Rosenblum, M. (1993) *Who Stole the News?* John Wiley.

They started with pigeons and the telegraph; now they're on the internet and both compete with and cooperate with bloggers.

News services – also called wire services or agencies – have been part of history for more than a century and a half;[1] now they are competing with their own customers and readers for attention and money.

Economics drove the founding of the services. No newspaper wanted the expense of having its own correspondents everywhere, yet no newspaper could afford to miss key news from outside its home market.

Agencies developed to service their customers with the raw materials of news, the building blocks of basic, factual stories that could fill space on their own, be the basis for rewrites, or be the tip-off services to guide further reporting.

Wire services were like the wholesale butchers of the information business, shipping great slabs of fact-based news like beef to newspapers-cum-restaurants around the world which then fashioned and served up the fillets, stews and tournedos of stories under their own brands and charged full retail price for them to readers and the advertisers who wanted those readers.

Now the question is to what extent the services should open their own restaurants of information, serving up news to a retail audience and getting paid directly by the advertiser or the individual instead of by an intermediate client.

The original economics seemed simple – like wholesalers in any business, the agencies relied upon scale. By supplying raw news to subscribers numbering in the hundreds and even thousands, they could afford a large bureau structure and the technological infrastructure to deliver news quickly.

But the world of the internet is changing the nature of competition and the economies of distribution, and confronting the wire services and their traditional clients with important questions that extend even to those of survival.

While founded for similar reasons and with basically similar editorial values and structures, the world's three major international agencies are very different commercially.

Associated Press (AP) is owned by its 1,500 newspaper clients (referred to as 'members' of the news cooperative) in the United States (AP 2007).

Agence France-Presse (AFP 2008), while chartered as a commercial business, has the French state as its major client and representatives of the government on its board.

Reuters (now Thomson Reuters) is a purely commercial business, listed on the London and NASDAQ stock exchanges, getting some 94 per cent of its revenue from selling news and information to banks, brokerages and other financial-services companies and 6 per cent from selling to the media (Thomson Reuters 2008a).

They have always competed fiercely with each other for clients and, most importantly, for the news.

Beating a rival may be important commercially, but make no mistake: for the men and women in the bureaus, it is an intensely personal competition. Winning a story by being the first or by being the best – or most satisfyingly yet, being best and first! – has from the very first days of the services earned correspondents first a telegram and now an electronic message of praise from editors; losing often results in a 'rocket' message of criticism with the editor demanding to know what had gone wrong.

Speed has been a key differentiator for the services, with each agency boasting of its 'scoops' when it beat rivals by days (when news was carried by boat, pigeon or telegraph), hours, minutes or seconds (the common margin in the current era).

So too has been international reach, with each agency bragging through time about its bureau network:

- 'The Associated Press is everywhere. Breaking news transcends borders and so does AP's coverage. The Associated Press has bureaus in more than 120 countries', states the AP (AP 2007b).
- 'AFP's worldwide network spans 165 countries, 110 of which are home to bureaus, and 50 of which are covered by local correspondents', says the French agency (AFP Worldwide 2007).

- And Reuters says it is the '[w]orld's largest international multimedia news agency – 2,400 editorial staff, journalists, photographers and camera operators in 196 bureaux serving approximately 131 countries' (Thomson Reuters 2008a).

All three agencies started as text services only; all three now have photography services as well. AP and Reuters run the world's two major video wholesale agencies, supplying raw television footage from around the world to stations and networks everywhere.

And from just supplying media clients, all three now have extensive web presences, sometimes feeding their own customers with news in web format and sometimes competing for the same viewers and the same advertising dollars with their own sites.

Since the agencies began by serving hundreds of different newspapers, each with a different editorial-page slant or proprietor with a political point of view, strict attention to facts and the avoidance of any hint of opinion became hallmarks of wire-service reporting and have remained so to this day.

'If your mother says she loves you, check it out', was the maxim of the now-defunct Chicago City News Bureau, a local agency for the American city. But it could just as easily have been the motto of any of the international agencies, where the 'two-source' rule requiring independent corroboration of facts and assertions has reigned supreme.

Reuters stated editorial policy is typical:

Reuters news operations are based on the company's Trust Principles which stipulate that the integrity, independence and freedom from bias of Reuters must be upheld at all times.

Reuters has strict policies in place to ensure adherence to these principles. We are committed to accurate and balanced reporting. Errors of fact are always promptly corrected and clearly published.

Reuters is the largest international multi-media news agency, reporting extensively from around the world on topics ranging from financial markets to general and political news.

Some Reuters coverage, including pictures and video, is of wars or conflicts during which all sides are actively promoting their positions and arguments.

We are committed to reporting the facts and in all situations avoid the use of emotive terms. The only exception is when we are quoting someone directly or in indirect speech. We aim to report objectively actions, identity and background and pay particular attention to all our coverage in extremely sensitive regions.

We do not take sides and attempt to reflect in our stories, pictures and video the views of all sides. We are not in the business of glorifying one side or another or of disseminating propaganda. Reuters journalists do not offer their own opinions or views.

The world relies on Reuters journalists to provide accurate, clearly sourced accounts of events as they occur, wherever they occur, so that individuals, organisations and governments can make their own decisions based on the facts. (Thomson Reuters 2008b)

The key question, though, is whether any of this history or these standards matter. The answer seems to be that the agencies, like the rest of the journalistic world, have a lot of work to do to prove that their ideals are real and relevant to today's readers.

A recent survey by the Pew Research Center for the People & the Press (2006: 48) showed a depressing trend in the credibility of the print media in the American public's eyes.

The very fact-based AP fared extremely poorly in credibility, behind some of its own owner-clients. And while no news outlet scored well, the more familiar big brands did better than the agency whose mission it is to serve those very brands.

Table 2.1   Trend in print credibility

Believe all or most of what organization says	1998	2000	2002	2004	2006
Wall Street Journal	41	41	33	24	26
U.S. News	–	–	26	24	21
Time	27	29	23	22	21
New York Times	–	–	–	21	20
Your daily paper	29	25	21	19	19
Newsweek	24	24	20	19	18
USA Today	23	23	19	19	18
Associated Press	18	21	17	18	17
People	10	10	9	7	8
National Enquirer	3	4	3	5	6

Notes: Figures are in percentages, based on those who could rate each. Dashes indicate figures not available.

Source: Courtesy of Pew Research Center.

One reason for this may be the anonymity of most wire-service reports, which are often reprinted in the newspaper or on the websites without the correspondent's byline. The agencies themselves, while serving so many communities, end up not having a strong independent identity in any.

A more important reason for the agencies' decline in standing is that the US public, at least, seems to be losing interest in the bread-and-butter coverage for the agencies – politics and international news.

The same Pew survey showed that weather and crime news beat politics, coups, wars and earthquakes every time (Ibid.: 41).

International news interests Americans, it seems, only when 'something is happening'; yet for news agencies something is happening somewhere every minute of every day as they churn out words and images by the hundreds of thousands for their clients.

Newspaper column inches are limited, and newspapers themselves are losing readers by the day. Local editors struggle to decide how much space in the columns they should turn over to agency-written material about far-away issues and lands.

Television news broadcasts too have limited time for international news, and anyway aren't the favourites of the advertisers' favourite audiences, the young and the wealthy.

Table 2.2   Trend in news interest

Type of news followed 'very closely'	2000	2002	2004	2006
Weather	–	–	53	50
Crime	30	30	32	29
Community	26	31	28	26
Health news	29	26	26	24
Sports	27	25	25	23
Washington news	17	21	24	17
International affairs	14	21	24	17
Local government	20	22	22	20
Religion	21	19	20	16
Science and technology	18	17	16	15
Entertainment	15	14	15	12
Business and finance	14	15	14	14
Consumer news	12	12	13	12
Culture and arts	10	9	10	9

Notes: Figures are in percentages. Dashes indicate figures not available.
Source: Courtesy of Pew Research Center.

These trends mean that the world of the web is the brave new horizon for agencies, where their thousands of stories a day can find interested readers eager to learn about niche areas or poised to make a financial killing somewhere in the 'long tail' of information.[2]

Here's just one example from Reuters that helps illustrate this phenomenon.

Through much of September 2006, the five most popular stories on the Reuters.com website were:

1 Natascha Kampusch, the kidnapped Austrian girl who escaped after eight years in an underground cell;
2 Steve Irwin, the Australian crocodile wrangler, who was killed by a stingray while he was filming a documentary;
3 France rejects war on terror;
4 Polar bears drown;
5 Paris Hilton wants a burger.

During much the same time, Reuters key financial services industry clients were reading:

1 Iran nuclear standoff;
2 Bank of England interest rate deliberations;
3 share transfer rules;
4 football (soccer) results;
5 United States Consumer Price Index movement.

Hundreds and thousands of more stories were written by correspondents, published by the agency to its media clients, on its website and through its specialized terminals for financial professionals ... and, in fact, read by both types of readers.

An agency that only published the popular stories would never survive. An agency that only had bureaus in the hot news centres of the moment would fail.

Much of wire-service work is about potential energy, having the resources ready when the news happens. Much, too, is about 'collecting string', building up awareness of impending stories before they hit the front pages so that alert readers and clients will be ready when the time comes.

The tale of the tail of information is a complex one.

No one but the agencies report and write about many of the world's crises. If it weren't for wire services first alerting the world to stories, the

Photographer Desmond Boylan transmits pictures watched by a US marine at a make-shift camp near Nassiriya in March 2003

Photographer Carlos Barria during a protest in Santiago, Chile, in September 2005

Reporter Adrian Croft works during a gas alert at a marine base at Jalibah, southern Iraq, in March 2003
PHOTO COURTESY OF THOMSON REUTERS

rest of the world's media wouldn't know where to send their far-smaller pool of correspondents or what to highlight on a front page.

And yet, the tug between pushing a story on an uncaring world and being pulled by the stories the world manifestly already cares about is a constant one for news editors and budget-minders.

News is a people business and an expensive business.

Salaries cost. Insurance costs. Communications cost. Housing costs. Transport costs ... and on it goes. The decision about how to staff a story (who to send, how many to send, how long to send them for), or whether even to staff a country or a city, is never an easy one.

The answer is in the nexus between push and pull: editors have to use their experience and instinct to know what is important to people, what they think should be important to people and what might be important and so better be covered for insurance.

Should we have a full bureau in Quito? Do we need to add an extra television reporter to Beijing? What's the right number of journalists to send to a G8 meeting?

These planning questions have their equal match in the post-mortem questions: 'How did we miss that story? Why was agency X three minutes ahead with the news? Why did they have that camera angle and we didn't?' And then the inevitable budget questions: 'Why was this story so expensive to cover? Did we really need to rent the helicopter? Could we have done as good a job with less? If we'd spent more, would it have made a difference?'[3]

The job of telling the stories falls to the men and women who are the correspondents, camera people, photographers and editors of the news services. All the major services have roughly the same structure of 'international' staff, who travel on assignments ranging from three to five years or more from place to place, and 'local' staff, who tend to remain in the place where they were hired.

Depending on the organization, actual nationality can have differing influence on the kind of career a journalist has; reporting skills, expertise, desire and ambition are key as well.

Crucial to the system is to get the best local contacts, information and understanding possible while overlaying a stateless, international perspective. Additionally, the agencies need to spread their values and standards to journalists who may never spend an hour in head office, while also providing stimulating career paths to those that want them.

Each of the major agencies has a particular style that shapes its report, based on its clients' needs: the AP, with its huge base of US newspaper owner-members, carries lots of US-oriented news; AFP has its strong French base; Reuters has to consider the needs of the financial services industry as well as the media.

These needs inevitably affect hiring, training and promotion.

Organizationally, the agencies operate similar systems of hub editing desks that take in and process copy from bureaus. That processing can range from light checking and coding to ensure that the stories reach the appropriate subscribers to heavy rewriting. Often the desks will have full responsibility for writing wrap-up stories while the correspondents concentrate on reporting.

Reuters, for example, edits Asian text copy in Singapore, Americas stories in Washington and New York, and those from Europe, the Middle East and Africa in London. Pictures are edited globally in Singapore and television in London.

Editors are either journalists taking time out from the field or those who have made it their profession and specialism to be on an editing desk.

Local correspondents are vital to getting the story right.

They know their areas; they have the expertise and the contacts. Many come from the best local media, so they have years of experience covering the story and the key players.

Many want to stay in their home countries and make a career in the place they know the best. Others want to join the international ranks and take their journalism chops and exercise them in a new place, either as part of a career that then moves from country to country or as an interlude before returning home.

This pattern is as true for an American who joins an agency in New York as for an Indian who joins in New Delhi; work as an agency journalist can include any combination of one country or many, one beat or several, one specialism or a handful.

At Reuters, we currently have journalists from 90 different nationalities represented at all levels of the organization.

In my own career, I joined as a locally employed staffer in Hong Kong, where I was living at the time. I was then posted on the international staff to Taiwan, China, back to Hong Kong and then finally to my home country of the United States, where up to that point I'd never worked as a journalist. I then made a move to London – and who knows what might be next! My experience is quite typical for Reuters; other agencies have somewhat different styles and career patterns.

All agencies are global in language as well as in staffing: at Reuters we report and publish in 19 different languages; AP and AFP have vibrant reports in different languages as well. The interplay between a local report and an international report, and between the different perspectives of staff members working for the different services, adds context and a healthy tension to the journalism produced.

In addition to the ranks of full-time staff members, all agencies use 'stringers' extensively.

A stringer is a journalist who has a more casual relationship with the agency. Some are used for only one story or picture. Some may be contracted to help cover a particular event. Others may have a closer relationship that calls for regular contributions over time.

An agency stringer may have a regular, full-time job at a local media outlet. Or the stringer may make a living putting together a series of 'strings' for various, non-competing organizations.

Some aspire to join an agency as a full-time journalist; others enjoy the freedom of being freelance and managing their workloads as they like.

Stringer contracts can vary from being on a piece rate to providing a retainer fee that guarantees both sides some stability in the relationship.

Agencies couldn't survive without stringers – they provide the flexibility in the system to help answer some of the key questions about juggling news and money posed above.

Stringers are used to supplement the regular staff; they often replace regular staff in places where the agency doesn't want to operate a full bureau. They can provide the news when it happens in places where the agency has never been and will never be again.

Without a formal staff relationship, however, issues of training and standards become more difficult to oversee. It is usually down to the local bureau chief to make sure that stringers are recruited well from established journalists and that their work is supervised. Agencies tend to have rules to make sure that stringer copy is handled carefully, insisting that it go through a staff member before going to a desk editor, for example.

Reuters rules state, among other things:

> Utmost care must be taken in hiring stringers that we use reputable journalists who are able and willing to adhere to our rigorous standards of accuracy, objectivity, sourcing and freedom from bias. No individual correspondent should hire a stringer without the explicit approval of the bureau chief or editor in charge. We must exercise the utmost caution in hiring ad-hoc stringers for individual stories. (Reuters 2007: 379)

Whether for staff or stringers, all agencies have strict rules about sourcing their reports. The AP's, which are typical, state:

> The AP routinely seeks and requires more than one source. Stories should be held while attempts are made to reach additional sources for confirmation or elaboration. In rare cases, one source will be sufficient – when material comes from an authoritative figure who provides information so detailed that there is no question of its accuracy. (AP 2006)

All agencies grapple with the question of anonymous sources, usually authorizing their use only when the information can't otherwise be obtained. In an age when the public is less trusting of the news media, the key defence agencies have against their critics is to be as transparent as possible about how their information is obtained and the standing of the sources they use.

Sometimes it is impossible not to use an anonymous source, however, particularly in reporting from many countries without a tradition of a free press. In places where giving a journalist information could garner a source a jail term, the journalist has an ethical and moral imperative to protect the source's identity – even if that weakens the resulting story.

How, then, does a correspondent get news in a place like China, where information that is commonly released in countries with a Western-media tradition can be considered a state secret? Here are some of the ways:[4]

- *Official media*: Correspondents spend a lot of time following the official media, either picking up announcements straight or 'reading between the lines' to understand subtle shifts in policy.
- *Official sources*: Even in countries that restrict information, officials release data and hold news conferences.
- *Business sources*: People in business are usually happy to talk about the work that they do, and that can give clues to many aspects of society and government policy.
- *Diplomatic sources*: Diplomats stationed in foreign capitals have a variety of official and unofficial contacts that can be helpful and illuminating.
- *Private sources*: All correspondents develop their networks of key people who can help them either with informal insight into how their country works or with hard information, ranging from facts transmitted orally to actual copies of secret documents. These can range from local journalists to well-placed academics to government officials or military officers.

As is true anywhere, the correspondent has not only to evaluate the character and veracity of the sources, but also to try to understand their motivations for giving information. And, sometimes, the correspondent has to protect the sources from themselves, making sure they understand the risks and consequences of giving information to a reporter for an international news agency.

Safety of sources is important; safety of journalists is too. To quote from the *Handbook of Reuters Journalism*:

> The safety of our journalists, whether staff or freelance, is paramount. No story or image is worth a life. All assignments to zones of conflict and other dangerous areas are voluntary and no journalist will be penalised in any way for declining a hazardous assignment.

Journalists on the ground have complete discretion not to enter any danger zone. While all reporting of conflict and other hazardous environments involves an element of risk, you must avoid obvious danger and not take unreasonable risks. Writers may be able to produce as good a story at a safe distance as from the front line. Camera operators and photographers need to be closer to the action but using their experience and training often can enhance their security through careful choice of position. (Reuters 2007: 382)

Chapter 10 of this book deals with safety in more detail; it is worth emphasizing that it is absolutely vital that only volunteers who are properly trained and experienced are sent into dangerous situations.

For a news service in a trouble spot like Iraq, for example, having a bureau involves a vast infrastructure of international correspondents, local correspondents, stringers, sources, cooks, drivers, security guards and security advisors.

Decisions about coverage are never made in isolation, but with constant regard to safety, with frequent consultation with security advisors, who are often ex-military, and senior editors who have ultimate responsibility for deciding from day to day what rules about movement and reporting should be.

All agencies have lost correspondents to conflict despite precautions; the striving to keep journalists as safe as possible remains a key goal.

At Reuters London headquarters and at key offices around the world, a book of remembrance to the many journalists from the company who have lost their lives covering stories so that the world may know what is happening stands in testimony to their bravery and sacrifice, and to the work that remains to be done on safety.

Journalists on the scene, risking their lives in unfamiliar places, bringing an unbiased, unvarnished view of the truth back to readers thousands of miles away – for more than a century and a half, that has been the model for news services in particular and the media in general.

Now it is being challenged.

In the twenty-first century, that one-way, hierarchical view of the world is being assaulted by a change driven by technology.

With self-publishing of blogs on the internet, everyone can be a journalist, anyone can be a chronicler of events mundane or monumental, and the journalist's privileged and exclusive role is no more.

The audience is starting to inform and entertain itself – so the professional troubadours, bards, jesters, reporters and chroniclers in the media must, in order to survive and be relevant, cement a unique position.

The media does have certain attributes that will help in this mission.

Professionals have access: as opposed to someone who happens to be in the right place at the right time, news services spend a lot of time and money ensuring that there are correspondents in key places. As correspondents, they have an easier time getting access to news makers and information than non-professionals. People want to tell them things because they have brand and they have the ability to reach a large audience.

Professionals have professionalism: by subscribing and adhering to codes of conduct and ethical behaviour, journalists can create a skin of trust around their reports – but as we've seen above, that skin is thin and must be buttressed.

Professionals have process: with a standard method of producing reports, from careful vetting of sources to note-taking, to trained writing and editing, journalists can write quality articles to scale.

Professionals have expertise: years of learning how to put events in context and how to understand complex phenomena can help readers.

Professionals have distribution: the power of having millions of readers readily available due to brand and tradition can garner access and make a journalist's reports powerful.

'Citizen journalists' – who are both a part of the professionals' audience and apart from it – have power, too, however.

They too have distribution, and with the democracy of the internet can quickly build a readership and create a movement.

And they have the advantage of ubiquity – chances are someone with access to the internet will be on the scene when and where news happens even if a professional journalist is not.

One of the most interesting phenomena has been blogs becoming severe media critics, holding the 'mainstream media' to account for errors of fact or for allegedly slipping into biased reporting. Criticism used to be confined to other professionals or to academics; now anyone with a grievance against a journalist or a news organization has a powerful platform readily available to make their comments known.

In a world where journalists' credibility is under assault, wire services and other media cannot either ignore these ad-hoc critics or simply bow to their attacks; each must be evaluated carefully and fairly, and if it is accurate, the agency must own up to its faults.

Remember, too, that in most of the world, being a journalist is a self-declared state. There are no exams to take, no requirements for a certain kind of degree. Journalists are those whose work adheres to certain forms and standards, who can point to a body of work as evidence of their qualification, and who have been selected by an organization to be part of its cadre of journalists – all but the last are, in fact, available to anyone who self-publishes.

This is an age, then, where blogs and citizen journalism must coexist with traditional journalism.

The dramatic photograph taken on a mobile phone may well be better than the professionally acquired one. The freely available blogged comment may well be more penetrating and useful than the factual news account. The eyewitness report contained on someone's website may well be more vivid than the one written by a staffer.

Or maybe it's just been made up. All the old rules on sourcing and checking and transparency about where information has come from take on a new urgency in a world where the organization's standards are no longer the only ones out there.

Blogs and user-generated content can partner the traditional news services. They can also compete.

The greatest competition of all is information overload.

There is the blare of audiovisual media. There is the profusion of blogs, with blogrolls about any topic stretching into the hundreds or thousands of sites.

There is the scream of emotional debate, with popular television networks in various places around the world sometimes seeming to be little more than hot-tempered invective poured from figureheads at opposite ends of the political spectrum.

There is the intense internet experience from Wikis to Google Search and Google News.

News services can add value, add analysis and add to the participative conversation. But they can never again pretend to dominate any part of the spectrum. The best thing they can do is help cut through the information overload, and help prioritize, organize and highlight key facts, readings and comment for the various audiences to read.

They started moving information via pigeons and the telegraph. But speed of bringing the world to their audiences can no longer stand alone in powering the next 150 years for the news services.

If facts continue to be important, news services will continue to exist.

If the economics of reporting means that only news services with their vast client bases can afford to have large bureaus around the world, then those services will continue to exist.

If having global standards of journalistic ethics and editing continues to be important, then news services will continue to exist.

If reporting the world continues to be important, then news services will continue to exist.

But it won't be the same. It can't be the same.

The relationship with the audience is changing forever, and that will necessarily change the process and the product.

The future will be about partnering, selecting, adding context and explaining.

And finding new ways to become relevant to an audience that wants its own voice heard and that wants to spend time reading what it finds important, and not just what an editor might choose for them.

Notes

1 Agence France-Presse (AFP) traces its roots to Agence Havas, founded in 1835 (http://www.afp.com/english/afp/?pid=history). The Associated Press dates from 1848 (http://www.ap.org/pages/about/history/history_first.html). Reuters was founded in 1851 (http://about.reuters.com/aboutus/history). These three are today the key global services; a fourth, United Press International, has faded from prominence after successive bankruptcies. Many countries have national agencies, sometimes extremely large, supplying their own newspapers in their own languages, but these rarely have extensive international sales.

2 The phrase 'the long tail' was popularized by Chris Anderson, who wrote an article for *Wired* magazine that he later turned into a book published in 2006. He describes how in a net economy businesses can prosper not just with the 'hits' at the fat end of the demand curve but by having the almost endless inventory of 'misses' that the web allows, satisfying the cravings from large numbers of niche buyers with tastes different from those of the mass.

3 If any of these questions appear on the final examination for your course, be assured there is no right answer – only lots of wrong ones!

4 This is based on my term as Reuters China bureau chief 1991–4 and as editor-in-charge, Greater China region, 1994–5.

References

AFP (2008) http://www.afp.com/english/home.
AFP Worldwide (2007) http://www.afp.com/english/afp/world.
Anderson, C. (2006) *The Long Tail*. Hyperion.

AP (2006) *What's New: The Associated Press Statement of News Values and Principles.* http://www.ap.org/newsvalues/index.html.

AP (2007a) Facts and figures. http://www.ap.org/pages/about/about.html.

AP (2007b) *AP International.* http://www.ap.org/pages/product/apinternational. html.

Pew Research Center for the People & the Press (2006) *News Consumption and Believability Study.* http://people-press.org/reports/display.php3?PageID=1069.

Reuters (2007) *A Handbook of Reuters Journalism: A Guide to Standards, Style and Operations.* http://www.reuterslink.org/docs/reutershandbook.pdf.

Thomson Reuters (2008a) Reuters media solutions. http://www.thomsonreuters. com/products_services/media/Reuters_Media_Solutions.

Thomson Reuters (2008b) Editorial policy. http://www.thomsonreuters.com/about/ corp_responsibility/workplace/editorial_policy.

Questions for students

1 David Schlesinger notes that recent Pew studies show a marked decline in interest in international news. In what ways can the news agencies continue to cover the world if readers, viewers and listeners don't seem to be interested in those stories?

2 How should news editors strike the right balance between publishing what is most popular and what is most important?

3 If the news agencies disappeared tomorrow, how would that affect the free flow of information around the world?

4 Do the news agencies have a role in the future of journalism?

3

Technology, Timeliness and Taste: The Battlefronts for the Twenty-First Century News Agency

Nigel Baker

Technology allowed news agencies to exist. Now technology has the potential to destroy them. But every threat is an opportunity – and technology is also enabling the international agencies to increase the speed and frequency of reporting from some of the world's most hostile and inaccessible locations.

In the middle of the nineteenth century the transmission of words by telegraph allowed the widespread distribution of stories to newspapers by both national and international news agencies.

A similar model endured, with relative comfort, for nearly 150 years. An agency covered a story once and sold it many times, usually to hundreds or thousands of customers on a subscription basis, pumping it out to customers via 'the wire'.

Then along came the digital revolution in the 1980s. Since then, technology, and primarily the internet, has changed the way news has been collected, distributed and consumed, as well as the nature of the competition. For the first time, in theory, the technology existed for anyone to start his or her own news agency.

The internet allowed the global distribution and collection of words at little, or no, cost. The falling price of cameras and ever-improving digital compression meant that photographs and video could be shared online with ease.

The effects can be seen in the twenty-first-century phenomenon of 'citizen journalism', with members of the public contributing to coverage of events – most noticeably on major stories like terrorist attacks or natural disasters.

But while news media are fragmenting into niches serving people of different interests or opinions, the news agencies, for the moment, appear to be keeping their position at the centre of the world's news eco-system.

Research by Chris Paterson of Leeds University, published in 2006, indicated that more reliance was being placed on agency coverage of international stories on the internet with little, or no, editing. Paterson concluded that 'discourse on international events of consequence within the global public sphere is substantially determined by the production practices and institutional priorities of two information services – Reuters and the Associated Press' (2006: 20).

Paterson discovered that, over the previous five years, the 'average amount of measurable verbatim news agency use' of international report-ing by the two main international news agencies, Associated Press (AP) and Reuters, had increased online.

Among six aggregators – AOL, Yahoo, Nando, Lycos, Excite and AltaVista – the verbatim agency use had risen from 68 per cent to 85 per cent of content studied between 2001 and 2006. Among seven original news content providers – MSNBC, CNN, BBC, ABC, Sky News, the *Guardian* newspaper and the *New York Times* – it had increased from 34 per cent to 50 per cent.

The reasons were not totally clear. There could have been several. In the post-9/11 period and during the 2003 US-led invasion of Iraq, there was a growing interest in international news. It could have been that the demands of providing more content on a greater number of platforms meant that mainstream media were spending less on international cover-age themselves. Or it could have meant that greater use was being made of agencies to update sites more frequently.

But, whatever the reason, it showed that there remained strong reliance on AP and Reuters for international coverage.

Research for AP by PQ Media shows that the global market for editorial 'outsourced content' – text, video photos and graphics – sold by agencies and syndicators is set to rise from $5.6 billion in 2006 to $7.8 billion in 2011.

Table 3.1   The global market for outsourced editorial content

Content	2006	2011
Text	3,533	4,539
Video	657	1,217
Photos	698	1,103
Graphics	720	940
Total	5,608	7,799

Note: Figures are in US$billion.
Source: © PQ Media.

Although the market for text remains by far the biggest, the highest growth rates are in video and photographic content, where the markets are set to nearly double.

While many traditional newspaper customers are taking a battering from digital challengers, it shows that agencies can have a successful future as long as they adapt to changing needs in the digital and TV markets.

The main international news agencies offer a model that is hard for others to replicate without considerable investment. They have a highly developed network of providers and can ensure the coverage is timely and produced to rigorous standards of accuracy.

The value of the agency brand in the twenty-first century hinges more than ever on accuracy and validation of news – ensuring that media companies know that in a world crowded with information, the agency coverage will paint a true and reliable picture of events.

As technology has reduced the barriers to entry of providing international coverage, the major agencies have also invested heavily in new technologies to ensure they can report more speedily from any trouble spot – however remote.

Diversification into video has been a key area of expansion to meet market demands and keep pace with the multimedia mood of the age. Being at the heart of the news eco-system in the twenty-first century requires providing video, as well as words and photographs, to the world's audiences.

In the digital world, news is consumed more on the move and has become 'ambient'. It is all around us rather than digested at fixed times in fixed places. The use of the image is of growing importance to point us to the main stories.

Timeliness and the Video Factor

There is probably something in our genes that predisposes us to attend to images, motion and noise; what once helped to ensure survival should now be exploited for effective attention management. (Thomas H. Davenport, 'Attention: the next information frontier')

The news agency of the twenty-first century is paying attention to the change in news consumption in a world where major events are now remembered more by moving images than words or photographs.

Whereas the written word was the staple of news agencies for 150 years, live video has become a major tool in delivering 'breaking news'. You cannot get faster than real-time.

The big stories of the first decade of the twenty-first century have been defined by the video images – planes flying into the twin towers of New York's World Trade Center during the 9/11 attack in 2001; a night sky boiling with flame as the United States bombed Saddam Hussein's Baghdad during Operation 'Shock and Awe' in 2003; the waves of the advancing tsunami devastating the coastlines of Asia in late 2004.

The founding of the video-sharing website YouTube in 2005 sparked its own wave of online video consumption, drawing millions of ordinary users into the creation and posting of moving images.

By 2006, there was a stampede by newspapers in the United States and Europe to have video on their websites – enabled by the increased penetration of broadband and the desire to find new revenues online as the numbers reading newspapers in the developed world continued to fall.

Since the millennium, AP and Reuters have become the main source of international news video for thousands of websites and portals. The agencies were only able to do it because they had spent the last decade of the old century preparing for the multimedia age.

Thomas H. Davenport is not a newsman but a distinguished American academic and expert in information management for business. He argued from the late 1990s that we now have so much information available to us that we have to be participants in 'the Attention Economy', where the best way to get a message across is with powerful video images.

Speed has always been a key prerequisite of the news business, but in the age of the internet and 24-hour TV news channels it has become more

Ellen Knickmeyer using a laptop computer, portable generator and sat phone in March 2003
PHOTO COURTESY OF ASSOCIATED PRESS/PHOTOGRAPHER LAUREN REBOURS

important than ever. Video can also be a live medium, delivering the story in real time and allowing it to unfold before our eyes.

But does it aid our comprehension, or give us only a superficial understanding of events? Are we in danger of reporting only what the camera can see, and ignoring important issues which don't immediately lend themselves to speedy coverage? Does the easier availability of video lead to new ethical and taste issues, where journalists and consumers are exposed to more graphic images – including the point of death – in wars, famines and executions?

Or is it as simple as this: journalists will always want their stories to be used, and compete to get the best and quickest access? In the twenty-first century, if news agencies don't provide stories in eye-catching video to the market as quickly as possible, they will become irrelevant to their customers and may cease to exist.

In the new millennium news agencies have to fight on three battle-fronts – timeliness, technology and taste.

- *Timeliness*: How are news agencies to continue being first to the story when anyone can access the technology to record events and distribute them over the internet?
- *Technology*: 150 years ago telegraphic distribution allowed news agencies to exist, but will the democratization of distribution destroy the model? Will news agencies be driven by journalism or technology?
- *Taste*: Can news agencies keep their jealously guarded reputations for accuracy, fairness and balance faced with a web audience that appears to want unmediated access to the news, where the shocking and the titillating takes precedence over the significant?

But, as the old joke goes, 10,000 lemmings can't be wrong.

The international news agencies have invested heavily in building television infrastructure since the early 1990s.

In 1993, Reuters took over Visnews, one of the two international TV news agencies in the world at the time. Previously, Reuters had been a part owner, along with the BBC and America's NBC.

In 1994, AP launched its own TV news agency, Associated Press Television (APTV), after being warned by its business advisors, the Boston Consulting Group, that it would struggle in the twenty-first century without a video component.

In 1998, AP acquired the only other international TV news agency, Worldwide Television News (WTN), to consolidate the market and form APTN.

By the twenty-first century, the two largest international news agencies, AP and Reuters, were both armed with video and prepared for the broadband age – but built on a bedrock of custom from traditional broadcasters.

Traditionally, the universe of customers for news agency video from AP and Reuters was around 500 national and international broadcasters. The agency service to them was akin to a TV news channel without the anchors or on-screen reporters. Each agency had a dedicated satellite network on which it sent a daily mix of the world's main news, sport and entertainment stories to its customers.

The footage generally had no commentary but separate script material was sent to broadcasters who used the images, for the most part, without crediting the agency source.

From Baghdad to Beijing, from the catwalks of Paris to the red carpets of Hollywood, most broadcasters were relying on the two main international news agencies for the bulk of their international coverage.

Partly this was an economic imperative: it was cheaper to pay an agency an annual fee to cover the world than do it themselves.

But also, the pace of change was such that technology was enabling more, and wider, coverage. It was impossible for all but a handful of international broadcasters to get to the stories in a timely way to satisfy viewers who anticipated real-time coverage on their growing number of news channels.

By 2007, AP had nearly 200 video cameras in more than 80 bureaus worldwide. Reuters also reported TV camera crews in more than 80 of their bureaus. By 2007, the third international news agency, Agence France-Presse (AFP), had also launched a TV service, AFPTV, with 40 video journalists and including 10 international bureaus outside its home territory of France.

Within AP it was estimated that a key video image of a major event like the tsunami could be seen by up to a billion people by the time it had been used by nearly all the world's national and international broadcasters.

It is little known, and even less recorded, that in the pre-internet world of the early 1990s, the news agencies played a key role in speeding up the way video was distributed around the world.

Before then, the two main news agencies gave most of the world only two 15-minute 'windows' a day of news coverage – short, edited versions of video from the world's main stories.

A TV company in Asia, for example, looking to a news agency for its international news footage, would rarely receive same-day coverage. Most of it was at least a day old, with some of the material shipped across the world to the agencies' London headquarters by plane before transmission to save expensive satellite bills.

Then, in the early 1990s, Visnews launched a service called Vis Europe, where it had a permanent 24-hour satellite to Europe, pumping stories 24/7 to the lucrative European market as soon as they were ready.

The launch of AP's television service in 1994 moved the market a step farther. AP put in place permanent, 24-hour delivery to most of the world – and their competitors, Reuters and WTN, followed.

So, by the mid-1990s, broadcasters in Asia and the Middle East were regularly beginning to receive same-day coverage from around the globe for the first time.

News agencies were becoming more vital to the eco-system of how video travelled round the world.

At the same time, the price of collecting TV news began to drop sharply. The launch of more satellites and the deregulation of telecommunications in much of the world meant satellites were cheaper to use for collecting news, so affordability meant coverage was provided at greater speed.

But in 1997 came a little-recorded event which I would argue set the scene for video to challenge the written word's supremacy in setting the agenda for international news coverage.

For the first time, compressed video could be transmitted down a satellite telephone from anywhere in the world, provided journalists had the basic equipment and a power supply.

Previously, video had to be sent to the agencies' main production centres from a TV station which had the capability to transmit to international satellites. The alternative was to transport up to two tons of portable transmission equipment to the site of a story – often impossible in remote war zones or where hostile regimes refused to allow access for the gear.

But once video could be sent via a satellite telephone, all the equipment involved could be fitted in an average-sized suitcase.

Suddenly, no part of the world was immune from same-day coverage, and hostile regimes could be circumvented.

Traditionally, totalitarian states had used the TV station as a point of control, from where the message to the domestic audience could be manipulated and any immediate TV coverage intended for the outside world could be censored or blocked entirely.

The new compression technology broke the stranglehold of the tyrant. For the first time, video could travel with almost the same speed and frequency as the written word – often with considerably more impact.

AP first used this to strong competitive effect in early 1997 in the former African state of Zaire, now the Democratic People's Republic of Congo. Rebel leader Laurent Kabila led his troops across an African state the size of Western Europe to topple the corrupt government of President Mobutu Sese Seko.

An AP television team kept up with his advance and filed regular same-day reports using the new compression technology and transmitting their video by a satellite telephone. Competitors withdrew because their material had to be taken to an airport and then flown hundreds of miles to Kenya to be transmitted – a time lag of up to three days.

While it was a competitive victory for AP, it had a wider significance. The technology opened up large areas of the world to more frequent international TV reporting.

Until then the formula had been simple. If an international story broke, usually in text form on the agency 'wires', a judgement had to be made by the TV wings of news agencies and broadcasters whether they were going to acquire any video coverage within a reasonable time frame.

Many stories went uncovered by TV cameras, or footage unused, because a decision was made that by the time the video arrived at London headquarters interest would have disappeared in the story.

But I would contend that, whether in Afghanistan, Iraq, Somalia or Ethiopia, the ability to transmit compressed video has transformed the assignment habits of TV news agencies and changed the expectations of broadcasters, and the public, as to what they could view from the world's remoter and more perilous places.

Since the turn of the millennium, video has increasingly been transmitted over the public internet from major centres of population, with two effects. First, the amount of video has increased because it is much cheaper than using satellites – so a news agency working to a daily budget can cover more stories. Second, the coverage is not subject to the same scrutiny by restrictive regimes, where previously the transmission point in the TV station was also a point of censorship.

The race, however, was by no means over. War often spurs inventiveness – and so it did in the first few years of the twenty-first century.

For a few hours, on September 11, 2001, hundreds of millions of viewers were transfixed by the live TV pictures of the Al Qaeda attack on New York's World Trade Center which left nearly 3,000 dead.

The raw drama of people's efforts to escape from the burning towers, and the buildings' subsequent collapse, was probably the most dramatic and sustained live news coverage of a single event that the world had seen.

As the story unfolded in the heart of the world's biggest television market, it appeared that TV companies were competing on immediacy, rather than depth, in their reporting of the story. Live TV eats significant resources, so the more money spent on creating it, the less there is to spend on the equally expensive investigative or enterprise reporting.

When the United States decided to invade Iraq in 2003, another battle took place – to make it the first war to be covered live from the frontline.

At times, the logistics of moving the technology needed to create live television from a war zone seemed almost as daunting and complex as the military operation.

While the larger broadcasters competed to find the best gadgetry to use for live reporting, there was a need for the agencies to respond – or not keep pace with the demands of the twenty-first-century news market.

AP created multiple live channels so any broadcaster could see the conflict unfolding in real time. From the 'Shock and Awe' bombing campaign on Baghdad, to the arrival of the first American troops on the streets of the Iraqi capital, to jet fighters taking off from US aircraft carriers in the Persian Gulf, each step of the conflict was provided live.

Of course agencies are open to the accusation – in the same way as any TV news channel is – that showing an event live does not convey a full explanation of events and may, indeed, show only one side of the story. Inevitably, this will happen on occasions, but the same could be argued historically about photographs. The difference is that the immediacy and reach of globally transmitted, live television may have greater impact.

As long as the real-time coverage is done as responsibly as possible and attempts are made wherever possible to provide live footage from both sides of a story, it would be unrealistic to think that agencies should not participate in the live television business.

To abdicate from this would eventually make them irrelevant to a large part of their customer base and would be denying progress. A desire for live coverage is a fact of modern life.

There is, of course, in video, as well as in text, the need to pause and make sense of the story in its entirety. Agencies have a duty to produce a balanced account of a story over time. Now live coverage is the norm for both of the 'big two' agencies and plays a key part in informing other areas of coverage.

Technology is only one aspect of timeliness by agencies. It has, of course, to be used by the right people in the right places to yield optimum benefits.

It is the 'journalism of access' that sets agencies apart from other news organizations. The world's news media rely on agencies to be 'first in, last out' on the big, breaking story and to keep a permanent presence in any major conflict area.

More than other news companies, agencies rely on 'local' staff – those recruited in the country they are covering, rather than staff 'parachuted in' from overseas.

Those 'local' recruits are often the most skilful, imperilled, but understated of the agency staff. They live with the story 365 days a year, mindful of the consequences for their family and friends if their reporting offends the ruling regime in their country.

They have to make a constant judgement call as to how far they report the story without provoking the regime to revoke their working credentials – always trying to champion the needs of the international news audience, usually within a state where press freedom is only a dream.

Since the early 1990s, technology has helped to make their jobs more possible. The internet and digital transmission equipment have helped them to get the message out with less monitoring at the point of dispatch.

However, the risk can now come after, rather than at, the point where they send the story. For example, a cameraman filming an anti-government protest in Zimbabwe transmitted his pictures. Shortly after they were aired on an international news channel, he was attacked and badly beaten by pro-government police, which he interpreted as an act of punishment. A generation earlier, if he had succeeded in getting his pictures out of the country, no international news channel would have existed and his pictures would not have been visible in his own country.

Likewise, restrictive regimes that may not allow free access to the internet in their countries are not averse to using it to search for negative stories about themselves. In the past, a story might have been more difficult to get out of a country but once in the 'free world' might have escaped notice by the subject of the reporting.

The technologies that have enabled greater reporting have, in many cases, brought about greater monitoring of adverse coverage. The technology has brought many benefits but has to be used carefully to avoid more risk to journalists.

Technology and Taste

The long-standing role of news agencies has been not just to report but to sift and sort; to work out what is happening in the world and be a primary point of setting the world's news agenda.

Journalists the world over rely on 'the wires' as an instant source of news to fill a page or a news bulletin. But new technologies have posed two phenomena which assail the traditional role of agencies as the central core of international newsgathering.

Agencies have long been used to having their judgements broadly accepted by a large section of the traditional news media. Now, however, pressure groups with a vested interest in discrediting the coverage regularly use new technologies to try to undermine coverage which conflicts with their points of view.

Even before blogs gave many a forum on the internet, agencies could be privy to smear campaigns by chain emails. Similar criticisms of a story have been known to emerge simultaneously in different parts of the world. A customary target for such campaigns has often been the Israeli–Palestinian conflict – with supporters of both sides using the tactic.

Of course, there are occasions when complaints of agency journalism have been legitimate – but they have been few. For the most part, the email campaigns and then those in the blogosphere have been mischievous, usually espousing rumour as fact or assumption as certainty.

This has been a test for agencies but all the more reason why they need to be meticulous with accuracy, to defend themselves against impish or malign allegations.

It is with moving images that agencies have faced their biggest test over taste in the past few years. With the growing amount of user-generated content, can agencies keep pace with monitoring the volume of material? If so, can its authenticity be guaranteed and can the agencies be sure of obtaining the copyright to it?

As a consequence, could the agencies' role shift from being the main trunk of the news eco-system to merely a branch?

The Iraq conflict encapsulated some of the most difficult issues facing news agencies in trying to make sense of the avalanche of video appearing in all areas of coverage within the bounds of taste. The conflict brought about video extremes – from the beheading of hostages to the execution of deposed Iraqi leader Saddam Hussein.

For the first time, combatants used video as a tool to get their own message across – managed in their own way.

The videotaped killing of American telecommunications worker Nicholas Berg in May 2004 heralded the first of a series of gruesome beheadings purported to have been carried out by groups linked to Al Qaeda.

Having accessed the video, a decision had to be made over how much of it to use. Could an agency running it on its satellite network inadvertently lead to broadcasters airing it in full by mistake? Could staff at an agency or customer reasonably be asked to handle such disturbing footage? If, however, an agency did not supply the video to its customers in full, would it be denying them the opportunity to describe clearly

Official Iraqi state television pictures of Saddam Hussein shortly before his execution, December 2006 (a–c); unofficial mobile phone images after Saddam's execution, later released by AP, December 2006 (d–e)

PHOTOS COURTESY OF ASSOCIATED PRESS

such an act of barbarism and be laid open to the charge of sanitizing the event?

This was uncharted editorial territory. The fact that the execution was videotaped was as much the story as the beheading itself. AP ran the video in full but with repeated advance warnings to its subscribers of its gruesome nature. In house, the number of people who had to deal with it was kept to an absolute minimum.

The feedback from customers was that they wanted to see it in full to make their own editorial judgements. In the event, different broadcasters around the world used it in different ways. Some ran the video at full length but obscured the execution. Others stopped the video before the execution. I am not aware of any which ran it in its entirety and unedited. The only recorded complaint was from a customer who had missed the video and failed to record it.

The material was run in full because of its uniqueness and to allow broadcasters to understand the nature of the incident so they could report a new phenomenon accurately.

However, having conveyed the reality of such an act, further similar incidents were distributed with the act of execution removed so as not to appear to encourage, or even glorify, such acts and also to minimize the distress to those who might have to deal with the videos in newsrooms round the world.

When Saddam Hussein was executed by the Iraqi authorities on 30 December 2006, official video was released of him being taken to the gallows. The material ended with the noose being placed round his neck and did not show the moment of death.

(d)   (e)

However, later that day, unofficial mobile phone video surfaced on the internet of his entire execution. Again, AP ran the latter as a matter of public interest. To a large part of the world – particularly a sceptical Middle East audience – it proved conclusively he had been hanged. The mobile phone video also revealed the taunts he faced from some of those present at his execution.

It would have been hard to validate the mobile phone video unless the official video – filmed by an Iraqi TV channel – had existed. Only by comparing the two was it possible to tell the mobile phone footage was apparently genuine.

In both these examples, an agency had to be the 'eyes and ears' of the world's news media – obtaining video in a timely fashion, endeavouring to validate it, and then having to become an arbiter of taste by deciding whether to distribute it.

Technology and Copyright

The internet has given rise to a new attitude to copyright by content users. The closest comparison with the news business is the music industry, where companies like Napster deconstructed traditional models by allowing free file-sharing. Most users do not respect the copyright of original content creators.

For news agencies to realize their worth, they have to be constantly vigilant as to how their content is being used across the web.

The establishment of Google News in 2002 brought a stark warning. Google aggregated 4,500 online news websites – producing a highly effective news site with no human intervention.

Again, a high proportion of the material originated from the agencies and a stand was needed to ensure agency copyright was not undermined. In 2006, AP and Google agreed a deal over the use of AP's material by the search engine – although Google maintained its public stand that Google News only used headlines, extracts and thumbnail images, so its site was reasonable 'fair use' of third-party copyright and linked through to news organizations paying for the agency content.

AP turned Google into a customer. But AFP chose another route by suing the search engine for $17.5 million over copyright infringement. Google responded by 'blacklisting' all sites containing AFP material.

After a two-year battle, they settled their dispute in April 2007 in an undisclosed deal with a statement which saw honour served for both sides. It announced the agreement would 'enable the use of AFP's newswire content in innovative, new ways' (Nuttall 2007).

Four months later, Google announced that it had done a deal with four news agencies, AP, AFP, the Canadian Press and the Press Association (the UK provider), to post their material directly on to Google News. It was seen as potentially provocative to the traditional news-agency customers who would be concerned that the move would mean less traffic to their own sites. Industry watchers questioned whether it was only a short-term win for the agencies – which could cause a backlash among their traditional clientele.

Like their customers, agencies are having to invest significantly to police the use of their content on the web. Techniques called 'watermarking' and 'fingerprinting' are being widely employed. Both techniques implant a digital signal in the content so its use can be tracked, and illegal users identified, and billed, accordingly.

Conclusion

Digital technology – particularly the internet – has had a profound effect on the way international news agencies operate, but provides the opportunity for growth as well as a threat from new entrants to the market.

The more crowded and faster moving the information world becomes, then, arguably, the greater the need for news agencies to be on hand to provide consistency and accuracy of coverage. AP's experience is that when a major story breaks, consumers revert to the known, 'mainstream' brands to get an accurate version of events even if under normal circumstances those same consumers have become cynical about 'traditional' media.

It pinpoints that whatever the interpretation or analysis of a major news event anywhere in the world, there needs to be an original content creator, like a news agency, to establish the facts and disseminate them rapidly and reliably. The news eco-system has to start somewhere.

Agencies, however, will need to continue to rise to serve a wider, faster global news agenda – able to tell the story compellingly in all media formats with images playing a greater part.

The famous first message sent by the inventor of the telegraph, Samuel Morse, in 1844 proclaimed: 'What hath God wrought'.

Today, many say the same about live news video, or video used in new and alarming ways as in Iraq. The signs are that, within the next few years, technology will enable live video to become more pervasive in news coverage.

It is in the nature of news agencies to use any tool possible to gather the news as quickly and as comprehensively as possible. Indeed, they will cease to exist if they ignore technologies available to potential new competitors.

I would contend that obtaining journalistic access to countries and events in the most visible way possible aids understanding and increases the accountability of political and military leaders.

Technology, therefore, can empower journalism and provide access to stories which in previous generations would have been left uncovered. It can help those stories be distributed in the timely way that news companies and their consumers require in a fast-paced, information-rich world.

Taste can mean different things to different cultures around the world. Some audiences may be more offended by nudity than bloodshed.

News agencies have a vital role to play in continuing to establish and maintain standards of accuracy, balance and fairness. There is a need always to think about the consequences of any coverage and to strive to give a balanced and fair account of events, wherever possible.

Technology has accelerated change in all aspects of news agencies. The coverage and images it can facilitate are likely to influence taste and what is editorially acceptable. But the role of the news agency is to ensure that technology continues to empower journalism – not replace it.

References

Davenport, T. H. (2000) Attention: the next information frontier. In *Mastering Information Management,* eds. Marchand, D. A., Davenport, T. H. and Dickson, T. Financial Times Prentice Hall.

Nuttall, C. (2007) AFP and Google settle lawsuit. FT.com, http://search.ft.com/ftArticle? queryText=AFP+and+google&y=8&aje=true&x=9&id=070406005834.

Paterson, C. (2006) News agency dominance in international news on the internet. In *Papers in International Global Communication,* No. 01/06, Centre for International Communications Research, http://ics.leeds.ac.uk/papers/cicr/exhibits/42/cicrpaterson.pdf.

Questions for students

1 What pictures would you have shown of Saddam Hussein's execution?
2 What are the ethical and taste issues that may result from video agencies being able now to publish far more graphic images of war, famines and suffering around the world?
3 Do news agencies have the responsibility to restrict the release of material that may be disturbing, or is it their role to acquire and distribute any and all newsworthy visual material and let their clients decide whether to publish or air it?

4

Freelance Journalism

Vaughan Smith

Introduction

JOHN OWEN

When you enter the Frontline Club for international journalists in London, you walk by a large framed collection of pictures of eight journalists – seven men and one woman. You look more carefully and you become aware that all are dead, all were freelance journalists, all were at one time or another working for the Frontline News Television agency and with one of its co-founders, Vaughan Smith.

Freelancers have paid a high price for their journalistic risk taking. Over the years 1996–2006, 94 or nearly one in 10 of the 1,000 journalists that the International News Safety Institute has identified as having lost their lives covering the news were freelancers (International News Safety Institute 2007).

Freelancers even more than agency journalists have never received proper recognition for their contribution to international newsgathering. Few networks or agencies have given them proper on-air credit for their pictures or reportage, let alone acknowledged their contributions inside the news industry.

In Britain, there has been a long tradition of former soldiers becoming freelance cameramen and using their training and detailed knowledge of conflict and war to great advantage over those without this expertise. After the Berlin Wall came down and we witnessed several years of nasty, bloody fighting throughout the Balkans, the former Soviet Union, Central America and many parts of Africa, it was freelancers who often provided 'exclusive' material that was coveted by the agencies and the mainstream networks.

But while the freelancers were eager to accept these assignments and take whatever risks others chose not to take, they resented how often they were not properly insured or issued the same quality of protective equipment. It was the death of one of the co-founders of the Frontline News Television agency, Rory Peck, in 1993 that led to the creation of a trust bearing his name that was established to provide financial compensation for the families of freelancers who were killed on assignment. What may still seem an insufficient amount of money for the families of freelancers living in Western countries is a substantial sum for those who lived and worked in developing countries and less affluent regions.

Even if freelancers are prepared to travel to cover conflicts in countries where their chances of being killed are far too great – Iraq or Somalia – in the view of broadcast news managers, should they still be supported to take those high risks? Some news executives argue that to do so is morally irresponsible; that if the story is too dangerous for their own staffers, why should they place freelancers at grave risk? But freelancers counter that it is the right of freelancers to take risks that others won't. They reject the oft-heard expression, voiced in chapter 10 of this book by former CNN International news boss Chris Cramer, that no story is worth the life of a journalist.

Today's freelancers are more likely to be local journalists in places like Iraq and Afghanistan. As Anthony Borden explains in chapter 9, many have been trained and supported financially by Western non-governmental organizations, such as the Institute for War & Peace Reporting.

Yet those who have been in the forefront of the freelancer movement led by Vaughan Smith argue that there is still a vital role for them to play in international newsgathering, exploiting the broadband revolution that makes it radically easier to distribute their material. But the question for Smith and other freelancers is how they make enough money in an era of YouTube and citizen journalism, where almost anyone with a camera or mobile phone is a potential free-lancer.

Vaughan Smith has a long history of confounding the experts. He's a fourth-generation army officer who bid farewell to his Grenadier Guards to become one of the most respected freelance cameramen. When he no longer thought the freelance business was viable, against all the odds, he created a restaurant and journalists' club in London that now has over 1,000 members and programmes documentaries and journalism debates almost on a nightly basis. And if all else fails, Smith can still shoulder his camera and go off to places like Afghanistan and provide first-rate pictures of that conflict along with incisive reportage and blogs.

Vaughan Smith filming Croatian soldiers, 1991
PHOTO COURTESY OF VAUGHAN SMITH

Reference

International News Safety Institute (2007) *Killing the Messenger: Report of the Global Inquiry by the International News Safety Institute into the Protection of Journalists.* INSI.

In all institutions that do not feel the sharp wind of public criticism (as, for example, in scholarly organizations and senates), an innocent corruption grows up, like a mushroom. (Friedrich Nietzsche, Human, All Too Human: A Book for Free Spirits)

Early in life I had noticed that no event is ever correctly reported in a newspaper. (George Orwell, Looking Back on the Spanish War)

If the newspapers are useful in overthrowing tyrants, it is only to establish a tyranny of their own. (James Fenimore Cooper, The American Democrat)

To work as a journalist employed by a broadcaster or publisher is to accept a compromise. In return for job security, the comfort of institutional and logistical support and easy access to an audience, individual independence and editorial control are relinquished. They must now be negotiated.

Working for the 'machine' becomes an investment in it and prospering requires a subscription and contribution to its collective approach and culture. There is a team to be supported and within that team loyalties and friendships can help determine the path of a journalist's career.

When the pay packet goes to support a mortgage, financial dependence is added to the matrix of ties that lock the journalist into the status quo, the corporate culture and risk aversion. There is a comfortable clutter that surrounds, but does not necessarily support, the journalistic mission.

The product is promoted as 'independent' journalism regardless of its link to the share price, its slavery to fashionable 'correctness' and whatever pasteurized news entertainment is currently popular with viewers. Criticism is directed outwards.

Of course news organizations vary in quality, particularly from country to country, and many journalists are able over time to build authority within their outfit and carve out a level of independence, even contribute to the editorial direction of their company's product. But it is still remarkable how many highly intelligent journalists lose their capacity for critical analysis when considering their own industry and profession. For which too few assume any responsibility.

That is not to say that journalism hasn't improved over the last century, if it really was as bad as John Swinton, a pre-eminent New York journalist, declared when the guest of honour at a banquet, believed to be in 1880, attended by the leaders of his craft. Someone who knew neither the press nor Swinton offered a toast to the independent press. Swinton outraged his colleagues by replying:

> There is no such thing, at this date of the world's history, in America, as an independent press. You know it and I know it. There is not one of you who dares to write your honest opinions, and if you did, you know beforehand that it would never appear in print. I am paid weekly for keeping my honest opinion out of the paper I am connected with. Others of you are paid similar salaries for similar things, and any of you who would be so foolish as to write honest opinions would be out on the streets looking for another job. If I allowed my honest opinions to appear in one issue of my paper, before twenty-four hours my occupation would be gone.

> The business of the journalists is to destroy the truth, to lie outright, to pervert, to vilify, to fawn at the feet of mammon, and to sell his country and his race for his daily bread. You know it and I know it, and what folly is this toasting an independent press? We are the tools and vassals of rich men behind the scenes. We are the jumping jacks, they pull the strings and we dance. Our talents, our possibilities and our lives are all the property of other men. We are intellectual prostitutes. (quoted in Boyer and Morais 1955)

More recently, the failure of the US and its allies to secure the promised quick victory in Iraq and to discover the weapons of mass destruction that were the pretext for the invasion have prompted many American journalists to be critical of US journalism.

> one of the enduring legacies of 9/11 has been this Administration's politicization of terror threats inside the United States, the media's lapdog hyping of the threats – its tendency to act as a megaphone instead of a filter, even in the wake of the Administration's clear record of distortion … news organizations remain much more willing to cheerlead terror warnings than seriously question them or put them in proper political context. (Boehlert 2006: 30–2)

> A handful of self-serving corporate fiefdoms controls practically all of our mass-market sources of news and information. GE now owns NBC, Disney owns ABC, Viacom owns CBS, NewsCorp. owns Fox, and TimeWarner owns

CNN; these five have a lock on TV news ... These aloof giants openly assert that meeting their own profit needs is the media's reason for existence ... Clear Channel.. (which owns ... a third of all the [radio] stations in America), opines that: 'We're not in the business of providing news and information. We're simply in the business of selling our customers' products.'

This single-minded mercenary focus combines with general corporate arrogance to bloat the egos of media chieftains ... 'We paid $3 billion for these television stations,' said an executive with Fox ... 'We decide what the news is. The news is what we tell you it is.' (Hightower 2004: 15)

Columbia University in the United States has been running its Project for Excellence in Journalism for nine years at www.stateofthenewsmedia. com. It claims to specialize in using empirical methods to evaluate and study the performance of the press.

They report that 'journalists are unhappy with the way things are going in their profession these days', that 'significant majorities of [US] journalists have come to believe that increased bottom line pressure is "seriously hurting" the quality of news coverage' and that 'TV stations owned by smaller media firms generally produce better newscasts' (Project for Excellence in Journalism 2004).

Amy Goodman, described by the *Los Angeles Times* as 'radio's voice of the disenfranchised left' (Braxton 2004), posed the question of the US press coverage of the 2003 invasion of Iraq: 'If we had state-run media in the United States, how would it be any different?'

'Government-supplied propaganda has become pervasive in mainstream media, from hiring journalists to write puff pieces to credentialing fake reporters to fawning reports from embedded reporters in Iraq. Where is independent media?' (Goodman and Goodman 2005)

Where indeed? Gone are the days when to call oneself a journalist one needed to work for a broadcaster or publisher at all. There is another way, but it is not for the faint-hearted. Freelance journalism takes considerable courage.

Working for an employer is likely to deliver better financial returns and considerably greater recognition; there will be a career path; the physical risks should be less; and there will be colleagues to learn from or imitate.

Working independently as a journalist commits you to a lonely professional life swimming against the current. Belief in yourself must be unshakeable because it will rarely be shared, and beyond this you will normally need to deliver better work than employed journalists to succeed. Whatever success you do have, others will try to mask or claim ownership of. You are not a member of the club.

But it is individuals who, by taking risks, change the society that we live in. Though this may be a necessary dynamic, it is the organizations, or institutions, that act to prevent or moderate the impact of that change.

Journalists can choose to work on the outside, and freelance journalism, unfiltered and unfettered, when conducted skilfully and with integrity, though its reach may be shorter, is journalism's highest form.

What is Freelance Journalism?

The freelance journalist aims to make a living in the media independently of the mainstream while retaining as much copyright and editorial control over his or her work as possible.

Freelance journalism is distinguished from citizen journalism by the fact that its practitioners have assumed journalism as a trade, fully subscribing to its professional responsibilities, but without accepting the authority of the news industry's broadcasters, publishers and institutions.

However, there are 'freelancers' who don't own the copyright of their work, or a share in it, and who therefore don't actually conduct freelance journalism. This leads to some confusion surrounding the term 'freelance', which is applied both to operators working independently and to industry workers who don't have secure contracts.

Further to this, many freelance journalists engage in occasional commissioned work or freelance crewing contracts where they may not retain their own copyright, and there are often arrangements where ownership of copyright may be split in some fashion.

There is freelance journalism in all disciplines of the trade: writers or bloggers, photographers and videographers. Many freelance journalists combine some or all of these skills in their output.

Since newspapers began, they have used 'stringers', or freelance journalists, paid for each piece of published work rather than receiving a regular salary. They mostly specialize in breaking news, and having stringers all over the world offers an inexpensive way to maintain a level of global coverage.

The term 'stringer' suggests a level of professionalism, or acceptance, while the term 'freelancer', which is more commonly used in television news, does not.

Winston Churchill

Men stumble over the truth from time to time, but most pick themselves up and hurry off as if nothing happened. (Winston Churchill)

Today's freelance journalists would recognize the contractual arrangements that Winston Churchill, a journalist before he became a politician and later British prime minister (1940–5, 1951–5), engaged in with the *Morning Post* and other newspapers of the day to cover the Boer War in 1899, and in his earlier journalism in Cuba, the Sudan and India's North West Frontier.

These arrangements were not dissimilar to the advances that he received as a writer for his books. However, his journalism was edited, though his books were not. Freelance writers have much in common with independent journalists.

Of course Winston Churchill's acceptance of his position as a prisoner of war in South Africa would not fit with contemporary ideas of independent journalism. He had been carrying a revolver when captured, as was common for correspondents then, and entirely identified with the British cause.

Magnum Photos

It's not enough to have talent, you also have to be Hungarian. (Robert Capa)

Independent journalism today owes its prime debt to the Magnum Photos agency, formed by Robert Capa, Henri Cartier-Bresson, George Rodger and David 'Chim' Seymour in 1947, two years after World War II. All were leading photojournalists of their time.

Robert Capa, the agency's dynamic leader and most celebrated war correspondent, was killed when he stepped on a landmine in Vietnam on 25 May 1954.

Cornell Capa, Robert Capa's brother, wrote about him that he

> lived and loved a great deal. He was born without money, and he died the same … his life is a testament to difficulty overcome, a challenge met, a gamble won except at the end. Born without the means to travel, with a language not useful beyond the borders of a small country, Hungary, he managed to experience the world through a universal means of communication, photography. He was thus able to speak to us all, then and now. (Whelan and Capa 1985)

Even after he had been recognized as one of the leading photographers of the century, Capa used to describe himself as a journalist rather than a photographer. It was as if he refused to acquire, or deliver, more photographic technique than absolutely necessary for the task of reporting. He never fully mastered the use of flashbulbs and was often very careless in the darkroom.

Some of his editors wondered whether he had intentionally found a way to incorporate some device in his camera to scratch his film. It was as if Capa somehow thought it obscene to make too fine a picture of human suffering.

In Paris in the early 1930s, Robert Capa and his friend Henri Cartier-Bresson both came under the influence of Andre Kertesz, one of the great pioneers of 35 mm photography. Together with their friend David 'Chim' Seymour they developed a photographic style that sought to capture what Cartier-Bresson called 'the decisive moment', and this style later became associated with Magnum Photos.

Magnum Photos was formed from their desire to work outside the formulas of the magazine journalism of the day and radically departed from conventional practice by supporting rather than directing its photojournalists. Copyright was to be held by the authors of the imagery rather than by the magazines that published the work.

This meant that Magnum photographers could cover the stories of their choice, without an assignment, and their work would be sold for a commission by the agency on their behalf to magazines all over the world. Magnum photographers were thereby able to escape the dictates of a single publication and its editorial staff and work for long periods of time on stories of their choice.

Magnum Photos took 35 mm photography and created photojournalism. It was an act that inspired generations of photographers and journalists to appreciate the value of their own work. You can still recognize traces of this extraordinary achievement in the independent, even insular, resourcefulness that still characterizes the best photojournalists today.

As Cartier-Bresson put it in one of his memos to the other photographers, 'Vive la revolution permanente'(Magnum Photos 2007).

Photojournalism Today

Since 1997, the photo-archive giants Getty and Corbis have bought up most independent photojournalism agencies. The most notable of the remaining independent photojournalism agencies, where the agencies are actually owned by the photographers themselves, are of course Magnum Photos and the much younger VII.

Despite the large structural changes that have occurred in photojournalism, it still has a large public following. Photography is such a popular hobby that its application in the most demanding of circumstances is compelling to people.

The photographer is still under pressure. Increasingly newspapers will take the first or the cheapest image over the best. But photojournalism still remains the best medium for the independent journalist to retain the greatest editorial control, short of the still unproven 'new media'.

The fact remains that the news photograph still has to be used as it was taken. Though it is technically possible to doctor photographs it is uncommon and still severely disapproved of. Picture editors can crop photographs but this rarely alters their journalistic messages.

In contrast, writers normally have their work subject to editing by sub-editors who were not there, and video cameramen normally work in teams. Many television journalists have their scripts approved by head office and their stories are still subject to further editing to fit in to broadcast schedules and editorial policies.

Photojournalism is still incredibly cool.

Frontline News Television

A small number of enterprising individuals, led by Gwynne Roberts, picked up Sony Video 8 cameras and tried to operate outside the television news machine in the mid-to-late 1980s, mainly working on foreign news stories that were hard to get to, like Afghanistan or the Sudan.

The first agency to organize itself to support the independent video journalism that came out of the availability of these cameras, mainly the much better Hi8 camera, was a London-based agency called Frontline News Television.

Peter Jouvenal, Rory Peck, Nick della Casa and I set up the agency while covering the Romanian revolution during Christmas 1989. BBC reporter David Loyn tells the story of the agency in his book *Frontline: The True Story of the British Mavericks who Changed the Face of War Reporting* (2006).

Other smaller agencies emerged and still survive today, the most influential of which is Insight News Television, created by executive producer Ron McCullagh. Together we built a new independent fringe of television news.

Frontline deliberately modelled itself on Magnum Photos. But while Magnum's founders had spent years working within journalism and photography before setting up their agency, at Frontline none of us had anything like this sort of industry experience.

Early Frontline freelances sought a quick and rewarding entry into television news backed up with some military experience.

Television news then utilized large Betacam cameras which until recently were in two pieces, requiring two operators as well as a soundman. A news crew might also include a producer as well as the reporter. Often a video editor would travel too.

Cameramen still expected to have to complete apprenticeships and to take long lunch-breaks. This was about to change as a significant number of Australian cameramen arrived on the scene with a wider range of skills and a completely different work ethic.

At Frontline we found that if our pictures were compelling we could sell our footage for about £750 per minute or part thereof, just to a British broadcaster. We could then get considerably more by selling to other broadcasters around the world.

If we filmed a complete story and made a competent edit of the material we could sell many minutes to one of the many news magazine shows around Europe and the US, hungry for good material.

At first, until we hired staff, the cameramen would trawl the world's dangerous places sending back videotapes and I would try to sell the film to broadcasters.

It was possible for an enterprising and smart freelance video journalist to make a living that compared to a successful television reporter's, but of course without the bother of all the hard work that went before it. It was thrilling, but dangerous.

All in our twenties, we thought we could make lots of money, spend it quickly, and live an exotic 'frontier' existence. We were independent, uncontrolled, free to roam and report. We would choose the rules. It was great fun. In Afghanistan we were looking for thrills. Then came the Balkans where we soaked in the reality of war.

To attempt to digest the breadth of human suffering that war delivers is astoundingly sobering. It is diminished by statistics, which cannot shine a glimmer of illumination on a quantum of lost lives, limbs, homes and hope. It was filling our lenses, and learning to convey it made us journalists.

We began to consider the dull cruelty of the disinterested viewer, people only separated from war by geography, time or perhaps the bravery of their grandfathers. We felt that it was almost our duty to engage – to immerse ourselves in our work and to be there, hoping that our films might make a difference.

We professionalized, improving our skills and developing a canny sense of what the news 'machine' might buy from us. We didn't just cover conflicts. In fact most of our work was on human stories from far-flung places that the broadcasters wouldn't often go to, or underground stories that were harder to find – stories like 'Chinese traders on the Trans-Siberian Express' or 'grannies selling drugs in Moscow'.

We would immerse ourselves in a story, often spending weeks with our subjects. Traditional news crews were rarely given the time to spend more than a few days on a story and presented a very much larger and intrusive footprint.

When we covered conflicts we would often go for stories that went against the grain, like 'UN corruption in Sarajevo', which other journalists had avoided out of concern for the effect that it might have on their future access to the story. During the Gulf War of 1991, when broadcasters and newspapers were heavily restricted, I disguised myself as a British officer to get footage of the conflict.

As it became more difficult to sell stories, we would take crewing jobs to get our costs covered and stay on longer to film our own work. Peter Jouvenal, our Afghan expert, filmed and helped fix access to an interview with Osama bin Laden for CBS.

By 2003, when Frontline News Television stopped taking new business, eight freelance journalists who had worked through the agency had been

Vaughan Smith, posing as a British soldier during the first Gulf War when he was the
only cameraman who witnessed the ground-level fighting, 1991

... and one of his exclusive images

killed. Two of them, Nick della Casa and Rory Peck, were among the original founders, along with Peter Jouvenal and me.

The others were Rosanna della Casa, Charlie Maxwell, Carlos Mavroleon, Roddy Scott, James Miller and Richard Wild. They were all killed during the course of their work.

Nick della Casa, Rosanna della Casa and Charlie Maxwell died in the northern 'Kurdish' part of Iraq in 1991. Rory Peck died in Moscow in 1993, Carlos Mavroleon in Pakistan in 1998, Roddy Scott in Ingushetia in 2002, James Miller in Gaza in 2003 and Richard Wild in Iraq in 2003.

Though the dreadful losses we sustained might not suggest it, we were pioneers in the news industry on the development of safe practice. We were consultants to the first industry safety course in 1993 and began promoting amongst ourselves a disciplined approach to taking risk where no reward was likely.

Nevertheless we continued to resist the ordinariness of the emerging industry safety policy, which put our lives so far before the suffering of large numbers of others.

After Rory Peck's death, his wife Juliet Peck and friend John Gunston, a photojournalist, decided to start a trust in his name. With the support of Frontline and many others, the Rory Peck Trust launched in 1995.

The trust aimed to create an award that recognized courage in freelance video journalism and start a fund to support the dependents of freelance cameramen killed in the course of their work. In the early 1990s freelance video journalists very rarely won awards for their film, because they didn't work for broadcasters.

The mid-1990s saw considerable changes in broadcasting. Hundreds of new private television channels emerged to compete with the older, mainly state, broadcasters. Budgets tightened as competition intensified. Magazine programmes closed, the Associated Press launched a television arm called APTN, and both they and Reuters expanded their wholesale output to broadcasters, much improving its quality.

By 1997 the use of small-format cameras was widespread, particularly by documentary makers. A new digital format had arrived called DV, standing for digital video, which delivered a significantly superior picture quality to Hi8.

As the price for news material fell, broadcasters were increasingly keen to promote their brand by having their own reporters on camera rather than buying in independent journalism. For all the expanded output that the broadcast news industry was delivering, it was subscribing to the same news agenda and morphing into an increasingly indistinguishable product.

Freelance video journalists had never been able to secure broadcast credits for their footage and this proved to be our undoing at Frontline News Television. The material we sold for our freelance video journalists was voiced by reporters working for the broadcasters and passed off as their own, whether they had been there or not.

This was the normal arrangement with Reuters and APTN content, disguising as it did the large wholesale content that goes into television news. It was impossible to maintain reasonable prices for our work in an industry that was ignorant about the extent of our contribution.

As fewer European and American freelances could make their television journalism support their work, the Rory Peck Trust, having failed to help enlighten the industry about the role of the freelance agencies, opened its award to a wider range of industry video freelances and determined to depend on the goodwill of the broadcast industry for its survival.

In 2003, Frontline News Television stopped seeking new business, but the Frontline Club was born.[1]

Technology

All the tangible advances in independent freelance journalism known to me have been spurred by technological advances in equipment that can be used for news acquisition.

The creation of Magnum Photos was enabled by the introduction of the portable 35 mm photographic camera, shortly before World War II.

Freelance video journalism thrived in the 1990s when independents picked up small-format cameras, sold on the high street, as tools for acquisition. The Hi8 camera, built first by Sony for a consumer market, delivered a very much poorer quality of picture than the much larger Betacam cameras used at the time, but it was enough of an improvement over the Video 8 standard so that if the content was compelling the pictures could be sold.

The internet and computer technology, although not 'acquisition' technology, now provide a platform for an individual to newscast without recourse to traditional news organizations at all. But this technology delivers the same opportunity to everybody, professional journalist or not.

While the internet, mobile telephony and 'new media' have yet to deliver a remunerative return that could fund a family and a London mortgage, they do seem likely to do so in time.

By combining it with some industry sales, I was able to make ends meet on a recent trip to Southern Afghanistan in September 2007. For the first time in my life as a journalist I was able to newscast myself, from the middle of the Afghan plains, taking full editorial control of my own reporting (except, of course, for the 'operational security' considerations determined by my military 'minder').

A sale of some of my film, including to the BBC's flagship news and current affairs programme *Newsnight*, on my return enabled me to make a profit on the trip. I wrote a video blog on fromthefrontline.co.uk and posted the video to YouTube. I used a social network called Twitter to keep the growing community that was following me linked and informed of my movements. I have not configured the website to generate any income but I have started to build my own audience, tuning in to 'Vaughan-cast'.

Freelance Journalism Today

> Network news is getting hit from all sides. Their corporate owners are squeezing them at every opportunity to increase profits by simultaneously skimping on costs, pushing for 'tabloid' stories and dumbing-down what's left. Viewership is declining … The future is clearly with narrow-cast networks, like Fox's right-wingers and Jon Stewart's fake-but-truer-than-the-real-thing news. (Alterman 2004: 12)

Narrow-casting evens the playing field. Freelance journalism is set to increasingly become a vibrant and necessary part of the professional journalism community and promises to complement the traditional industry and share the 'new media' space with it. The clock cannot be turned back.

At the same time the trade has broadened away from Europe and the United States. The wars in Iraq and Afghanistan have pushed media skills into the Middle East, and media non-governmental organizations have been funding the development of these skills internationally.

The freelance journalist of tomorrow will come from any and all countries. There will continue to be many more amateurs than professionals, but whatever freedoms our children, and their children, enjoy will be secured and maintained as much by the freelance journalist as by any body or entity.

But there is an overwhelming imperative to promote professional integrity and fairness in reporting as widely as possible, to prevent all good journalism from sinking beneath the potential for fog and mission-less chatter presented by the blogosphere.

Note

1 The Frontline Club (www.frontlineclub.com) is dedicated to those who have lost their lives covering conflicts around the world and promotes freedom of expression for journalists everywhere.

References

Alterman, E. (2004) Anchors aweigh: The refs are worked. *Nation*, 1 November.

Boehlert, E. (2006) Politics, the media and 9/11. *Nation*, 25 September.

Boyer, R. O. and Morais, H. M. (1955) *Labor's Untold Story*. United Electrical, Radio and Machine Workers of America.

Braxton, G. (2004) She has opinions, will travel: Left-wing radio's Amy Goodman takes her views on the road. *LA Times*, 21 April.

Goodman, A. and Goodman, D. (2005) Un-embed the media. *AlterNet*, posted 8 April, originally published in *Baltimore Sun*, 7 April.

Hightower, J. (2004) Just because they could. *Texas Observer*, 30 July.

Loyn, D. (2006) *Frontline: The True Story of the British Mavericks who Changed the Face of War Reporting*. Penguin.

Magnum Photos (2007) 1950s and now. http://agency.magnumphotos.com/about/1950s.

Project for Excellence in Journalism (2004) *The State of the News Media 2004: An Annual Report on American Journalism*. http://www.stateofthenewsmedia.org/2004.

Whelan, R. and Capa, C. (eds.) (1985) *Robert Capa: Photographs*. Faber and Faber.

Questions for students

1 If freelancers are prepared to take risks to cover stories that news organizations feel are so dangerous that they won't send their own staff journalists, should they be encouraged to do so?

2 What are the advantages and disadvantages of being freelance?

3 Is it morally defensible to refuse to support financially a freelancer before he or she pursues a highly risky story but promise to consider buying their video material if it's newsworthy?

4 Vaughan Smith claims that freelancers can pursue stories that staff journalists won't, as staff journalists have to self-censor because of the commercial or corporate interests of their media owners. Is he right?

5

Letter to a Young Photographer

Gary Knight

Introduction

JOHN OWEN

A little Vietnamese girl, her clothing incinerated by a napalm bomb, screaming in agony and running naked trying to escape the explosions from an air attack mistakenly launched by a South Vietnamese plane on her village. Who will ever forget that picture taken by Associated Press (AP) photographer Nick Udt of Kim Phuc, forever ingrained in our memories as a defining image of the Vietnam War?

'Falling Man', the image that we can never shake from our consciousness when we recall the nightmare of 9/11, the Al Qaeda air attack on the World Trade Centre. AP photographer Richard Drew snapped the picture of a man whose identity would not be known for some time but whose free-falling body, shot in parallel with one of the Twin Towers, haunts us.

On a poorly reproduced poster blu-tacked on the back of my 18-year-old daughter's bedroom door 'The Kiss' – the enduring image of the end of World War II. An American sailor takes an American nurse into his arms, and famed *Life Magazine* photographer Alfred Eisenstaedt caught the moment that will live forever marking Victory Over Japan day.

South Vietnamese forces follow after terrified children, including 9-year-old Kim Phuc, centre, as they run down Route 1 near Trang Bang after an aerial napalm attack on suspected Viet Cong hiding places in June 1972

A man falls from the North tower of New York's World Trade Center in this September 11, 2001, file photo, after terrorists crashed two hijacked airliners and brought down the twin 110-storey towers

PHOTO COURTESY OF ASSOCIATED PRESS/PHOTOGRAPHER RICHARD DREW

Those are just three images that came to mind when writing the introduction to this chapter about photojournalism. In fact, I could close my eyes, as anyone can, and bring to mind countless pictures that recall things dramatic and disturbing, as well as things trivial and joyous.

Photojournalism has always captivated us, in part because photography is something that most of us practise in some form or fashion. Yet professional photographers, especially the men and women who record the conflicts and natural disasters around the world, have a special hold on us, in part because many of the photographers themselves were larger-than-life characters, such as Robert Capa and Tim Page, or, like Horst Faas of AP, a two-time Pulitzer Prize winner, admired for his intelligence and all-round journalism.

Most students of media and photography point to the founding of the Magnum agency in 1947 in Paris as the seminal development in photojournalism. This cooperative, driven by Capa and Henri Cartier-Bresson, established the tradition of independent photographers retaining control over their images, committing themselves to stories that mattered as well as earning them and their clients money. Said Cartier-Bresson: 'We often photograph events that are called news'(Magnum Photos 2007).

Before television provided instant visual imagery, it was highly produced, richly visual magazines such as *Life Magazine* in the United States, *Stern* in Germany and *Paris Match* in France that combined reportage with gripping photojournalism and glossy snapshots of the stars and newsmakers.

But while *Life Magazine* and many other big-circulation magazines would fade away (not *Stern* or *Paris Match*), photojournalists still risked their lives to take pictures that were published in serious major newspapers and newsweekly magazines.

Then two developments changed everything: the internet and new technology. By 2001, photo editors in major newspapers were trying to track as many as 2,000 digital images a day streaming into their computer workstations from all over the world. While photojournalists used to shoot their rolls of film, then develop and transmit their pictures, a process that could take days, digital photojournalists today on assignment in most parts of the world can record and email from their laptops within seconds. Santiago Lyon, director of photography for AP, estimates that a newspaper probably receives more than 6,000 images a day, including 2,000 from AP and another 4,000 from other agencies such as Reuters and Agence France-Press. Not only are today's digital photojournalists working constantly to update their newspaper or agency's websites, which feature up-to-the-second photos from around the world, they are also running greater risks, staying longer than they might have in the past. It is a trend that worries Lyon.

A dilemma that has always confronted photojournalists and their editors is how much reality readers and viewers should be shown. When is a graphic picture necessary to illustrate the reality of a brutal battle or catastrophic natural disaster?

Hot-button digital photo taking reduces the time frame for judgements about what violates any editorial guidelines about taste and

Guardian photographer Sean Smith documents the aftermath of Israeli air-strikes on the Lebanese town of Qana during the conflict between Hezbollah and Israel in 2006
PHOTO COURTESY OF SEAN SMITH

decency. Back home in newspaper offices, editors have to decide whether what goes into the paper or on the website is driven by sensibilities about their readers or commercial fears of alienating advertisers.

What to publish or not to publish is often these days related to images provided not by the professional photojournalists but by amateurs, or what is now classified as 'user-generated content'. Many of us no longer even carry cameras but instead rely on our mobile phones equipped with sophisticated cameras that shoot stills and record video. Amongst the images flooding news operations – in television and newspapers and magazines – are those provided by the public. The most memorable images of the tsunami and the London bombings were those provided by 'citizen journalists' on their cameras and phones.

But trained and talented photojournalists are still essential to professional newsgathering. The enduring photographs are still those taken by photographers with a passion for storytelling and an appetite for adventure and risk taking. Unlike television reporters, who can 'package' stories and leave the impression that they are on location, or print reporters, who can file without being present, photojournalists have to bear witness to take the picture. And Robert Capa's often-repeated adage 'If your picture isn't good enough then you are not close enough' is as true today as when he took his memorable photographs of the Spanish Civil War in the 1930s.

While Capa's Magnum remains an elite photojournalism powerhouse, there is now a rival group also based in Paris. The VII group (it had seven founding members) formed in 2001 days before 9/11 and includes such international star photographers as James Nachtwey and Ron Haviv.

British photojournalist Gary Knight was its driving force and chaired the VII board during its initial three years of operation. Knight began working as a photographer in South East Asia in the late 1980s. But it was the war in Bosnia that solidified his reputation. It was also where Knight began documenting what became recognized as crimes of war, in the shared belief that journalism could contribute to helping hold accountable anyone with responsibility for actions that violated the norms of war and the Geneva conventions.

Later as a contract photographer for *Newsweek Magazine*, Gary Knight took his cameras to Africa to record its many brutal wars but also to keep faith with the VII credo: 'What unites VII's work is a sense that, in the act of communication at the very least, all is not lost; the seeds of hope and resolution inform even the darkest records of inhumanity; reparation is always possible; despair is never absolute' (VII Photo Agency 2006).

But Knight was in deep despair in 2007 after completing an assignment in Darfur with correspondent Rod Nordland for *Newsweek Magazine*. At a time when thousands continued to be displaced from their villages, Knight and Nordland were the only Western journalists covering what other prominent journalists and high-ranking government officials had labelled a genocide.

Yet Gary Knight retains his passion for photojournalism and the power of the photographer to record images that can make a difference in the world.

References

Magnum Photos (2007) History of Magnum. http://agency.magnumphotos.com/about/history.

VII Photo Agency (2006) About VII Photo Agency. http://www.viiphoto.com/photographer.html.

Photojournalism is not for the faint-hearted but I can think of few interesting things that are. I have been reading about its demise for practically all my working life, usually from grumpy, middle-aged men. (You know the type; they tell you how they used to walk 10 miles to school in wooden clogs in horizontal rain!)

Trust your eyes, look around you, and on magazine stalls or on the internet you will see that the truth is somewhat different, for photojournalism is still thriving, and the commitment and maverick nature of the men and women who are the most accomplished photojournalists makes me believe that it will be around for a long time to come.

What these old folks were really announcing was the death of a few tired and irrelevant business structures that sold photographs to the media; the demise of their own jobs; the demise of irrelevant magazines; or they were berating technological advancements in the field of image capture and distribution that they did not understand. I am not sure what any of this has to do with photojournalism. Photojournalism is storytelling with photographs; it is not a technological or commercial endeavour, although an understanding of both areas is essential.

When I look at photographs in the newspapers, magazines or agency archives of the 1960s and 1970s I am not generally inspired. I have been told that these were the golden days of photojournalism, but it's hard to see why. Of course I remember the great work; the iconic images of the Vietnam War, the struggle for freedom in the USA and South Africa, the thoughtful and penetrating work of photographers like Larry Burrows, Don McCullin, Philip Jones Griffiths and others, but the photographic fare delivered daily to your newspapers and websites today is far improved in practically every way over that of yesterday if we remove the filter of nostalgia. The challenge now is that photographs are commonplace and readers are less easily moved by them.

The future is bright for photojournalism, and, at its best, it is still without doubt the purest and noblest of all contemporary forms of journalism.

Objectivity versus Having a Point of View

Objectivity is the rack upon which many a journalist has been stretched and a word that should not be confused with having a point of view.

A journalist without a point of view is neither interesting nor useful and photographers should not shirk from the responsibility of expressing an opinion. Hiding behind the misused creed of objectivity is not courageous, nor is it useful. Without a point of view we are reduced to the role of surveillance cameras. In this, photographers are no different to anyone else in the media. Photojournalism is not illustration: that is why 'journalism' is tacked onto 'photo'.

Photo by Gary Knight, Kosovo, 1999
PHOTO COURTESY OF GARY KNIGHT

Photos by Gary Knight, Zaire, 1997

Amateur Photography in the Media

What differentiates a professional newsgatherer from an amateur one is that a professional should have a universally recognizable credibility by virtue of accountability, experience and track record, and in a perfect world, by adherence to the conventions of good journalism; that is by trying to be principled and honest.

The use of amateur photography in the media is not unreasonable on those occasions when an event of great magnitude occurs without other witness, like the Asian tsunami of 2004 or the underground bombing in London in 2005. But the daily purveying of citizen photography by large media organizations who charge the public to submit images is a marketing gimmick and a means to obtain free content, and should be regarded as nothing more than that. It is not a challenge for you.

Ethics

It really should not have to be said, but it is incumbent upon everyone who seeks to portray himself or herself as a member of the media to be honest, and to demonstrate the integrity that we so desperately want the public to believe we still have.

Photographers do not deserve an exception to this fundamental rule and need to be especially careful. Distorting the truth, manipulating events, manipulating negatives or digital images are commonplace and have been since the early photographers stepped onto the fields of the Crimea with a plate camera more than 150 years ago.

Don't cheat. Don't lie. Try to tell it as you see it. The primary purpose of the photographer is to challenge the audience to think about the issue that is being photographed and to respond to it. You need to inform your audience so that they can act. To fabricate images or to photograph these issues in a way that is only self-serving is gutless and disgraceful and if you do it once, everything you ever do can, and probably will, be called into question.

There are photographers who have taken costumes to war zones for their subjects to wear, pay people to re-enact scenes they missed and scream at soldiers in training to look more scared so that the photos look more convincing, and they have won kudos for doing so. The responsibility for this behaviour lies primarily with the photographers, who should know better, but such individuals are weak characters driven by avarice and ambition, and the editors and the agencies that represent them must shoulder a great deal of the responsibility for encouraging, condoning or turning a blind eye to this behaviour.

Photojournalism is not the place for the vain and ambitious. The poor and downtrodden deserve more than to be used as a palette for the fragile egos of poseurs and dilettantes making pretty pictures for their own deification.

If photojournalism is in a crisis it is not one of money and magazines but one of honour and integrity. Photography, like writing or broadcast journalism, is fairly straightforward. What makes some photojournalists exceptional is not their artistry but their point of view and the conviction and integrity with which they deploy the language of storytelling. Artistry and style are important tools but without storytelling substance they are insufficient.

Explicit Images

My friend and colleague James Nachtwey addressed a seminar in New York recently and said that he would not censor himself any more than he would allow anyone to censor him, and generally, I think that is a wise guiding principle. James was responding to a question I had answered where I said that there were occasions where I would either not take a photograph, or not print it.

I know James would agree that neither of us would want the family of a deceased soldier or civilian during war to learn of the death through one of our photographs, so occasionally such photographs are best held until the relatives have learned of their loss by other means. There have been times when I have been confronted by such despair that I have chosen not to print – for example – close-up images of maggots falling out of the exposed brain of a young child crawling across a hospital floor in the Congo. That particular image was one of many I took that day that could convey the appalling horror and barbarity suffered by civilians at the hands of soldiers. I chose to use others.

It is really just a question of exercising one's best judgement at the time and ensuring that the images one makes available to the public are an accurate and fair representation of the events. You might consider that being a member of the media often gives us privileged access to the most intimate despair and suffering that strangers endure, often through a belief on their part that we can help them. In these cases that privilege brings with it a responsibility; to tell the story as you saw it, to hold people to account, to demand justice and reckoning, but with respect for the people one is photographing. I always ask myself whether what we are about to publish is for my benefit or theirs.

Herds and Instinct

Beware of the herd, trust your own instinct and judgement and do not be afraid to make mistakes by the act of trying. It's better than doing nothing at all.

The company of colleagues is usually a pleasure socially but beware of being seduced by peer pressure when working on a story that attracts many of them. Over the course of your career you may find yourself on a major news story with hundreds or even thousands of other journalists. Some of these events, like natural disasters, are spontaneous. In this case one usually has no option but to make spontaneous decisions with minimal information. They are pretty straightforward and the art is in moving fast, getting to the heart of the matter and being organized sufficiently well to dispatch your work on time. Planned events like Western governments going to war pose different problems, not least of which is the time one spends around colleagues who all have an opinion on the best way to cover the story and the outcome of events. I don't recall any occasion when anyone I listened to ever predicted the outcome successfully, myself included!

One of the most effective tools that governments and militaries employ to keep you away from the sharp end of a story is to convince you that you have no chance of getting there without them. They often promise that, if you cooperate with them, you will get everything you need in due course. Many of your colleagues will be only too happy to comply and, in time-honoured fashion, will try to persuade you of the folly of going it alone, of being a maverick. Photographers are often accused of being foolhardy mavericks, usually by colleagues who are trying to make sure you won't get the story because they are too cautious to try. Take it as a compliment.

It is your responsibility to get to the place where events are unfolding and record them, not to talk to others who were there before you, so I urge you to find your own way, gather your own intelligence and when the event starts, be sure to be at the front and let everyone else worry about catching you up. Whether you carry half a ton of gear or a bag of beans, be nimble of mind. When wars start there is always a small window of opportunity to get to where the story is and if you miss that opportunity you can spend days catching up. In pretty well every case I've been involved in, those who followed the herd failed to get the story.

Waiting in Kuwait for the onset of the 2003 invasion of Iraq, many people, military and media alike, tried to convince me and other photographers to wait for the US military to take us in. Instead we hired four-wheel-drive cars, packed them with fuel and food, covered them in oil and sand and went and hid under trees and in farm houses on the border for days, so that when the barrage started we could cross no man's land behind the first wave of combat troops. About 20 of us made it across, leaving several hundred waiting for days in Kuwait City for the Coalition forces to take them in. They missed the first few days and were left far behind the forward troops, which is where the best story was.

Safety

There are a number of 'hazardous environment courses' now available to the media. Indeed, many news organizations will not hire you unless you have done one. I would always recommend them if you can find someone to help you pay for it, but bear in mind that some stories are dangerous and no amount of training will change that. These courses help lessen the danger by making you more aware, but a significant number of journalists die in wars, and many of them are young. If you cannot deal with the fear, there is no shame in that. Just get out and go home. If you are going to go to war you owe it to the people you are photographing, the people you are working for, your audience and yourself to get the job done properly.

The Boring (but Important) Business of Photography

There is no point in trying to tell a story without an audience, which means that distribution and the relationships you build with agencies, newspapers, magazines, publishers and curators are all going to be crucial to achieving your aims and avoiding the status of an impoverished but well-intentioned super-tourist.

It may be very tempting to be aloof and disdainful of commerce but, unless you are sitting on a trust fund, there is no avoiding the reality that, like any tradesman, you will need to sell your wares. The photojournalism marketplace responds to the laws of supply and demand just like any other and is currently fairly well endowed. I know it is hard to take this on board, but no one owes you any favours and although you may think your photographs are poignant and powerful, you may not find others who will subscribe to that view beyond your immediate family. Don't overestimate yourself and don't underestimate the market.

Gilles Peress[1] once told me that I had to make a choice between being a utility photographer and being an author. I interpreted that as meaning I could either be a jack of all trades, an illustrator available to anyone for anything, or I could concentrate on a small number of issues that I care about and, by virtue of commitment, focus and understanding, earn legitimacy for my work. You should consider whether it is the photography, the lifestyle or the issues that are most important to you and choose your own path. Once you have made that decision you can begin to put together an array of structures and relationships that will help you sell your work and reach the appropriate audience.

By the time you read this, new agencies and publications will have been created and some that I am looking at online from my hotel room will have expired, so I cannot recommend a list. Even if I could, I would not, as what works for me may not work for you. I have found that the best agencies are those with whom you form the best relationships. Whether they are famous or not, large or small, is of little importance. If they understand your work and have a strong relationship with the publications that are appropriate for your work, you are off to a good start. If they have a business plan that makes sense and will pay you on time, they are probably worth considering. The addition of the words 'VII' or 'Magnum' after your name will not change the quality of the work, and it is that quality with which publications generally concern themselves, at least the ones you should aspire to work for.

Freelance photographers are represented by agencies, photographers do not represent agencies. Do not forget this, especially when you negotiate terms with an agent.

Agents are in business to make money, like car salesmen, and you need to make sure that the deal they offer is worthwhile for you. Do not be intimidated by them, and make sure you have them explain how they intend to develop their business and what your role in that will be. A significant part of your financial well-being will be in their hands.

When you approach clients don't show them too much. It's better they ask to see more rather than roll their eyes with boredom halfway through your portfolio. Don't bombard them with emails containing unsolicited photos. It will usually be treated like SPAM. When you show your work make sure it represents where you are going rather than where you have come from. No one is interested in what you have done in the past if it does not represent what you are trying to persuade them to buy from you in the future.

When I first started in this business it was all conducted by a handshake. There was something rather charming about that and it rarely went wrong. These days things are rather different, but rather than rue the past you need to deal with the present, and at some point you will be asked to sign a contract so that an editor can work with you. Most contract negotiations start with a client presenting you with something that works to their benefit but may not work to yours, and this usually comes in the form of copyright and usage rights. I would recommend that you never sign anything that gives away or shares your copyright. Those rights represent your future economic well-being, and low editorial day rates acknowledge that you will be able to exploit your images after the first publication. Don't be afraid to negotiate contracts, and if you can, try to do so through the collective pressure of an agency or an ad-hoc group of photographers who share common interests.

Stories

Some clients, like *Vanity Fair,* will conceive their own stories, but by and large assignments come from ideas photographers conceive by themselves or with writers.

Beyond the Media

Magazines and the media are only part of what is available to you in your quest to change the world. They are not the end game. The media have limitations both in terms of audience reach and in terms of what the media themselves find acceptable or interesting. In general, any given publication will have a point of view that may well diverge from your own, and publications are sometimes afraid of challenging the status quo because of commercial considerations. What they can do is allow you the means to get to the story. What they can rarely do is give you the means to tell it the way you want to. To this end you need to consider publishing your own work, as it is one of the few ways you can tell the story the way you saw it. The easiest and one of the most effective ways of doing this is on the internet, on your own or an agency website.

Publishing a book and producing an exhibition further increases your reach and, if managed well, can bring in money to help you pay for your next project. Both are time consuming and take a lot of planning, in most cases years.

Equipment

You are better off with a few dollars in your pocket and an air ticket in your hand than you are with a bag full of new gear, watching something happen on TV.

Alex Majoli of Magnum, one of the most interesting photographers working today, uses a couple of digital compact cameras that cost less than lunch at a smart restaurant in London. Antoine d'Agata, also of Magnum, has a different happy-snappy hanging around his neck every time I see him. Cameras don't make pictures.

It is worth mentioning that you must have the equipment you need to get the job done. I once walked into a Bosnian enclave called Gorazde during the war in the 1990s with Peter Northall of Associated Press, Andrew Reid of Gamma[2] and a small number of other journalists. It was a memorably nasty experience that involved walking for 16 hours over-night in a blizzard, sometimes under mortar and machine-gun fire across mountains, in a pair of Levis and Timberlands. A number of the Bosnians we were walking with froze to death on the way when they sat down in the snow exhausted, and I only survived because Peter absolutely refused to let me sit down and die. At some point during the journey Andrew decided to put his cameras on a passing donkey because he couldn't use them at night and he couldn't carry them any longer. An uncharacteristic momentary lapse of reason. We all laughed when we arrived and found out the donkey had fallen off the mountain and died, but not as much as we laughed when we realized we had no choice other than to use another donkey to ship our film out of the enclave to make our deadlines.

The moral of the tale – other than beware of donkeys that pass in the night – is two-fold: don't take more than you can carry and go to any means to get your photos out.

Notes

1 Gilles Peress is an award-winning photojournalist and author and a member of Magnum Photos.
2 French agency, founded in 1967.

Questions for students

1 Does journalism need less impartiality and more clearly identified points of view?
2 What distinguishes professional photojournalism from citizen journalism? What are the advantages and disadvantages of both?
3 Gary Knight identifies his red lines for not taking or not printing a photograph. What are yours? Or should there be no red lines, no self-censorship?
4 Is there a crisis or conflict in the world that if photographed might arouse international awareness? If so, discuss why there have been no photographs.
5 Analyse one conflict or crisis around the world which has been influenced by photojournalism.
6 Construct a narrative based on the pictures displayed in this chapter.

6

Diplomacy and Journalism

Bridget Kendall

Introduction

JOHN OWEN

Do journalists 'give peace a chance', to borrow John Lennon's anti-war anthem words? Is mainstream journalism so focused on war and conflict that it invests far fewer resources in reporting on those who advocate non-violent solutions? That's the considered view of one school of journalistic thought advocated by a British journalist-academic named Jake Lynch. His 'reporting the world' approach calls for the appointing of 'peace correspondents' who would have equal weight in their news organizations with the high-profile and usually award-winning 'war correspondents'. Lynch, now a peace journalism trainer at the University of Sydney's School of Peace and Conflict Studies, is researching examples of the media inflaming conflicts.

But many of us who accept Lynch's well-argued critique, replete with case studies, reject his prescribed 'peace journalism'. The idea that journalists should somehow take upon themselves the responsibility to pursue proactively solutions to world crises smacks of the 'civic journalism' that was in vogue for a while in the United States.

Instead of 'peace correspondents', what journalism needs more of is skilful diplomatic reporting that examines what efforts are being made by governments to avoid war in the pursuit of non-violent solutions. Note that I said 'governments', because too often diplomatic journalism is associated with propagating the views of 'your' government without helping viewers and readers understand how a disagreement or potential conflict is seen through the eyes of the other country. Journalists covering their foreign offices or state department are often given or denied access on the basis of how 'friendly' they are in their coverage. There is also an assumption that they will respect the rules of engagement for covering the offices and their activities. When Henry Kissinger was national security advisor to President Nixon and dominating the then secretary of state William Rogers, Kissinger insisted on being identified as a 'senior White House advisor' in briefings and leaks to correspondents. Only the general public was denied knowledge of this open press secret. The same fiction was practised recently during the Blair government in Great Britain. Alastair Campbell, Tony Blair's powerful press advisor, insisted on being identified as a nameless 'senior Downing Street advisor' when spinning skilfully those covering Westminster and the Blair government.

In recent decades, we have witnessed less and less of the Kissinger-era-styled 'shuttle diplomacy' and more of what became known as the 'CNN effect'. This translated into leaders of countries considered unfriendly or hostile to the United States appearing on CNN instead of engaging in any meaningful negotiations with high-ranking American diplomats, envoys or emissaries.

Then Al Jazeera became the dominant broadcasting voice in the Arabic world, and soon it, not CNN, was the satellite channel where leaders needed to appear if they wanted to send a message to other Arab leaders or to the so-called 'Arab Street'.

Today in the instantaneous world of internet communications and global television satellite links, some question the value of traditional diplomacy. One of Britain's leading journalists, Jon Snow, the main presenter for Channel 4's influential nightly news programme, argues that there's been a 'sea change in the whole world order' because of the polarizing effects of the American-led War on Terror and wars in Iraq and Afghanistan. Snow claimed that in a dispute between Iran and Britain that resulted in 15 British sailors being held in custody, it was his *Channel 4 News* interview with a senior Iranian official that helped to free the sailors. Snow's comment was made during a debate held in New York staged by the London-based Frontline Club. Another participant, the *New York Times* correspondent at large, Roger Cohen, rejected the idea that journalists should see themselves as latter-day diplomats.[1]

Central to this debate was the issue of whether journalists should seek out the views of those who are sworn enemies of 'your country', including those who practise terrorism and belong to groups branded as terrorists. Some fellow journalists and many viewers in Britain condemned the BBC and its correspondent David Loyn for airing the views of the Taliban as part of his reporting from one of their strongholds in southern Afghanistan. Loyn took great risks to get to the Taliban at a time when British soldiers were increasingly under attack. There was a similar controversy over a British documentary that probed the views of British Muslims who were linked to the bombings that killed Londoners in July of 2005.

For all of the misgivings about traditional diplomacy and the value of reporting on it on a regular basis, most respected newspapers and broadcasters still consider diplomatic reporting an essential part of their newsgathering operation. At the BBC, Bridget Kendall has been for nearly a decade its leading diplomatic correspondent. She came to that post after extensive reporting in other countries, with her special area of expertise being Russia, where she was posted for five years during the 1980s. As a fluent Russian speaker, she was able to host on two occasions live-interactive phone-in radio programmes (simulcast on the internet) with Russian president Vladimir Putin. She also knows American politics well, having reported out of Washington for five years.

In her chapter, Bridget Kendall reflects on how the post 9/11 world, the 'breaking news' culture of 24-hour news channels, and new technology have changed dramatically the role of the diplomatic correspondent.

Note

1 The 'Talking to the Enemy' debate was held at the Frontline Club's inaugural New York event on 16 April 2007.

There is no getting around the fact that the art of interpreting international diplomacy is often arcane. Negotiations get bogged down in intricate detail. Yet a reporter's job is to understand subtleties and boil them down into an accessible form for an often bewildered audience, all the while conveying myriad points of view that more often than not are never reconciled.

If that sounds boring – do not believe it. Close up you'll find the ways our political leaders deal with each other on the international stage are intriguing and sometimes downright bizarre.

A few years ago I followed the British foreign secretary and the French foreign minister on a joint trip to several African countries. Their jaunty intention was to show the strength of the Franco-British *entente cordiale*. What emerged was just how different French and British diplomacy can be.

As usual British officials were preoccupied with protocol: talking points, ceremonial trimmings, delegation lists and what publicity the trip might generate. French concerns went further.

'We met up with the French to finalize the guest list for the garden party in Kinshasa and it took three hours', complained one British diplomat in the capital of the Democratic Republic of Congo. 'All they wanted to talk about was the menu.'

Does that sound like unfair national stereotyping?

Food is a crucial part of French diplomacy. That was why they isolated Serb and Kosovo Albanian negotiators for three weeks in a French chateau in 1999: in the hope that French haute cuisine and premier cru wines would lull the Balkan antagonists into a peace deal. It was a misplaced hope. The dispute erupted into a full-scale air intervention by NATO – which just shows that a faintly comical diplomatic dance can swiftly metamorphose into a blockbuster tragedy without warning.

Diplomacy is about people, personal passions, national obsessions, misunderstandings and sometimes pure coincidence. It is as much a soap opera as any other aspect of human life. You just need to peel away the bland speeches and polite comments, and get at what lies underneath.

Journalistic Challenges

Think ahead

The first challenge is to find out what is really going on. When faced with 'megaphone diplomacy' – where officials use the media to trumpet positions in public – this is not a problem. But more typically talks are held behind closed doors by diplomats with cards clenched to their chest. They have no interest in spilling the beans and they are supremely busy. You cannot just barge in, or pester them by telephone and email. You must seek out information by other means.

It took me some time to realize that the solution was to think ahead. Before a crucial meeting, governments – whether British or foreign – often arrange media briefings to talk up or play down expectations. If you get in ahead of that, before the topic has become 'hot news', you may well learn more. Officials have more time. Their comments are less guarded. You can ask what they hope to achieve and then measure their response against the final outcome. All too often a summit ends with a nondescript statement. Properly armed, you can gauge whether the end result falls short of or exceeds expectations.

Non-governmental sources, think tanks, charity organizations, human rights groups and other lobby groups are another rich source of information. They may speak more frankly and in less 'air-brushed' terms than government officials. They may tip you off about something which is coming up. They may put you in touch with eyewitnesses to some crucial event or crisis. They may highlight the gap between a government's interests and those of ordinary people. Overall, even if they represent an interest group with an axe to grind, they offer a vital corrective to the rather enclosed, rarefied world of diplomats.

Keep your distance

The second challenge is to beware of taking information at face value, especially if it comes 'off the record', where the source does not want to be quoted directly. An official who offers to speak candidly but without attribution does so for a reason. It might be an honest desire to make sure you understand the intricacies of a negotiation. It may equally be a calculated attempt to bend your ear, or feed you distorted information. Even a person who sincerely believes he or she is telling you the truth can be wrong. Keep reassessing your sources, checking their reliability against reality.

There is another reason to keep your distance. Diplomacy rarely deals with one truth. More often it is a complex, multi-faceted puzzle. Sometimes negotiations end with different parties or countries inadvertently or deliberately misunderstanding each other. So instead of unravelling threads to make it all crystal clear, your report may need to expose a tangled muddle, or a deliberately fudged set of conclusions that could be heading for diplomatic disaster. All to be explained in lucid, clear terms that a general audience can understand – never an easy task!

One good example is the diplomacy in the run-up to the 2003 invasion of Iraq. For weeks in the autumn of 2002 diplomats representing the 15 countries on the Security Council of the United Nations worked their way through every word and comma to thrash out a text that all sides would agree to. Finally in November 2002 the entire Security Council voted in favour of Resolution 1441, which required Saddam Hussein to allow UN weapons inspectors to return to Iraq to search for evidence of illegal weapons programmes.

At the time the unanimous vote was seen as a diplomatic triumph. In fact the text contained significant ambiguities. It included a critical caveat that if Iraq was found to be in breach of UN demands, it could face serious consequences and the Security Council would consult on further measures.

French politicians immediately declared that there was no way this could be used as a trigger for war, since there was a reference to further Security Council consultations. But US officials argued differently. The resolution mentioned 'consultations' but not a second vote, they said, so the threat hanging over Saddam Hussein was indeed of possible military action.

Britain took a middle position: 'Of course we'd prefer to get a second resolution before going to war, but we're hoping it won't come to that', British diplomats briefed us with misplaced optimism.

As months went by and it became clear that the US president was intent on invading Iraq even without UN approval, this difference of opinion proved crucial. France and others insisted that without a second resolution an invasion would lack international legitimacy. President George W. Bush, backed by Tony Blair, disagreed.

These divisions over the Iraq War were to cast a shadow over the whole operation and cause deep damage to the Transatlantic Alliance. Yet with hindsight you could see that they were already deeply embedded in that UN Security Council Resolution No. 1441, at the time hailed as a great example of diplomatic unity.

Predictions

Did I see that diplomatic crisis coming? I confess I did not. But then, nor did most diplomats.

The challenge for any reporter is to 'call' a story right, accurately predicting what might happen.

But when you are dealing with high-wire diplomacy, you rarely get access to enough information to be confident of making hard and fast predictions. Even if your sources are highly placed, they may not be best able to guide you.

'We are not thinking about failure. All our efforts are focused on making sure we get a success', was the abrupt response of one British diplomat when I once asked about the prospects of a certain diplomatic initiative ending in failure.

Experience helps sharpen your awareness that all may not go according to diplomatic plan. But beware: recalling past diplomatic failures may be helpful, but it can also make you unduly sceptical.

Amassing background information which you may never use but which informs your judgement is the real key. Often what you write or say on air may be only the tip of the iceberg of what you know.

And if you cannot confidently be wise before the event, then avoid sticking your neck out and guessing. If the future looks murky and your information is limited, keep to a more modest ambition: coming up with a report which you will not forever after remember as 'the story I got completely wrong'.

Closed societies

International tensions and crises often involve countries with closed societies and little access for journalists. So if you are covering negotiations involving, for instance, the Democratic Republic of North Korea – a notoriously closed regime – how do you balance your report to ensure their side is also reflected?

There is no easy solution. A call to the North Korean embassy is worth a try, but it may get you nowhere. 'We are not talking to the BBC', was the response I got when I first phoned them.

The alternative is to build a picture through a variety of official and indirect sources.

One advantage of a country with a tightly controlled media is that media reports often give a clue to official thinking. Some commentaries may be deliberately placed propaganda pieces, aimed at influencing public opinion. Again, the more background information you have, the easier it is to interpret what at first glance may look like official gobbledegook.

Ask local contacts how they interpret what is being said. Check the views of well-regarded academics, diplomats and aid workers. Match the language against other reports put out on the official media. As I discovered when I was correspondent in Moscow in the final days of the USSR, if you make a habit of scrutinizing official government pronouncements often enough, it is amazing what you can read between the lines! (The BBC's Monitoring Service, based at Caversham near Reading in the UK, which monitors and translates media reports from around the world, is an invaluable resource if you can get hold of it.)

But you need to be sure you understand the parameters of a country's media scene before assuming a journalist is a mouthpiece for a government. It is not unusual for a country to exert tight control over national television, but to allow a lively and wide-ranging debate in newspapers, on the radio or on the internet. (Russia and Iran both spring to mind.)

As in all journalistic endeavours, you need to understand the context in which information is being offered. Only then can you evaluate its usefulness.

Reading the code

Part of the trick of diplomatic reporting lies in learning to read the code. I must confess that no one ever sat down and taught me how to interpret 'diplo speak'. But you soon pick it up. 'A frank exchange of views' means they had a blazing row. A meeting which was supposed to conclude an agreement but instead appointed a committee 'to look into the issue' is a pretty good hint that it ended in stalemate. A joint statement suggests a modicum of agreement, though sometimes it only goes as far as the wording of the press release. The absence of any joint statement or the failure of participants to appear at a joint press conference may mean there was no meeting of minds at all. But beware: if a meeting of several foreign ministers breaks up and they all depart in haste without saying a word, it does not necessarily signal disaster. Sometimes these are just busy officials with planes to catch who are sufficiently relaxed in each other's company to leave it to the host country to speak on their behalf.

Sometimes it is the venue or tone of voice used that gives you the clue to the real mood of a meeting. An awkward press conference where one speaker shows irritation or interrupts another speaks volumes. And watch to see how closely they – or their officials in the front row – monitor each other's words.

Sometimes a journalist's blunt question at a televised press conference plays an important role – by forcing an answer to a question never asked in the all too short private meeting that has just ended; or by revealing whether someone is prepared to repeat in public a pledge made in private. Once a promise has been made publicly on camera, it is much harder to break it.

The code can involve gestures as well as words. I covered the Reykjavik summit in 1986 which brought together the Soviet leader Mikhail Gorbachev and the American president Ronald Reagan. This was a rare encounter between a US and Soviet leader who between them controlled most of the world's nuclear arsenal, at a time when Cold War tensions were still strained. Though the agenda of their talks had not been made public, it was clear to all that the consequences could be momentous. As the talks dragged on excitement grew. Journalists and officials, both Western and Soviet, gathered in a big hall to await results. Big screens displayed the live camera shot of the doorway from which the two leaders were due to emerge.

Soviet leader Mikhail Gorbachev and President Ronald Reagan in Reykjavik, Iceland, October 1986

PHOTO COURTESY OF ASSOCIATED PRESS

I stood next to the Soviet Foreign Ministry spokesman, Gennady Gerasimov. He too was excited. 'If they come out and shake hands, then there is a deal', he told me in an undertone.

In the event the two leaders came out, waved at the cameras and left. Thanks to Mr Gerasimov, I immediately knew the lack of handshake meant that there had probably been no agreement.

Though quite what had been at stake took longer to emerge. It turned out the deal the Russian leader had been suggesting was to rid the world of nuclear weapons altogether – but only if President Reagan would scrap his Star Wars plan, which he refused to do.

Attributing sources

Like much political reporting, diplomacy is often about dealing with 'off the record' sources. Public comments by named officials are becoming more common. These days British ambassadors regularly give 'on the record' interviews. But many government employees prefer not to be quoted directly. This does not mean they will not talk to you. But you have to agree a code in order to use the information they give you.

The same goes for other sources – politicians for example – who may often be willing to be quoted in full, but may give you more interesting information if you disguise their identity.

If the rules are not spelt out ahead of time, then strictly speaking their comments are 'on the record'. But if you intend to use them as a source in the future, you may think twice before going public with their name and position without explicit permission. In these circumstances it may be better to agree the ground rules beforehand.

The codes for referring to sources differ slightly from country to country. So be sure you know what they are. If an American official tells you his or her briefing is on 'deep background' and you are not sure what that means, ask for an explanation. Mostly it is a question of common sense.

In London if you refer to a 'senior Foreign Office official', it is clear the source is a senior official or politician in the Foreign Office, so it may not be very difficult to work out who you have been talking to. Sometimes that may not worry your source. But sometimes they may prefer to keep their identity more opaque and ask you to refer to 'Foreign Office sources' or 'British officials'. When dealing with multilateral negotiations involving several countries (at the United Nations for example), a British diplomat may ask you to refer to 'European diplomats' to hide which country the information is coming from.

Some BBC reporters use the term 'I understand' as a code to disguise information from a reliable source who does not want to be traced. It is a useful convention, but best used only when it is unavoidable. Most of the audience will not have a clue what 'I understand' is code for. Far better, if you can manage it, is to come up with direct quotes from named sources to back up your information.

On occasion officials will say that their information or analysis is not for direct quotation, that it is just 'stuff you know', to be used without any attribution. There are various ways of dealing with this. In the informal context of a live radio or television interview, for example, you could dress it up with 'I wouldn't be surprised if …' or 'You could also argue that …'. But the critical judgement that you as reporter need to make is: if your source will not be quoted, how far can their information be trusted?

The challenge of spin

'Government spin' has become a notorious term, synonymous for many with the practice of using distortions, omissions or even blatant lies to mislead journalists and through them the public. The hostile reaction to this sort of systematic manipulation is hardly surprising. Once someone realizes they are being deliberately deceived, the bond of trust disappears and is difficult to replace. So for those who practise it – and for those journalists who fall prey to it – spin is a dangerous game.

To some degree, it is also probably inevitable. When an official or any other source goes out of their way to brief you, offering information and explanations, of course they want you to put extra emphasis on their point of view. Your job as a journalist is to make sure you never forget they have an agenda.

On the diplomatic beat, spin may amount to an attempt to distract: a phone call from a press officer, for example, who tries to shift your attention towards a marginal event and away from something else – perhaps a new report that contains embarrassing statistics, perhaps a scandal which they know (but which you do not) is about to break. So a good rule of thumb is to ask yourself what this person's motivation may be: why are they so keen to give you this steer?

The danger is that you become cynical. Once or twice I have discarded information on the grounds it is probably spin and therefore worthless, only to regret the fact when it turned out the tip-off was about an event that was far more interesting than I had expected.

Sometimes blatant spin can be useful. Getting a government's message straight is important. An official who doggedly feeds you the party line without seeking to disguise it can be quite helpful. He will prove less misleading than the more sophisticated diplomat whose spin is harder to detect.

One type of 'spin' is the early leaking of bad news to weaken the shock of a later announcement, and to gauge – through journalists' reaction – the likely impact on the public at large.

In February 1999 negotiations in the French town of Rambouillet between Serb and Kosovo Albanian leaders were on the point of collapse. I well remember standing in a cobbled car park as two British officials quietly slipped out of a side door of the chateau and headed towards me. Their message was that the talks had got nowhere, but they would try again in a couple of weeks' time. I remember saying: 'This is disastrous. If you let both sides leave now, they will never reach an agreement.' They did not disagree. Less than a month later the failure of diplomacy paved the way for a NATO bombing campaign – unsanctioned by the United Nations – which lasted some 70 days. I later concluded the diplomats' main purpose in coming out to talk to us – and leak the outcome – was to test the waters ahead of a planned press conference by seeing what our reaction was.

Another sort of briefing which can prove tricky is when officials insist that what happened in public is markedly different from what went on in private. But how do you know who is telling the truth?

Ahead of the Iraq War, for example, President Putin made his reservations about using force against Saddam Hussein abundantly clear. In the autumn of 2002 Tony Blair paid a visit to Moscow to try to sweet-talk Mr Putin into modifying his opposition. But at a joint press conference at the Russian president's country villa, surrounded by hunting trophies dating back to the era of the former Soviet leader Leonid Brezhnev, President Putin refused to budge. He dismissed British intelligence reports on Iraq's weapons of mass destruction as 'propaganda', and looking pointedly at Mr Blair declared that Russia was not a 'bazaar' where allegiance could be bought or sold. We journalists listened in amazement. Relations between Mr Putin and Mr Blair had been good up to that point. But, it seemed, no longer.

Afterwards a rather anxious Downing Street official came running after me to say that behind the scenes Mr Putin had been much more affable than in public. 'His belligerence was just for the Russian press', he said. 'In fact we are very pleased with the meeting. They got on well.'

So was the Downing Street official spinning me a line, or was President Putin playing a double game with Mr Blair?

Certainly later President Putin joined France in opposing the Iraq invasion and has continued to criticize it ever since. In retrospect it was his public comments at that 2002 meeting which were a better guide to where Russian diplomacy on Iraq (and towards the UK) was heading.

Wars and diplomacy

Diplomatic correspondents, you would think, deal with peace, not war. But the threat of force often backs up diplomacy. Sometimes diplomacy is even seen as a pretext designed to lay the groundwork for the use of force. And once a conflict is under way, relations between journalists and government often come under considerable strain. How you handle the information that comes your way can raise some stark issues.

Over the past 10 to 15 years the role of the media in what is known as 'the battle for hearts and minds' has become more crucial. Recent conflicts – in Iraq, Lebanon and Afghanistan – have shown that superior airpower where bombs do not discriminate between military targets and civilian victims means the side using air-strikes risks losing public support by its actions.

These days it is not enough to crush your opponent with military power. You need to win the argument. And in an era of continuous and global news, where television footage of battles can be broadcast live as they happen directly into people's living rooms, cafés, computers and mobile phones the world over, how you report on what is happening on the ground becomes a pivotal element of the so-called 'information war'.

The failure to find weapons of mass destruction in Iraq and the use of intelligence to help make the case for war were hugely controversial. Since then the erosion of public trust means any heavy-handed 'spin' by government officials risks backfiring immediately.

It was a very different mood in 1999 during the NATO campaign against Yugoslavia over Kosovo. The British government was anxious to make its case for what it saw as a humanitarian intervention on behalf of Kosovo Albanians, hundreds of thousands of whom were fleeing their homes to seek refuge elsewhere. The government was quite open about its desire to use the media as a tool to back up its military campaign.

I very rarely felt that I was being misled deliberately. But on one or two occasions I did wonder.

I will never forget one afternoon when I received an unsolicited call from a senior British official. He claimed that intelligence information had just come across his desk which suggested a recent attack on a refugee convoy of Albanians was probably the work of the Serb army. I asked how he could be sure the attack was not the result of a mistake by NATO pilots, since an investigation at NATO headquarters was already under way. He replied that the intelligence looked good, but hastily added that I could not quote him and that there was to be a Pentagon briefing by Americans in a few hours' time.

I asked if he expected the Pentagon to confirm what he had told me. He prevaricated. So I told him I could not use such controversial and unsubstantiated material and would wait for official confirmation – with good reason, as it turned out.

Within days NATO apologized for what they said had been a terrible and unintended mistake.

Perhaps the official had been carried away by his own conviction that this was a 'just war' and he wanted to persuade people of that. Perhaps he was cynically trying to mislead me. In either event it did not matter, as I did not use the information. It taught me that it is wise to be meticulous about attributing sources where possible, and if not, think twice about using the material.

Withholding information

There can be moments when withholding information seems the right thing to do. But this can raise difficult dilemmas.

No one wants to cause distress to family members by broadcasting the name of someone who has just been killed or injured before relatives have been contacted.

In an era of raised security threats, government officials may well ask you to withhold information – for example by not publicizing the foreign travel plans of government ministers ahead of time.

But there are occasions when it suits the government to use the security argument for political purposes. Saying nothing about a senior politician's trip to Afghanistan is fair enough. But what about a speech nearer home where the concern might be that protestors could throw a tomato? Careful judgement is needed.

Hostage videos released by insurgents to global news networks pose another problem. When videos of British hostages began to appear from Iraq, it prompted an intense debate among UK television broadcasters. How far should these videos be used and shown on news programmes?

Some argued that this was a legitimate news story that needed illustration, and to ignore the videos might be to deny those being held the publicity needed to keep up pressure on governments to work for their freedom. Others argued that seeing hostages pleading for their lives could be distressing and possibly humiliating for victims and their families. And the worry persisted that by airing the video material, broadcasters might be doing the insurgents' work for them, promoting their cause and reinforcing their message of terror.

At the BBC the decision was taken to use the minimum, sometimes using only stills pictures while the story had news value, but trying not to repeat the material gratuitously. When the practice of issuing hostage videos began to subside, that seemed a good call.

It also raised the question of what material one should use in other contexts.

How far, for example, should we show pictures of other prisoners of war or – in the case of Guantanamo Bay – 'non-lethal enemy combatants', as the US described them?

Where do you draw the line between your duty to inform the public, and your responsibility not to inflame a situation?

Many years previously I faced this particular dilemma in another context. I was based in Moscow for the BBC, and had travelled to Chechnya on a short trip to meet its separatist leader, a former Soviet bomber pilot called Djokhar Dudayev.

The Soviet Union had just collapsed. Chechnya had been one half of a small autonomous republic inside the Russian Federation. But General Dudayev wanted to gain the same independence from Russia for his people that had just been achieved over the border in Azerbaijan and Georgia. The place was chaotic and tense, but there was little hint of the Islamist agenda that was to develop in Chechnya later. And though Russia was to fight two wars against Chechen rebels during the next 10 years, there was not yet much violence.

Late one night General Dudayev summoned me to his palace. He wanted to give the BBC an interview. During the long, rambling discourse that followed, he declared that if Russia refused to let Chechnya break away, he would hijack planes and use them to bomb Russia's nuclear power stations.

I was not sure he was serious. He was something of a showman, who sported a waxed black moustache and black fedora hat and was given to flamboyant gestures. At the time, I decided there was a chance this incendiary statement might be used as a pretext by one side or the other, and I did not think I should allow my interview to be turned into a mouthpiece for making threats of this nature. So I edited it out.

Some 15 years later, I wonder if I did the right thing. Nowadays we watch and listen to audio- and videotapes containing terrorist threats from Al Qaeda leaders, and most people consider it is important to be informed about them. Was I too cautious in 1991? Or have times changed and we are now all a bit more immune to the troubling notion of terrorist threats and attacks, tragically such a dominant issue in the first decade of the twenty-first century?

Avoiding bias

Can you be neutral when reporting on international issues? Or will your report always be coloured by your own interests and experiences, nationality and place of origin? I think inevitably it will.

On occasion I would expect my report to sound different depending on where I was. It is a question of how you frame it. You can make judgements and 'call' stories in different ways, depending on how close you are to the action or – in the case of diplomacy – participants in negotiations. In Moscow, your report might well reflect the inside nuances of Russian government thinking. In Washington, your views probably will be coloured by what you have heard from American officials.

As long as you are aware of this and take other points of view into account, and signal to the audience that they should recognize this is a 'view from', I do not see anything wrong with it. What is important is to retain your ability to keep some objectivity from the story, and try to put your own personal preferences and interests to one side.

This does not mean you need to sound bland. Indeed some events (mass murder and other atrocities, blatant lies) require a strong response. But my view of my own style of journalism is that if you let yourself get too angry or emotionally involved, then you risk undermining the impact of what you are saying.

Technological challenges

One aspect of journalism has changed dramatically since the early 1990s, when I first became a foreign correspondent: the technology.

In many ways it has made a journalist's life considerably easier.

On that same trip to Chechnya in late 1991, I was only able to file radio reports to London by a convoluted route that required considerable technical ingenuity. It involved me unscrewing my hotel phone, attaching leads and clips to my tape recorder, then getting the hotel operator to patch me through to a kindly Chechen post office assistant who stayed up till midnight to help me book a late call through to the BBC Bureau in Moscow (no direct dial from Chechnya in those days), where a producer linked me via another phone line to a call he had booked to the newsroom in London.

Nowadays a journalist would flip open a satellite dish or mobile phone or laptop computer and get through to the London newsroom within seconds from anywhere in the world, no matter how remote the location. It removes much anxiety and uncertainty from the business of reporting from abroad. It means you can also access information globally. At a tap of a button you can check facts or updates to put your own material into context.

But the upgrade in technology also raises a host of new issues.

24-hour news

The pressure of '24-hour news' requires a journalist to make swift judgements. Sometimes you may need to report live on an event that is still unfolding. How can you assess the importance of a press conference given by the US president if you have only heard half of it?

It is not just the broadcast media that face these pressures. Newspaper journalists are not immune either. Any 24-hour online newsroom needs constant updates. Under these circumstances it is hard to think a subject through, to ensure balance and accuracy.

As global communications become ever swifter and more mobile, this challenge will only get greater. The key, as ever, is preparation, both journalistic and logistical.

New sources of journalism

How will traditional journalists fare in a world where they must now compete with blogs and so-called 'citizen journalism'? The internet has opened up a plethora of new opportunities for people to express their views and interact with each other.

For traditional journalists – diplomatic reporters included – it is both an opportunity and a challenge.

It is already creating a more questioning, challenging environment. Public scepticism of officials has increased. So has suspicion of journalists who rely on officials as an information resource.

On the other hand 'spin' and traditional propaganda are being rethought. When emails home from soldiers describing conditions on the ground can be circulated round the globe electronically, the pressure mounts on governments and military commanders to avoid exaggeration or concealment, since any manipulation of facts is likely to be exposed all too easily.

All electronic information, especially if unsolicited, needs to be treated with caution. But the internet also keeps us journalists on our toes. Gone are the days when you could report on a far-away country and risk a rash judgement, secure in the complacent knowledge no one there was likely to read or hear it. Now within minutes you may receive an email holding you to account for your words and opinions. One misjudgement or error has the potential to escalate overnight into a cause célèbre. All local journalism is now global, instantly available internationally.

Conspiracy or 'cock-up'

The new world of electronic journalism also, however, fuels misconceptions, inaccuracies and conspiracy theories. All too often there is an assumption that any political or diplomatic turn of event must have been planned, the result of a sophisticated calculation that someone in power has secretly plotted.

I too have been guilty of suspecting conspiracies where actually there probably was none. Observe diplomats and politicians for a while and you soon realize they are fallible, prone to the same mistakes and guesswork as the rest of us.

Never rule out the 'cock-up' factor in international relations. It is always quite possible that some piece of diplomacy fails or succeeds by luck or for some trivial and banal reason: a key politician refuses to play ball because he or she is jet-lagged or badly briefed or has the flu. Conversely two international statesmen may suddenly unlock their disagreement by discovering a shared passion for fishing.

Why Diplomatic Reporting will Endure

Diplomatic reporting will, I am sure, endure. Specialist journalism which relies on face-to-face contact and the constant checking of information from reliable sources will always be needed alongside the multiplying open sources of electronic information.

The challenge is to come up with original analysis that not only gets beneath the surface of events, but correctly identifies where the world is heading.

Trying to keep up with global developments day by day is daunting. I often joke that my job is like constantly revising for an examination which I know is coming, but have not been told what the subject is. As one of my former colleagues advised me when I started this job, 'You'll feel like a butterfly, going from flower to flower, but rarely staying long enough to become properly immersed in the subject.'

In return, though, you get the chance to develop a global overview – highly relevant in an era where so much is interconnected. You have opportunities to probe sources and weigh information which many others do not get access to.

The key is to prepare adequately by making time to do research and cultivate contacts. Read as much as you can. Take every opportunity to travel and immerse yourself in a particular situation or country. Historical and geographical context is invaluable. Cast your net widely. No place is too small or subject too esoteric for a crisis of mega-proportions that may suddenly hit the headlines. It is a subject that never palls, a job that is always reinventing itself.

Questions for students

1   What are the dangers of relying too heavily on official sources? Cite examples from recent coverage, including the run-up to the war on Iraq.
2   Do ordinary consumers of news understand clearly enough how information exchanged between sources and reporters is 'coded'? Is it important that they know what it means when something said is 'off the record' or 'for deep background only'? How does this affect the understanding of the story and its sourcing?
3   Do you agree or disagree with Bridget Kendall that it is not possible to be 'neutral' when reporting on international issues because your views will always be 'coloured by your own interests and experiences, nationality and place of origin'?
4   Is the Jake Lynch argument right or wrong: do we need proactive 'peace reporting' to counter the influence of 'war reporting'?

7

Non-Stop Deadlines: 24-Hour News

Nick Pollard

Introduction

JOHN OWEN

Back in July 1989, the year the Berlin Wall came down, we at CBC TV News launched NEWSWORLD, the world's third all-news and information channel. Five months earlier, Britain's Sky News, Rupert Murdoch's answer to Ted Turner's CNN, went on the air with the slogan 'We're There When You Need Us!' Murdoch described the launch of Sky as the dawn of a new age of freedom for the viewer.

But Turner's CNN was the world's leading all-news channel by a long shot. It had been in existence since 1980 and it had transformed television news and global communication. The world's leaders used it to short-circuit diplomacy. Senior officials found out more from CNN than they did through traditional diplomatic channels. That point was made most tellingly by journalist Warren Strobel recounting how the then US ambassador to the United Nations, Madeleine Albright, reacted to the bloody bombing in the Sarajevo marketplace during the Bosnian conflict in 1994: 'I did what everyone else would do', she said. 'I turned on CNN. For the rest of the day, I sat in my living room, watching television, telephone in hand.'

There was what many called a 'CNN effect' to describe its power and influence to pressure government leaders, especially American presidents, to react to world events as shown in 'breaking news' coverage on CNN. David Halberstam tells the story of President Bill Clinton (again in 1994) goaded by CNN's chief correspondent Christiane Amanpour in a live 'town hall' meeting being aired around the world on CNN. Amanpour, highly charged and emotional from her reporting of the Bosnian war, standing in Sarajevo where she had witnessed so much suffering, pressed Clinton on why his administration hadn't yet formulated a policy on Bosnia and accused him of 'flip-flops'. Clinton was described as livid about his treatment and furious that his inaction had been so exposed (Halberstam 2002: 283).

For all of CNN's dominance and the obvious imperative to go to 24/7 all-news television, there was no global stampede to compete. The costs were prohibitive. Satellite transmission was hugely expensive, as was the technology inside the newsrooms and outside for global newsgathering, not to mention the added expense of hiring staff to work around the clock, especially in news organizations governed by collective bargaining agreements with trade unions. Moreover, the audiences for all-news channels, broadcast on cable or by satellite, remained small and spiked only when there were huge breaking stories. The mainline channels and stations argued that they still had the power to capture big audiences by suspending normal programming in times of crises and providing rolling news coverage produced by their own news teams. But breaking into lucrative high revenue commercial programming was difficult to do. And many viewers objected to their favourite soap operas or sitcoms interrupted by live news coverage. (Yet all-news channels themselves weren't free from the tyranny of regular programming. Then and now, 24-hour news channels worry about interrupting regularly scheduled documentaries or Larry King-styled call-in programmes to provide rolling news coverage of what are often less than dramatic news stories.)

Critics of all-news channels, and there are many of them, question just how much of the 24 hours a day at news channels' disposal is actually used to cover a range of stories beyond what you get in any regularly scheduled news bulletin. Those who have studied this issue – and what appears to be the most systematic analysis is the American

Pew Foundation's annual review of the American media – have found the claims of ' all news, all the time' to be bogus. The Pew studies have found that two-thirds of the stories on American all-news channels – CNN, MSNBC and Fox – are basically recycled versions of the same stories, and only 10 per cent are 'meaningfully updated'. The Pew analysis from 2005 (Project for Excellence in Journalism 2005) con-cludes: 'What does that mean? With hours of air time and numerous correspondents, resources are devoted much less to gathering new information, or going deeper with background reporting, than to being live and appearing to be on top of three or four big stories of the day.' (Sky News in its early days did develop a reputation for updating its stories often but the main motive was not to update the story but to cor-rect it – so much so that its critics used to lampoon Sky as 'Sky News: Not Wrong For Long'.)

British historian and writer Timothy Garton Ash, a self-proclaimed TV news junkie, in a 2005 interview, made the same point as the Pew study:

> It is extraordinary that in a multi-media, multi-channel world we can somehow only have one event at a time. [During Hurricane Katrina], there was nothing else on CNN and Fox, 24 hours a day. You could have had three revolutions going on in the world and they never would have made it [into the running order].

For Jeremy Paxman, the star presenter of BBC's flagship nightly cur-rent affairs programme *Newsnight*, the major failing of 24-hour news channels is that there is too much frenzy and too little understanding: 'What's happened is that we have a dynamic in news now that is less about uncovering things than it is about covering them. It doesn't matter whether it's a war in Lebanon or floods in Doncaster, it doesn't really exist until there's a reporter there in flak jacket or wellingtons, going live' (Paxman 2007).

No discussion of the history of 24-hour news channels would be complete without mentioning the truly revolutionary impact of Al Jazeera, the first non-English-language satellite channel to become a major international news player and a force in the political world. If there was a CNN effect in the 1980s and early 1990s, after 1996 when Al Jazeera (meaning 'the Peninsula' in English) began broadcasting from its world headquarters in the tiny Gulf state of Qatar, there was an Al Jazeera effect. You didn't have to be an Arab-language speaker to grasp why it was so profoundly significant that for the first time an estimated 250 million Arabs had their own channel and voice.

But rather than patterning itself after the BBC, where most of its journalists were trained and early on worked for the short-lived BBC Arabic channel, or CNN, Al Jazeera copied Fox News and its programmes built around outspoken, highly partisan hosts such as Bill O'Reilly. Its most highly rated programmes became *Islamic Law and Life* and *Opposite Directions* (that programme a variation of CNN's *Crossfire*, the often-contrived clash of views). It also gave the Arab world something it had never had before: the opportunity for anyone to express himself or herself on a call-in programme.

But Al Jazeera gained its greatest notoriety for being the channel of choice for Osama bin Laden. When bin Laden or, in more recent years, his deputy, Ayman al-Zawahiri, released their videos, it was Al Jazeera that would first air them and then make them available to other channels to decide whether they too would show them.

In the Arab world, Al Jazeera was gaining popularity for its fearless reporting on corrupt practices. In many countries, Al Jazeera was forced off the air or shut down temporarily by governments unhappy about its reporting. But after 9/11 and the war in Iraq, Al Jazeera became Washington's least favourite broadcaster. Its Kabul bureau was destroyed by an American missile in an attack that has yet to be fully investigated or officially explained to Qatar. Nor has the Pentagon ever satisfied Al Jazeera with its explanation of how on 8 April 2003, the US Air Force fired a missile that wiped out the channel's Baghdad offices and killed its correspondent Tariq Ayoub, who was on the roof filing live reports.

Just as CNN had to take on big network challenges internationally from Sky News and BBC World (created in 1991) and then found itself knocked out of first place in cable news ratings by Fox News, so did Al Jazeera find itself with some substantial competition. The main challenger became the Dubai-based Al Arabiya, backed financially by the Saudis, whose ruling family detested the emir of Qatar's sanctioning of a channel that was considered politically unfriendly. Al Arabiya positioned itself as a more balanced and impartial channel than Al Jazeera.

After a few real attempts at English-language channels – few because of the costs involved – there has been in recent years a veritable explosion of new domestic 24-hour news channels along with higher-profile international ones. In India, there are an estimated 30 channels broadcasting in a blizzard of languages, including English, throughout that vast country.

No longer were the costs of technology prohibitive. One of the most travelled media consultants advising countries on how to launch their channels is a former CNN executive, Ken Tiven. He advises prospective 24-hour-channel owners on how to avoid paying for extravagant technology that isn't required to power their channels. He told the *New York Times*, 'Today if you have a Mac laptop, just about everything you want to do is in that laptop. You feed your video into the computer. You edit your video and you output it back to a videotape or a network server' (Carvajal 2006).

But money really hasn't been an issue for governments that have decided that bankrolling a 24-hour channel is no different from opening an embassy or trade office. They also opted for English-language channels that could compete in the marketplace with the established players, or at least offer an alternative to what many argued was an American- or British-biased view of their own countries. From 2005 to 2006, Russia created its Russia Today channel, France launched its France 24, and in Venezuela, President Hugo Chavez spearheaded a new pan-Latin American channel, Telesur, with the governments of Uruguay, Cuba and Argentina. Its new director proclaimed, 'Today we are beginning to see ourselves with our own eyes' (Aharonian 2005).

The most anticipated of all, and far and away the most ambitious and costly (delayed in large part because of the complex and expensive requirements of launching in high definition), was Al Jazeera International. But for all of its journalistic firepower and high-profile stars recruited from major networks in Britain and the United States (David Frost, the celebrated talk-show host in Britain and the US, was given his own programme), Al Jazeera has been unsuccessful in finding a cable distributor in the United States.

Technology once again may come to the rescue of channels like Al Jazeera that may be frozen out of the highly political cable channel universe. It is now available online, like so many other channels, the beneficiaries of the broadband revolution. Once broadband is successfully integrated into our television habits and easily accessible through the TV as well as our computers, so the argument goes, channels such as Al Jazeera International, France 24 and Russia Today will find new and more internationally minded audiences that want an alternative viewpoint on the world.

The next two chapters are devoted to the history and operation of all-news channels. First, British journalist Nick Pollard, who was instrumental in making Sky News one of the world's most emulated all-news channels, explains the history of Sky and examines the challenges facing 24-hour news then and now.

In the following chapter, Tony Burman, who recently stepped down as CBC's editor-in-chief, makes the case for global perspectives on international news. Burman was at the helm of CBC News from 2000 to 2007 and held every senior position during his 35 years with Canada's public service broadcaster.

When I asked whether, in a world of 24-hour news channels, citizens are exposed to a reality that is closer than ever to the truth, Timothy Garton Ash said 'There is no question that citizens of the developed world today are much better informed about what is going on in the rest of the world than they have ever been in human history. And I see a whole generation of deeply engaged citizens, bloggers, journalists, and activists who live on this extraordinary information feed.'

References

Aharonian, A. (2005) Quoted in 'A Latin Al-Jazeera?' *Newsweek*, 4 July.

Carvajal, D. (2006) All-news channels abroad look to their future in English. New York Times nytimes.com, http://www.nytimes.com/2006/01/11/arts/television/11engl.html?_r=1&pagewanted=print&oref=slogin.

Garton Ash, T. (2005) Interviewed at the 2005 NewsXchange conference '24-Hour News: Rolling News and Big Events'. http://www.newsxchange.org/newsx2005/rolling_news_01_05.html.

Halberstam, D. (2002) *War in a Time of Peace: Bush, Clinton and the Generals*. Scribner.

Paxman, J (2007) MacTaggart Lecture. Telegraph.co.uk, http://www.telegraph.co.uk/news/main.jhtml?xml=/news/2007/08/25/npaxspeech125.xml&page=3.

Project for Excellence in Journalism (2005) *The State of the News Media: An Annual Report on American Journalism*. http://www.stateofthemedia.org/2005/narrative_cabletv_contentanalysis.asp?cat=2&media=5.

It's hard to believe now but there used to be a time when we didn't have 24-hour rolling news. And hard for some of us who worked in those days to imagine what we did all day!

But it's true. There really was an era before CNN, before Sky News, News 24, Al Jazeera and Fox News and, of course, way before today's tidal wave of news online, video on demand, headlines sent to your mobile phone, extra channels streamed to your set-top box and impossible-to-escape news on screens at train stations and in the back of taxis.

Back in those good old days, in the dark ages, broadcasters and viewers knew their place. It was simple. The viewers waited until the broadcasters were ready to tell them something and then they watched in large numbers. There were fixed times for news. The viewers (we didn't regard them as 'customers' in those days) knew exactly when to switch on – half an hour or so at lunchtime, 15 or 20 minutes while you were having your tea, and then a solid half-hour of the day's news in the evening. If news happened in between those times, well, you just had to wait until the next bulletin came along to hear about it.

Ah, those were the days – a golden age when audiences were huge, reporting was always mould-breaking and budgets were something you worried about once a year.

And yes, it did seem a bit like that. Viewing figures for the commercial network ITN's flagship news programme *News at Ten*, when I joined from the BBC in 1980, were gigantic by modern-day standards. On the nights when we followed blockbuster shows we might inherit an audience of more than 15 million, and hang on to a good proportion of them through to our famous nightly '… and finally …' story.

Naturally we liked to have our cake and eat it – when viewing figures for *News at Ten* soared we patted ourselves on the back and took the credit. Whenever they fell we blamed a poor inheritance from whatever show ITV had screened before us.

And there was some terrific journalism too. My recollection is that the BBC newsroom, despite having some top-class staff, was a rather sleepier place than ITN for most of the eighties. *News at Ten* ruled the roost and was regarded as the country's top news show.

There were outstanding correspondents too, on both ITN and the BBC.

Both sides seemed to have money to burn. No one held back on coverage of the big stories of the day – the Iranian Embassy siege, the Falklands, Lockerbie, Zeebrugge, Piper Alpha, war in Lebanon, the Brighton Bombing, the year-long miners' strike over pit closures. We spent what it took and the network made up any shortfall at the end of the year with (it seemed to us non-managers at the time) hardly a grumble.

And then there was the lifestyle. Just as it may be hard for young journalists today to comprehend a world without continuous news, it seems incredible that in those days the natural order of things was that work, for most of us, was something to be fitted in around the day's lunching and drinking.

The very idea that lunch might consist of a sandwich eaten at one's desk so as not to break the flow of a busy day would have been regarded as a vaguely unnatural practice. Rather, it was a full three courses at a good restaurant.

The closing words of the 5.45 p.m. news (a brisk 12-and-a-half-minute canter through the events of the day with no story ever longer than a minute and a quarter) were always drowned out by the crashing of chairs and thunder of footsteps as the newsroom emptied in the general direction of the local hostelry.

It was an accepted part of ITN 'custom and practice' that you returned at least 20 seconds before the 7 p.m. final briefing meeting for *News at Ten*, a meeting that was believed to exist solely to force people to come back from the pub.

Now here's the odd thing. It never occurred to any of us that we weren't working both very hard and very effectively. For one thing, exactly the same culture, to a greater or lesser degree, was followed in virtually every other newsroom, whether broadcast or print, in the UK. For another, our programmes were actually very good and recognized as such.

One reason why the quality of *News at Ten* seemed pretty high was that we had all day to prepare. We genuinely did put a lot of effort into coming up with the right approach to stories. Themes and scripts got mulled over pretty carefully (though we never went as far as the American practice of 'script approval', where every correspondent had to submit their words, even for a piece to camera, for scrutiny by the programme editor).

There was also very little 'liveness'. The modern custom of following virtually every story with a live update from a reporter on the scene hadn't reared its head. And there were at least two pretty strong reasons why it couldn't or wouldn't have happened, even if someone had suggested it. First, we didn't have the range of equipment, and second, with a total running time, minus the advertisement break, headlines and so on, of about 25 minutes, we simply had too much to get in.

It's worth just recalling a few other things that were markedly different from today. For one thing satellite time was at a premium. It was limited and expensive. By and large, satellite uplinks were only really available from big Western cities and a few other major world capitals. You booked a segment of 15 minutes (or 10 if you could get away with it) to feed your package. If you missed your slot, the chances were you wouldn't get another one and your perfectly crafted, but now useless, piece wouldn't make the programme.

Plenty of material was still 'shipped' or hand-carried back to base from overseas. It's another sign of how much the times have changed that you could turn up at virtually any airport in the world, find a friendly passenger or crew member, and get them to carry back a package of video or film for collection by another complete stranger at the other end. (Imagine trying that today: 'Whatever you do, you mustn't open this metal canister and look inside. Just take it on the plane and all will be fine!')

As a result of this generally low-tech approach, news, or at least pictures of it, often took far longer to reach the viewer than it does today. And there are certainly those who would say that was no bad thing, giving journalists more time to consider their words, their images, and the effect of both on the viewer. It could also be argued that really dramatic stories, when they reached air, had a far greater impact because of the absence of today's rich and deep 'soup' of information.

There was another big difference too. Television news was very highly unionized, both at ITN and at the BBC. Restrictive practices were rife. Shift patterns, particularly for camera crews, tended to be arranged for their convenience rather than the needs of programmes, and it was standard practice for the less enthusiastic crew member to demand a meal break just when the story was getting interesting.

Network time, of course, was like gold dust and the ITV controllers were very reluctant to give any more to news than was in the schedule. When the SAS stormed the Iranian Embassy in London to free hostages on 5 May 1980 (a national holiday in the UK), the ITV network controller insisted on showing the last few minutes of the long-running soap *Coronation Street* before switching to the astonishing live coverage.

Despite all this, as the eighties wore on, coverage got more imaginative and bolder. Technological boundaries were pushed and the makings of today's television news could be seen emerging.

Enterprise was the key. Though satellite uplinks remained amazingly bulky – and expensive to ship – they were increasingly deployed in the field: to Normandy for the fortieth anniversary of D-Day in 1984; to China two years later for historic pictures of the queen walking on the Great Wall; to Zeebrugge for the aftermath of a ferry disaster in 1987 (with amazing pictures beamed back live from a rowing boat carrying the presenter alongside the sunken ship); to Afghanistan in 1989 to see the Mujahideen celebrating the dramatic departure of Soviet troops; and to Germany later that year for the fall of the Berlin Wall.

All this time, pretty much unnoticed in the UK, the seeds of a different type of revolution were being sown across the Atlantic in Atlanta. The farmer was Ted Turner, an entrepreneur and multi-millionaire who once skippered the winning yacht in the America's Cup and had made his fortune in radio and billboard advertising. In the early sixties he bought a string of loss-making local TV stations, turned them profitable, and used his money to launch CNN, the world's first 24-hour TV news channel, in June 1980.

As most truly innovative ventures are, it was widely derided by those with most reason to feel threatened. It was famously dismissed as the 'Chicken Noodle Network' by a rival, partly as a result of Turner's use of young, non-union staff to fill most of the technical posts. And even though Ted Turner's self-confidence was the stuff of legends, he and his executives were never completely sure that the fledgling channel would survive, particularly in the face of a competitive 24-hour news operation launched immediately afterwards by ABC and Westinghouse. In 1983, however, Turner bought out his struggling rival and never looked back. By 1985, CNN was in 30 million American homes and turning its first profit. It came spectacularly of age during the first Gulf War of 1990–1 with continuous live coverage of the nightly Western air attacks on Baghdad.

It's worth pointing out that back in the mid-1980s no such channel could possibly have been launched in the UK; the broadcast capacity simply didn't exist. That situation changed dramatically in the late eighties with the launch of two competing satellite services: the government-approved British Satellite Broadcasting (BSB) and Rupert Murdoch's Sky Television with the world's second – and Europe's first – 24-hour news channel, Sky News.

A ruinous battle between the two nascent services followed, with massive losses building for both sides. Eventually, with BSB on the point of collapse, a merger – in reality a takeover by Sky – was agreed, and BSkyB was born.

World News Headquarters, Sky News, 2007
PHOTO COURTESY OF SKY NEWS

In those early years, back at the start of the 1990s, Sky had the 24-hour news field very much to itself in the UK and it started to make its mark journalistically – though because of low subscription numbers, viewing figures were pretty small. Like CNN, Sky News was initially derided by its bigger rivals, BBC and ITN, but it scored some notable hits with its own Gulf War coverage and a spectacular success with its live pictures of the dramatic verdict in the O.J. Simpson trial, the only UK channel to show it, pulling in an amazing million-plus viewers. At the time of writing it remains the third biggest audience in Sky News's history.

As multi-channel television took hold in the UK, first analogue, and then digital, it became clear that continuous rolling news was not only here to stay but would play a major part in the future of broadcast journalism.

In 1997, the BBC got into the game, launching its own rolling news channel, News 24. It got off to an unhappy start. Despite the corporation's unequalled journalistic resources, it seemed to lack the fleetness of foot and viewer-friendliness that Sky had mastered. Its first set was a masterpiece of awkward angles and mismatched materials. Viewers found themselves distracted by newsroom staff munching lunchtime sandwiches or wearily putting on coats to head home. Most damaging of all, it was scorned within the BBC by some pretty senior figures, both on and off screen, who regarded it as 'not proper journalism'. Inevitably, Sky News looked a much more polished and modern product in comparison.

But the BBC's new channel struck one immediate and lasting blow against Sky News – it completely undermined its commercial basis. Until News 24's launch, Sky News had been charging the UK's cable operators about £6 a year to supply the channel to each of their three million customers. With the BBC service given away free, it was clear that that price would have to plummet and it did, with Sky News revenue from cable disappearing completely within weeks, pushing the channel from profit into loss.

But Sky News continued to set the pace in journalistic enterprise and ratings. The trial of the British nanny Louise Woodward in 1997, accused of murdering a baby in her care in Boston, USA, proved to be Britain's 'O.J. moment' and showed that viewers would stay hooked for hours if the subject were engrossing enough. The death of Diana, Princess of Wales, in 1997 gave audiences a week-long single-story boost and brought Sky News a share in the gold-standard Royal Television Society award for news coverage.

Increasingly, technology and enterprise became the battlegrounds. Through the 1980s, newsgathering equipment had become smaller, lighter and more mobile, with a technological rush triggered by the switch from film to videotape. Editing in the field, rather than shipping raw footage back to HQ, became the norm. Just as significantly, satellite uplinks became cheaper and more portable, either fixed to the back of small trucks and sent on the road, or packed in a couple of flight cases and flown with reporting teams to far-off lands.

The first Gulf War had shown something of the potential of mobile uplinks, with American and British teams racing to be the first to set up their satellite links in newly liberated Kuwait after the defeat of Iraqi forces.

But it was the Kosovo conflict that took that mobility, and the journalistic freedom it provided, to new levels. It also demonstrated how difficult it would be in future for military authorities to physically control and censor broadcasters by rationing access to resources on the battlefield.

As NATO troops prepared to enter Kosovo from Macedonia in June 1999, media minders from the British Ministry of Defence believed they had limited broadcasters' ability to report by authorizing only a single satellite truck to travel with the troops – with even that kept well to the rear.

However, in the preceding weeks Sky News had driven four of its own satellite trucks across Europe to the south of Italy, shipped them by ferry to Greece and driven them north to Macedonia, from where they were ready to drive in, accompanying the NATO troops as they crossed the border into Kosovo. The result was a remarkable day's broadcasting with two of the satellite trucks stopping to transmit live coverage while the other two drove ahead to set up further down the road. The first two vehicles then 'leapfrogged' ahead to set up further still along the column of troops, guaranteeing the ability both to provide continuous coverage and to keep up with the advance itself.

Technological developments like these drove an increasing demand for 'liveness', which became one of the dominating features of the medium and a hotly debated issue within the TV news industry. Put simply the question is this: does the ability to 'go live' at the scene of a news story add much, or indeed anything, to the quality of coverage?

Much depends on the story, of course. No one would argue, I think, that there is not real value in seeing an event genuinely unfold in front of the cameras, whether it is scenes of historic importance such as the September 11 attacks, the arrival of US troops in Baghdad or a new prime minister taking office in Downing Street, or even less weighty matters.

But there clearly is room for debate about the now-routine inclusion of live reporting from the site of nearly all news stories, particularly when little fresh is happening. One strong argument against this reliance on 'liveness' is that it prevents reporters from getting on with real journalism. The complaint (voiced by plenty of reporters themselves) is that there's a real danger of them ending up as 'satellite jockeys', tied to a live presentation spot and unable to go off and gather fresh facts.

The Omagh, Northern Ireland, car-bombing of 1998, which killed 29 people, prompted us at Sky News to address this and we came up with a rule of thumb for working out how many staff to send to really major stories such as that one. We put together a team with a journalist, producer, camera crew and technical support – and then multiplied it by four. The thinking was that the first team would provide continuous live coverage while a second team busied themselves behind the scenes gathering information, interviewing witnesses and preparing fresh reports – a task that simply couldn't be undertaken by the first 'live' team.

The justification for teams three and four was straightforward: after 12 or 15 hours the first two crews would simply get too tired to carry on, so if you wanted genuine 24-hour coverage you needed to replace them with fresh people. In Omagh, as at other major story venues such as the Asian tsunami of 2004, this approach worked well, though it is, of course, extremely labour intensive and expensive, especially if you need to ship dozens of staff members and tons of equipment across the world. The crucial thing is that it does genuinely allow a TV news operation to carry out some real journalism rather than simply commentate on unfolding events.

Rolling news is a ferociously competitive business and the leading channels are always looking to new technology to give them a vital edge against their rivals, particularly in coverage of wars and other major stories.

The next major conflict after Kosovo, in Afghanistan, required a different approach. It wasn't possible to drive satellite trucks there, so mobile uplinks were flown in, mounted on hired lorries and trundled around the dusty roads to where the action was happening. The BBC outwitted everyone by breaking an uplink down into a couple of dozen smaller packages, strapping each one to the back of a donkey, and taking the whole caravan through the mountains to the outskirts of Kabul for live coverage of the capture of the city by the Northern Alliance and their Western allies.

The Afghan conflict also saw the first really large-scale and imaginative deployment of new 'videophone' links, which used mobile phone technology to send a compressed and inevitably rather grainy live picture without the need for a satellite uplink. Viewers back in Britain were thereby able to see some remarkable live action from places that simply would not have been accessible with a conventional satellite link.

The Iraq War that began in 2003 became one of the biggest journalistic, technical and logistical operations in broadcast history. Audiences for rolling news channels soared around the world and technological boundaries were pushed even further. The American broadcaster NBC stunned its rivals by unveiling an amazing converted tank-recovery vehicle bearing a stabilized satellite uplink, allowing the channel's correspondents to broadcast live, in vision, while the behemoth bounded along, Mad Max-style, across the Iraqi desert with the US army.

Television coverage of the Iraq War generated intense debate within the industry and the wider world. In particular, the use of 'embedded' reporters accompanying troops raised the question of whether they could ever be really impartial while relying on the military for safety, transport, food and shelter. Critics also questioned the value of such reporting when correspondents and camera crews were not free to roam beyond the immediate vicinity of the unit they were stationed with.

But most Western broadcasters accepted the notion, arguing that with 20-plus reporters embedded with UK forces, all pooling their coverage, and dozens more with American troops, plenty of valuable – and highly visual – material would emerge, which it did. Broadcasters also pointed out that none of the major news organizations relied on embedded reporters alone. Others were sent as 'unilaterals' (or 'mavericks', as the army preferred to call them) and were able, with difficulty and great danger, to undertake a certain amount of independent journalism on the battlefield. There were other layers of coverage too, with correspondents reporting live – and with great bravery – from Baghdad and from the other major centres of the war: Kuwait, Bahrain, Doha and the Kurdish areas of Iraq.

The Afghan and Iraq wars saw a steep increase in the number of journalists killed on the battlefield, some caught in crossfire, some in 'friendly fire' and others in accidents. It was also clear that journalists no longer had the 'protected status' they had enjoyed in other wars and other eras. In many areas of conflict they would be just as likely to be attacked, kidnapped or murdered as soldiers themselves.

In the UK rolling news market, things were changing. ITN had launched its own 24-hour channel in 2000 with the clear intention of displacing Sky News as the market leader. It had, though, struggled from the outset, with poor ratings keeping it resolutely in third place despite some strong programming. More alarmingly, the economics of the industry, with the BBC's channel still distributed for free, effectively ruled out forever the chances of anyone else making a commercial proposition from 24-hour news. In the end, ITN's ultimate paymasters, ITV, decided enough was enough and closed it down at Christmas 2005.

BBC News 24, after a painful first few years, was getting stronger, both editorially and in ratings. The Corporation's hierarchy finally accepted that the channel had to have a pivotal role in the news department. It received a real boost with the success of Freeview, a multi-channel offering to households who preferred not to have a satellite dish or cable connection. While satellite viewers still tended to watch their rolling news on Sky, Freeview homes strongly opted for News 24, and with Freeview heavily outselling satellite, the BBC channel slowly overhauled Sky News in the ratings. However, journalistic rivalry between the two organizations remained intense.

In America, an entirely different battle was being played out between the now venerable CNN and an aggressive and ambitious rival, Fox News, owned by Rupert Murdoch's News Corporation, with a third channel, MSNBC, striving valiantly to keep up with the Big Two.

Fox News was launched in 1996 to counter what Murdoch saw as liberal bias in America's news media, including CNN, and pursued a conservative and strongly patriotic agenda though maintaining its coverage overall was, to quote its own slogan 'fair and balanced'. News Corporation pulled off a masterstroke at the time of its launch by offering cable operators $10 per subscriber, up front, to carry Fox News, neatly undermining efforts by Time Warner (owners of CNN) to restrict Fox's carriage. By 2007 Fox was in more than 90 million US homes, reaching the vast majority of Americans, and was the most-watched news channel in the country.

So how does the future look for 24-hour news? Predictions abound but even those piloting the big news organizations admit there's no single, clear road ahead. It is, though, possible to sketch out a few main trends.

It's likely that the imminent demise of all traditional media, prophesied for several years now by the high priests of e-futurology, will be more gradual than feared (by some) and hoped for (by others). Just as radio didn't kill off newspapers and television hasn't smothered radio, so online offerings won't make network TV obsolete just yet. However, it's clearly impossible to imagine a reversal of the steady decline in audiences for nationally networked, simultaneously viewed news broadcasts both in America and in Britain. Similarly, it seems clear that sales of newspapers will continue to fall as their readers find electronic alternatives elsewhere.

But rolling news channels alone won't provide a complete alternative, or anything like it. Indeed it's already been argued that the basic 24-hour channels are becoming obsolete as viewers move away from linear – in other words passively watched – offerings to more interactive services. The main weakness of continuous news channels, at least in the UK, is their reliance on big breaking stories – by definition impossible to plan in advance – to provide audience 'spikes' or peaks in viewing figures. Efforts to attract audiences to 'appointment to view' programmes built around individuals and specific themes haven't been a success here.

That's not the case in the US, where big-name presenters such as CNN's Larry King and Fox's Bill O'Reilly are the star draws, in Fox's case helped by a much freer regulatory attitude towards powerful opinion than would be allowed in the UK.

It's clear that all organizations that want to be major players in news will have to offer their products through a whole range of outlets – and most already do. This means having – for the moment – networked programmes, a rolling news service, a strong internet presence (a news website), plus a selection of streamed channels and news items to a set-top box, headlines and clips sent to mobile phones, and probably a radio service as well.

This sounds like a dizzying set of requirements but actually, with modern newsrooms arranged the way they are, it's relatively easy for broadcasters. These days all content sits on powerful video servers – rather than reels of videotape as it would have done five years ago – and so can be easily accessed and used ('repurposed' is the industry term) by teams or individuals preparing news services for all these different outlets. The cost is increasingly in the generation of the material in the first place rather than the work of chopping it up in varying ways and sending it on to the customer.

Newspapers are determined not to be left behind. They recognize that they can no longer satisfy their customers simply with words and some dramatic photographs (certainly not just once every 24 hours). They, too, need to be developing more rounded offerings including, ideally, news video clips and constantly updated stories. The more far-sighted of them are already redesigning their newsrooms so that the traditional print function sits side by side with the online team, with all material shared. It's quite easy to envisage now the newspaper of the not-too-distant future – a flexible, electronic sheet (imagine a very thin, foldable laptop screen of tabloid size or smaller) onto which can be downloaded text stories, still photos, video clips, animating maps etc. You might read this on the train going to work, leave it in your briefcase during the day, then take it out for the return journey and read a completely updated version with new content downloaded five minutes before you boarded the train home.

How to pay for all this is a tough question, harder, in many ways, than the issues of the technology and the content. For those organizations which generate most of their revenue from subscription, like Sky, or, in the BBC's case, from the licence fee, it's not too much of a problem. The online offerings can be used to give 'added value' to subscribers and perhaps to justify increases in payments.

But to others, like newspapers, that get most of their money from individual sales, it's a real headache. The internet is a vast pool of free news and information and users are wedded to the idea of not paying for it.

There are huge 'aggregators' of content like Google News, which claims to offer the best of more than 4,000 news services from around the world, all constantly updated and all free. Google itself doesn't generate a single story, take a single photograph or shoot a single piece of video, but it does act as a giant clearing house for every news outlet under the sun. Unless you are a very specialized or high-value news operation, like, say parts of the *New York Times* or *Financial Times*, trying to charge people to access your site seems like a non-starter with so many free alternatives available.

Online advertising, therefore, looks like the only substantial source of revenue and all news outlets compete fiercely for it (though with Google mopping up a huge percentage of it, it's hard to see that there'll be enough to go round for everyone else).

So how does that leave the business of continuous news? Well, in one form or another it's clearly here to stay. The one thing that won't diminish is the public's hunger to know what's going on in their world, to absorb well-informed opinion and explanation about it, and to have their own say as well. That's easier than it's ever been, but my own view (perhaps coloured as much by wishful thinking as by genuine foresight) is that real journalism is going to be just as vital in the future as it is now, maybe even more so. For all the technological advances, for all the ever-improving means of distribution, the best bit of kit to deploy in the field remains an experienced, dedicated, healthily sceptical journalist with whatever backup and support they need, ready to report what they've seen with their own eyes or have learnt from sources they know and trust. When it comes down to it, that's all there is to it, really.

Questions for students

1 Thanks to new technology, 24-hour television news can 'go live' almost anywhere, any time. But as Nick Pollard notes, there is a major debate about whether 'the ability to "go live" at the scene of a news story add[s] much, or indeed anything, to the quality of coverage'. What do you think?
2 What can continuous news channels do to capture viewers and attract advertisers when there are no big breaking stories to cover?
3 What are the dangers and advantages of 24-hour television news channels?

8

World Perspectives: Ignoring the World at our Peril

Tony Burman

Why does the rest of the world matter to us more than ever before? Why do we need to report other people's cultures and alternative perspectives to better understand our own? And, on the most practical level, how can we make *international* news seem *local*?

For many of us, the events of September 11, 2001, and their aftermath have so far defined this first decade of the twenty-first century. But that is not how this stage of history was expected to be.

After surviving two world wars and many smaller ones, the twin scourges of fascism and communism, and a potential nuclear catastrophe during the Cold War, much of the world had hoped the beginning of this exciting new century would be marked by relative peace and stability. Even better, many thought, it would be an opportunity to deal finally with the many pressing North–South issues that had been evaded during decades of East–West tensions.

The conditions seemed right. Weary from the battering it took throughout most of the twentieth century, the world appeared more interdependent than ever before. And so vulnerable and small. In much of it, an information and technology revolution had begun which promised unprecedented access to places and ideas that up until now had been closed. At the centre of this – or at least this is what many journalists hoped – would be the world's proliferating news media spreading high-minded ideas and, perhaps, even a semblance of democracy to all corners of the planet.

For example, if there were only three major all-news television networks at the end of the 1980s – CNN, Britain's SKY TV and Canada's CBC Newsworld – there were nearly 100 of these channels worldwide a decade later.[1] And this gave rise to high expectations. The press, wrote famed American journalist Walter Lippmann in 1922, should be 'like the beam of a searchlight that moves restlessly about, bringing one episode and then another out of darkness into vision' (1922: 229). As we entered the twenty-first century, the worldwide information explosion raised hopes that journalism's noblest goals were actually attainable.

But this was premature. The turbulence of this decade, not its tranquillity, has defined this period. In many cases, the news media have been passive, at best, or even complicit, as world events spiralled out of control: growing conflict in the Middle East, spreading religious and political extremism, increased worries about climate change, fears about immigration and vanishing borders, the spectre once again of potential nuclear conflict and – of course – the deepening poverty and despair in many developing countries – the list goes on.

As a consequence, many in the world's industrialized countries – particularly in the United States and parts of Europe – have turned inward. Instead of greeting this new century with openness and hope, they have become more protective of what they have and more fearful that in this uncertain future they may lose it.

The response by the world's news media to these events has been mixed, even contradictory.

- In the developing world, there have been aggressive efforts to expand coverage of the world and provide alternative voices to the Anglo-American monopoly (CNN, BBC, etc.) that has long dominated the world of international journalism. The most notable example has been in the Middle East with the creation of the Al Jazeera network and its newer competitors, a development that is inspiring similar initiatives in Africa and Asia.
- In contrast, many of the world's largest commercial news organizations – particularly the major American broadcast networks – have mirrored their sense of the perceived public mood by reducing world coverage. Although still rich by most measurements,[2] these companies have reacted to pressure from shareholders and to apparent indifference from audiences

CBC cameraman Sat Nandlall on assignment in Afghanistan, 2002
PHOTO COURTESY OF CBC NEWS

by drastically cutting back their international bureaus and shrinking the relatively small amount of space and airtime they devote to 'foreign news'.

In the full sweep of history, one could argue this is precisely the time when understanding other cultures is a necessary prerequisite to truly understanding your own. If information is power, ignorance can be dangerous. As recently as June 2007, a national public opinion poll in the US indicated that as many as four in ten Americans (41 per cent) still believed Saddam Hussein's regime was directly involved in financing, planning or carrying out the Al Qaeda attacks on 9/11, even though no evidence has been produced to support such a connection (Newsweek 2007).

As a justification for reducing costly international coverage, it has been irresistible for some media companies to blame the victim – in this case, the audience – as in ' people don't actually care about foreign news'. But this is self-serving. Although it tries to absolve journalists and programmers from blame for boring or confusing their audiences, there is considerable research in North America suggesting that superficial coverage of the world is the most important contributor to public apathy.

What is also being ignored is another crucial role of news organizations: to provide news they believe the public *needs* to know to become better-informed citizens. This assumes that journalists in the end should be more than mere order-takers. There used to be a time when major American media companies saw it as their public duty to maintain strong, well-resourced news divisions as a form of 'pay-back' for access to the public airwaves and the immense profits this produced. This was perhaps best summed up in the 1950s in the United States when Bill Paley, founder of CBS, said something to the effect of 'I make money on Jack Benny so I can afford to do the *best* news.'

So what is the *best* news, the news the public *needs* to know? Well, we know what it isn't. A consistent drumbeat of 'good guys, bad guys, those who are with us and those who aren't' is cited by many in surveys as a major negative in the coverage of world affairs.

Beyond labels and name-calling, the public needs to know – and, arguably, *wants* to know – who these leaders are and how they gained power. And what can we learn from this? Why did Iranians turn away from their established leaders and vote in Mahmoud Ahmadinejad as president? Is he delivering on his promises in the minds of Iranians or being seen as too preoccupied with the US and Israel? The public needs insightful and detached reporting about who he is and what he represents. In Palestine, why did Hamas oust Fatah after Arafat's death? Why were so many people surprised at Hamas's election victory? Moving beyond labelling them as 'terrorists', what is the meaning of their popularity? And what explains Hezbollah's support in Lebanon? Or Chavez's importance in Venezuela?

Why? Why? Why?

Turning the world off may be therapeutic to some, but it is no long-term solution. The long march of history shows us that. It is instructive to examine the media's two different directions more closely to identify a strategy that would turn the world back on.

Lessons from Abroad

Al Jazeera is the largest and most controversial Arabic news channel in the Middle East and it originates from the tiny state of Qatar in the Persian Gulf. It is one of the most widely watched news channels in the world, with an estimated audience ranging from 30 million to 50 million (Lynch 2006; Miles 2006; Zayani and Sahraoui 2007).

Apart from creating waves in Washington since the post-9/11 emergence of Osama bin Laden and Al Qaeda, Al Jazeera is being watched closely throughout the developing world – particularly Africa – as a possible model for the creation of new international news channels.

It was created in 1996 by the emir of Qatar as a satellite channel that would project a progressive image for his small state and an alternative perspective on world affairs. Since then, Al Jazeera and other new satellite competitors in the Middle East have transformed Arab politics. By shattering state control over information and encouraging open debate by a range of voices, Al Jazeera has transformed itself from a little-known regional broadcaster to a multi-channel, multi-lingual, multi-service international enterprise.

In December 2006, it launched a separate English-language news channel (www.english.aljazeera.net). But the irony is that this service is widely available throughout most of the world – except the United States and Canada. The Al Jazeera English network is not carried on any major American satellite system in spite of the hundreds of channels that are offered.

Part of the reason is the controversial reputation of the Al Jazeera Arabic service, but it is also because of the hammerlock that profitable non-news channels – including gambling and sex channels – have on the US satellite system. Of the three English-language international news channels launched in 2006 (Al Jazeera English, BBC World and a new French joint venture, France 24), none has been able to break into the US satellite market.

With more than 500 journalists worldwide, both the Arabic-language and English-language Al Jazeera networks are notable for their extensive coverage of the developing world, including parts of South America, Africa and Asia that are rarely seen on British and American news channels. In a 'North–South' world, the Al Jazeera networks consciously make an effort to project the perspective of the 'South' on major stories, not only on regional issues but also those which are international in scope. They don't always succeed, but they often do.

Its Arabic-language network is particularly known for the vigorous debate of its talk shows, introducing a range of opinion that had never before been allowed publicly in the Arab world. Al Jazeera's original slogan, translated from the Arabic, was 'The Opinion ... and the Other Opinion'. Its English-language channel promotes 'Setting the News Agenda'.

Wadah Khanfar, Al Jazeera's director general, suggests that there should be no surprise that the network has created controversy both within the Arab world and beyond, since that was its intention from the start:

> From the very outset, Al Jazeera found itself confronted with sharp dualities: official versus non-official, centre versus periphery, mainstream versus margins. It was necessary for Al Jazeera to feel its way through this reality, reaching out to both power and those who remain outside its realm. How can we use the camera to shed light on all that is darkened by power ...? While the official Arab media considered the viewer as a mere receiver of official political propaganda, Al Jazeera chose from the beginning to be the 'voice of the voiceless', thus curbing the deeply rooted impulse of the power towards control and dominance of the media. (Khanfar 2006: 11)

Al Jazeera's success as a broadcast operation surprised most industry observers. Apart from creating a radical opening for democratic debate in the Arab world – something which was praised by the US government in the network's early years – it had lessons for broadcasters in other parts of the developing world. No longer was it assumed that a network needed to be close to the corridors of power to be successful. In fact, Al Jazeera's popularity with so many people largely came from its perceived distance from established power.

In 2005, Philip Fiske de Gouveia, director of a leading European think tank, the Foreign Policy Centre in London, published a paper titled *An African Al Jazeera? Mass Media and the African Renaissance*. He urged the British government as well as African and European Union members to explore ways to create an independent, pan-African broadcaster, and made the connection with the Al Jazeera experience:

> Lessons can be learned from the experience of the Arab satellite television news channel Al-Jazeera. This station, which only began broadcasting in 1996, has already had a real impact, for example, in improving transparency and accountability across the Middle East. As a consequence state media, which have previously tended towards uncritical 'protocol news', are now being forced to improve their own coverage. It seems probable that a pan-African broadcaster would have similar consequences ... Opportunities for factional media to incite violence, for example, as in Rwanda in 1994 would be more easily limited. Media which act as an alternative to established western broadcasters, and better present Africa to itself, will improve the continent's 'self-confidence'. (Fiske de Gouveia 2005: 15)

In 2006, an African consortium led by Salim Amin, chairman of the Mohamed Amin Foundation,[3] announced plans for the creation of A24, a

24-hour news channel run by Africans for Africans. Mr Amin is the son of legendary cameraman and journalist Mohamed Amin, who was the first to film the Ethiopian famine in 1984 and died in a plane crash off the Comoros Islands in 1996. With its planned focus on regional coverage, Salim Amin has compared this new channel to the new Venezuelan-based Latin American news channel Telesur and the Arabic-language network of Al Jazeera:

> By presenting the real Africa as a place of good and bad, honesty and corruption, economic vibrancy and poverty, eager entrepreneurs as well as those who still rely on foreign aid, A24 will present to Africans the truth about their world. A24 will empower Africans with knowledge to help them decide who they want their political and social leaders to be, where they want to invest their hard-earned money and how they want to move forward in their own Continent … this, for me, is the greatest social purpose the media can achieve … information is power and, for too long, the power has not been in the hands of the people of Africa. (Amin 2007)

There are common aspects in these different projects that have relevance beyond their borders. They clearly portray themselves as serving the interests of their viewers, not advertisers or politicians. Not only do they promise authentic regional coverage that is actually rooted in the location, they overtly identify with popular interests without any self-consciousness. They make no claim of being the audio–video service of the rich and powerful. To the contrary, they make an aggressive effort to tap into the public's widespread feelings of powerlessness. And in a more basic way, they try to respond to the public's apparent growing appetite for news and information that shape their world.

Turning the World Off

In addition to the political dramas, this twenty-first century has ushered in an exciting new era in media. In the past few years, there have been as many changes in the way that news is 'produced' and 'consumed' as we have experienced in the entire history of broadcasting. The ground is changing beneath our feet. As our societies gradually transform themselves through greater immigration and multiculturalism, so too does our world of media.

The key elements have included the explosive growth of the internet, the emergence of 24-hour cable news and the digital revolution, which is empowering audiences and enabling interactivity in ways that are redefining journalism.

Does it follow then that the public's apparent ambivalence about understanding the wider world is also undergoing change? The answer to that is mixed, depending on what part of the world we're talking about. There are signs that the appetite for international news in the developing world, in Europe and in Canada is increasing, but not yet, it appears, in the United States. And this is ironic given the ubiquitous international influence of the world's last remaining superpower.

In August 2007, the Pew Research Center for the People & the Press published a revealing analysis by US political scientist Michael J. Robinson of *Two Decades of American News Preferences: Analyzing What News the Public Follows – and Doesn't*. The two decades covered 1986–2006, and examined Pew's annual News Interest Index for the past 20 years.

Its conclusions were striking: in terms of news preferences, the American public's embrace of the status quo has been unrelenting:

> Although the size and scope of the American news media have changed dramatically since the 1980s, audience news interests and preferences have remained surprisingly static. Of the two major indices of interest that are the focus of this report – overall level of interest in news and preferences for various types of news – neither has changed very much. This has been especially true for news preferences; Americans continue to follow – or to ignore – the same types of stories now as they did two decades ago ... Foreign News – news from abroad unlinked to the U.S. – engenders the least interest. [It] has consistently been at, or near, the bottom of the index for 21 years. (Robinson 2007: 2–4)

What is extraordinary in this Pew study is the list of 'page one' stories buried within these overall categories. The 20-year period that began in the mid-1980s was quite breathtaking in its news significance. And many of these news stories had unmistakable American fingerprints on them. But in spite of this, the broad American public seemed indifferent:

> Only the most monumental developments in 'other nations' register with the general public. Most of the important stories from abroad that lack an American connection go practically unnoticed. The arrest and extradition of Chile's Augusto Pinochet (1998) was followed very closely by 3% of the public. Tony Blair's election (1997) in Great Britain, ending 16 years of Conservative Party control, was followed very closely by 5% of the U.S. audience. The peace agreement in Northern Ireland, in 1998, ending decades of The Troubles, eked

out an index score of 7%. The vote in 1992 to end more than four decades of apartheid in South Africa: 13%. The return of Hong Kong to Chinese authority in 1997: 14%. Even negotiation leading directly to unification of East and West Germany was followed with great intensity by only 21% of the general public – five points below the average for all stories. (Robinson 2007: 31)

So what's going on? Why would one of the world's most educated and sophisticated countries – with so much at stake in major international issues – be seemingly so uninterested in world affairs? Another Pew study – this one published in June 2002, the year following 9/11 – offered a clear answer. It suggested that the media, not their audience, should take the rap:

The survey offers powerful evidence that broad interest in international news is most inhibited by the public's lack of background in this area, Overall, roughly two-thirds (65%) of those with moderate or low interest in these stories say they sometimes lose interest in these stories because they lack the background information to keep up. The poll finds fewer people explaining their lack of international news interest in terms of repetitiveness of overseas news, its remoteness, or excessive coverage of wars and violence. (Pew Research Center for the People & the Press 2002: 2)

A similar survey taken in Canada in 2003 for CBC News showed similar results (Canadian Broadcasting Corporation 2003). A majority of those surveyed felt that 'the news' in all media was often confusing and superficial, ranging from 'just so much noise and static' to outright 'incomprehensible'.

Historically, of course, Americans – and their governments – have often been reluctant to engage with the wider world. To many, 'America' is an island unto itself, and that's just fine with them. After all, only 20 per cent of Americans actually own a passport. But the 2002 Pew study and others examining this issue suggest a reason that is rarely debated in newsrooms today: that journalists themselves should assume much of the blame. By marginalizing international coverage and reinforcing public stereotypes – all on the assumption that the 'public doesn't care' – many news organizations have created a self-fulfilling prophecy that simply ensures continuation of the status quo. For that reason, even the catastrophe of 9/11 seemed not to change US media 'preference' patterns in the end.

Dr Susan Moeller at the University of Maryland has written about the media's tendencies in their treatment of international news. She argues that since most of the media assume the public is not interested in international news, 'there is a perceived need to hype the coverage of "foreign" events to an even greater extent than domestic news'(Moeller 1999: 1). Dr Moeller is the director of the International Center for Media and the Public Agenda at the University of Maryland, and author of several books including *Compassion Fatigue: How the Media Sell Disease, Famine, War and Death* (1999).

In that book, she outlines her view of the 'four habits of international news reporting' that help explain the problem:

1 *Putting forward a formulaic chronology of events*: 'Americans like to think of things in terms of good guys and bad guys' (1999: 1).
2 *Employing a sensationalized and exaggerated use of language*: 'It takes more and more dramatic coverage to elicit the same level of sympathy as the last catastrophe' (1999: 3).
3 *Referencing certain metaphors and imagery that resonate with Americans*: [This] 'can be an extension of [the media's] tendency towards sensationalism, but it can also be an attempt through vivid shorthand to replace complexity with a known quantity' (1999: 4).
4 *And emphasizing an American connection*: 'With the general cutting of news budgets, the media (television especially) can't afford to cover all the disasters that occur. So they choose chauvinistically ... Africa, South America and much of Asia get short shrift in this equation' (1999: 5).

It is these very 'habits' in many news organizations, writes Dr Moeller, that reduce complex and often fascinating international stories to the superficial.

Turning the World Back On

There is a circular pattern that becomes evident when examining the treatment of international news by many American news organizations – particularly the three major US television networks as the most influential medium.

Coverage is very costly, therefore it is limited.
Being limited, it is superficial and often confusing.
Being all of that, the public turns off.
Since the public turns off, costs are even more reduced.
And the self-fulfilling pattern plays on.

There are alternative approaches, and not only in the Middle East, Africa and Europe. Some of them are pursued by the top newspapers in the United States, such as the *New York Times* and *Washington Post*, or by National Public Radio. In their own way, they resemble the 'go aggressive' stance of Al Jazeera, but they are the exception, not the rule.

Another intriguing example is in Canada, where the views about international news – and the media's central role in it – appear far different from their southern neighbours in the United States. And their experience suggests a different model.

In 2003, the Canadian Broadcasting Corporation undertook a major CBC News Study into Canadians' attitudes towards 'news' and 'information' in this new century. It was the most extensive of its kind in Canada. The study was prepared by two respected independent research companies and drew on the views of thousands of Canadians from all across the country, surveyed in a multitude of settings and circumstances. CBC programmers then produced an alternative 'news strategy' that was designed to respond to the public's preferences.

The surprising headline in the study was that, contrary to conventional wisdom, a majority of Canadians indicated they wanted *more* international news, not *less*, and believed more than ever that what happened beyond their borders matters a lot. But they wanted 'international made local' – global stories told in more relevant, local, accessible ways:

> The world is growing smaller and the issues of the world have become our own. This was a common thought pattern throughout the CBC research. In some cases, it is because we simply can't get away from the world anymore and in others because technology and 24/7 news coverage has made the world accessible and fascinating. There is a sense among most people that global issues are, in fact, their own. People seem easily able to make connections, even if the story is something totally outside of their realm of experience. The world is now on our doorstep and like it or not, having to deal with global conflicts and other issues is now an inescapable fact of daily life. This has both heightened the sensitivity to international news and whetted the appetite for it. To many Canadians, connecting internationally has become just as important as connecting locally and the distinctions between the two are seen as irrelevant. They want 'international news made local'.

The study also identified general weaknesses in news presentation – including with international coverage – that were associated with all media, not just television:

- International news is often defined too narrowly, focusing on 'bad' news that is of little relevance to most people. Journalists use language that is often confusing, and frequently choose stories that interest them more than their audience.
- News is often presented as a passive act instead of focusing on those stories which reveal meaningful change that can stimulate a meaningful response. Too much of today's news is only 'of passing interest', or like 'ambient static'.
- Journalists should deliver more 'issue-based' stories that illuminate and provide understanding, background and context – and rely less on empty, contrived 'events'.
- And the audience is saying it wants to hear *all* sides of the story, not just two. They want an end to a simple black-and-white world, and want increased exposure to more divergent views and perspectives.

The study showed that many people are becoming as interested in the world as they are in their back yards. And that's because so many things have changed.

The world has changed. In a post-9/11 environment, people seem to value world news and its impact on their lives increasingly. They distrust any effort at short-changing coverage. Audiences expect both context and dramatic storytelling, and want journalists to make world issues as familiar to them as what is happening in their own communities. They want it made as real as if it were 'local'.

Society has changed. Increasingly, it is becoming a multicultural world with people having ties all over the globe. Immigrants are anxious to hear 'news from home'. Families often move back and forth from their place of origin. And world conflicts are often reflected in the tensions, aspirations and struggles evident in our cities.

And audiences have changed. More than ever, people talk about their desire to know about meaningful change at home and around the world. They want to know what people around the world are thinking and what motivates them. They want to know in a more insightful way than what is currently offered.

The CBC response in 2007 to this study was comprehensive. The air-time devoted to international news was increased, with a particular focus on 'international made local'. A regular international segment – titled 'Our World' – was added to the CBC's national nightly newscast. On the CBC's all-news network, Newsworld, an hour of international news each evening was added in prime time. And many of Newsworld's top-rated programmes were documentaries about international issues.

The CBC also increased the number of its international bureaus. When I worked abroad in the 1980s as a news and documentary producer for CBC News Canada, I worked side by side with the American TV networks. I always admired the dedication and skill of the American journalists and production crews working abroad, but I was even more envious of their resources. In the 1980s, each of three major American networks (NBC, CBS and ABC) had about ten times the number of journalists abroad that the CBC had. That's not a surprising ratio given that the US population is about ten times greater than that of Canada.

But today, in spite of the many budget cutbacks that Canada's public broadcaster has experienced in the past 15 years, CBC News now has more journalists covering the world than each of the major American networks. Or, to put it another way, CBC has 14 international news bureaus – which is about the same number as the three major US networks *combined*. This is an amazing fact when one considers how important the American presence is in the world compared to Canada's.

Other networks and news organizations have also expanded their coverage of the world as a response to today's tensions. The BBC, for example, now has about 50 international bureaus with more than 250 foreign correspondents – the largest of any news organization in the world.

In Whose Interests?

As we scan the wreckage of this first decade of the twenty-first century, there is an issue that urgently needs debate: *Whose interests should journalists serve in deciding how much of the 'world' will be presented to the public?*

For those of us who believe that this shrinking world is crashing down upon us – in a way that affects everyone's day-to-day life – these are challenging times. We are now part of a 'news culture' where stories about celebrities like Paris Hilton or Anna Nicole Smith receive more coverage than the staggering tragedies such as Darfur. It is about time that we all reflect on why.

The Pew survey I referred to earlier (Robinson 2007) lists 'Tabloid' and 'Foreign' news as the areas of *least* interest to the public over the two-decade period 1986-2006. Coverage of 'foreign' news has certainly shrunk in recent years, but not so 'tabloid'. It has significantly *increased* across the board. But in spite of this, public interest in 'tabloid' stories is still small and has not grown in recent years.

So why the increased coverage? The study concludes that the motivation for more tabloid coverage was not to respond to widespread public appetite, but was due to commercial and competitive reasons – in other words, to appeal to smaller 'niche' audiences that will improve ratings and please advertisers.

The study examined the three-week saga in 2007 involving the death and interment of American celebrity Anna Nicole Smith. Many news organizations, particularly US cable, blanketed that story, devoting 22 per cent of their entire news programming to her. On the day of Smith's death, CNN tripled its audience of the day before, and this was hailed by beaming TV executives as a response to public interest.

However, the Pew study presented a different interpretation:

> how big a shift is this in terms of the national audience? On CNN, the audience initially increased by a factor of three, an increase of approximately a million people – less than a single Nielsen ratings point. And from the sociologist's perspective, that shift represents less than one half of one percent of the nation. All this helps explain how it happened that the most competitive news system – cable, above all – would become frenzied in covering the Smith story. And how, from a commercial perspective, based in ratings, news organizations were 'right' in doing so. But this calculus, based in commerce and ratings, does not account for the broader reality – that most of the national audience was, according to the polls, either indifferent to, or disapproving of, that coverage. (Robinson 2007: 9–10)

Let me repeat the study's point for emphasis: It concluded that a tabloid story which increased ratings by a mere million people – in a country with a population of 300 million – ended up filling nearly a quarter of US cable's news programming for that period.

In whose interests are these editorial decisions being made? Is it a mystery, therefore, that surveys in the United States indicate the current credibility of journalists and news organization among the public is lower than it has been in living memory?[4]

This probably would have come as no surprise to the late Neil Postman, the American media and cultural critic who in 1986 wrote his provocative analysis of television, *Amusing Ourselves to Death*. In that book, Mr Postman argued that television – particularly TV news – treats serious issues as entertainment, and demeans political discourse by making it less about ideas and more about image. 'When a population becomes distracted by trivia, when cultural life is redefined as a perpetual round of entertainment, when serious public conversation becomes a form of baby-talk, when, in short, a people become an audience and their public business a vaudeville act, then a nation finds itself at risk: culture-death is a clear possibility' (1986: 161).

Many years from now, when historians reflect on this decade, I believe their judgement of the media's performance during these years will be harsh. Looking at the current state of the world, it is difficult not to conclude that disastrous decisions have been made by political leaders in an environment of ignorance and hubris. And these disasters were condoned by a public that largely chose to look the other way and a news media that was at various times complicit or incompetent.

That's certainly not how this decade was supposed to turn out. And as the world becomes more dangerous, this should give us all motivation to set it right.

Notes

1   With the explosion of the internet, there are now hundreds, perhaps thousands, of news sources available worldwide. In terms of TV specialized networks dedicated to 'news', there are an estimated 20 public channels and 75 private news channels in the world. But a growing number of people are now relying on news websites to get their news. These include major sites such as Google, Yahoo and MySpace as well as countless sites associated with newspapers and broadcast organizations – often providing audio, video and text – not to mention thousands of blogs of varying quality which focus on news.

2   One of the major challenges facing the American news media is the series of budget cuts rolling through the industry, resulting in the elimination of thousands of journalistic jobs. Media companies cite unprecedented financial pressures on their bottom line, yet most of these companies still experience profit margins of around 20 per cent. This is an extraordinary level of profit when compared to almost any other business sector. So what's the problem? Many observers blame the 'tyranny of Wall Street' – excessive expectations of shareholders and investors (see Project for Excellence in Journalism 2007). In February 2007, former CBS news anchor Walter Cronkite gave the keynote address at a media conference at Columbia University's Graduate School of Journalism. Mr Cronkite warned that pressures from media companies to generate ever-greater profits threaten the

very freedom the nation was built upon. He said today's journalists face greater challenges than those from his generation. No longer could journalists count on their employers to provide the necessary resources, he said, 'to expose truths that powerful politicians and special interests often did not want exposed'. Instead, he said, 'they face rounds and rounds of job cuts and cost cuts that require them to do ever more with ever less' (Cronkite 2007).

3   The Mohamed Amin Foundation is a broadcast television training centre set up in 1998 for young Kenyan and East African television presenters (http://www. moforce.com).

4   A US national survey by the Pew Research Center, conducted 25–9 July 2007, 'underscores the fundamental change in basic attitudes about the news media that has occurred since the mid-1980s. In the initial Times Mirror polling on the press in 1985, the public faulted news organizations for many of its practices: most people said that news organizations "try to cover up their mistakes," while pluralities said they "don't care about the people they report on," and were politically biased. But in the past decade, these criticisms have come to encompass broader indictments of the accuracy of news reporting, news organizations' impact on democracy and, to some degree, their morality. In 1985, most Americans (55%) said news organizations get the facts straight. Since the late 1990s, consistent majorities – including 53% in the current survey – have expressed the belief that news stories are often inaccurate. As a consequence, the believability ratings for individual news organizations are lower today than they were in the 1980s and 1990s' (Pew Research Center for the People & the Press 2007).

References

Amin, S. (2007) Using the media for social purposes. Speech at the Commonwealth Broadcasting Association conference, Nairobi, 18–21 February.

Canadian Broadcasting Corporation (2003) *CBC News Study: What Canadians 'Want' and 'Need' from their News Media, 2005–2007.* Internal CBC News Canada publication, http://www.cbcnews.ca.

Cronkite, W. (2007) Media reform: Is it good for journalism? Keynote address, www. journalism.columbia.edu.

Fiske de Gouveia, P. (2005) *An African Al Jazeera? Mass Media and the African Renaissance.* Foreign Policy Centre, www.fpc.org.uk.

Khanfar, W. (2006) The Al Jazeera spirit. In *The Al Jazeera Decade: 1996–2006*, http:// english.aljazeera.net/English/archive/archive?ArchiveId=38302.

Lippmann, W. (1922) *Public Opinion.* Free Press/Simon and Schuster.

Lynch, M. (2006) *Voices of the New Arab Public: Iraq, Al-Jazeera, and Middle East Politics Today.* Columbia University Press.

Miles, H. (2006) *Al Jazeera: How Arab TV News Challenged the World.* Abacus.

Moeller, S. (1999) *Compassion Fatigue: How the Media Sell Disease, Famine, War and Death*. Routledge, http://www.frameworksinstitute.org/products/fourhabits.pdf.

Newsweek (2007) Poll by Princeton Survey Associates International, 18–19 June. www.msnbc.msn.com/id/19390791/site/newsweek.

Pew Research Center for the People & the Press (2002) Public's news habits little changed by September 11. Pew Research Center for the People & the Press, http://people-press.org/reports/pdf/156.pdf.

Pew Research Center for the People & the Press (2007) Internet news audience highly critical of news organizations. http://people-press.org/reports/display.php3?ReportID=348.

Postman, N. (1986) *Amusing Ourselves to Death: Public Discourse in the Age of Show Business*. Methuen.

Project for Excellence in Journalism (2007) *Annual Report on American Journalism*. www.stateofthenewsmedia.org/2007.

Robinson, M. J. (2007) *Two Decades of American News Preferences*. Pew Research Centre for the People & the Press, http://pewresearch.org/pubs/574/two-decades-of-american-news-preferences.

Zayani, M. and Sahraoui, S. (2007) *The Culture of Al Jazeera: Inside an Arab Media Giant*. McFarland.

Questions for students

1 Is Tony Burman right in arguing that the Pew study of 'news prefer-ences' (Robinson 2007), showing poor understanding of significant international stories, demonstrates that 24-hour continuous news channels have failed to use their airtime in a responsible manner?

2 In giving saturation coverage to stories like the O.J. Simpson trial and the disappearance in Portugal in 2007 of the 3-year-old British child Madeleine McCann, are news channels giving viewers what they want or has the balance of news coverage tipped to excessive coverage of tabloid stories?

3 What difference has Al Jazeera made in changing the international news agenda? Would an African all-news channel do the same?

4 Take one current story and analyse how the coverage differs between different countries.

9

Local Heroes

Anthony Borden

Introduction

JOHN OWEN

It's not all gloom and doom out there in the world of international journalism. Contrary to what journalism students are being told far too often about the state of the media, there are – thanks to the internet and the new technology – exciting possibilities for covering the world beyond crisis and conflict. But if Anthony Borden, the executive director of the Institute for War & Peace Reporting (IWPR), has it right, the real key to inspired reporting on the world is a well-trained, well-supported local journalist who has finally been empowered to tell his or her own story.

Those who tend to be the most pessimistic about the state of international reporting are former correspondents and producers who had the privilege of working for big-budget television networks and newspapers. They travelled the world in style, lived exceedingly well, and if posted abroad, worked in well-resourced foreign bureaus. (I was one of those. I ran the CBC London Bureau for six years in the 1990s. While we had a fraction of the budget of the American networks and BBC/ ITN, we were a major player on the international scene.) When a big story broke, they spent whatever money was required to get wherever they needed to go and to get there first. They often hired the best local journalists available to work as their 'fixers' and translators. Local journalists could make more money in weeks working for the international networks than they could in an entire year at their local newspaper or state-run broadcaster.

The emergence of the local journalist has taken place against the backdrop of the big networks and major newspapers closing their foreign bureaus and reducing their international coverage (in the United States) except for stories related to the wars in Iraq and Afghanistan and anything pegged to the War on Terror. In London, anything having to do with the Royal Family or the martyred Princess gets attention well out of proportion to the merits of the stories.

For some former war correspondents, such as the *Guardian* newspaper's Maggie O'Kane, the shift to reliance on local journalists is long overdue: 'The traditional model of the foreign correspondent is a pretty colonial approach. Usually we're only as good as our local fixers' (quoted in Cockburn 2007). O'Kane now heads up the *Guardian*'s Film Division, which trains local journalists to produce documentaries about stories and issues in their countries. Part of her argument also centres on the inability of Western correspondents, usually white and Anglo-American-Canadian, to practise their journalism in Muslim countries or in the developing world without fears of being taken hostage, attacked or even killed. (Swedish freelance photojournalist and video journalist Martin Adler was murdered in 2006 in Mogadishu, Somalia, at what was ostensibly a rally to celebrate a peace agreement. Adler had worked extensively in Africa. Also murdered in Mogadishu a year earlier, soon after she had arrived to produce the BBC's news coverage, was its seasoned Africa producer Kate Peyton. In late April 2008, an American missile attack killed the man American authorities claimed was responsible for ordering her killing. According to news reports, Aden Hashi Ayro, described as a senior Al Qaeda operative, was targeted by American forces and killed with as many as 30 others (Gettleman and Schmitt 2008). For local journalists in Somalia, it's also become a nightmare trying to report and stay alive. Nine Somali journalists were murdered in 2007.

Not only are local journalists being turned to increasingly by the news agencies and other news media, they are also providing the textured reportage and analysis on international news websites run by not-for-profit groups such as IWPR (with centres in London, Washington, and Johannesburg; www.iwpr.net), the Prague-based Transitions on Line (www.tol.cz), Human Rights Watch (headquartered in New York; www.hrw.org) and Brussels-centred International Crisis Group (www.crisisgroup.org). While these groups fall somewhere between professional news organizations and campaigning charities, they can rightly claim to cover the world in a more systematic way than do most broadcasters and newspapers.

There is also an argument to be made for aspiring journalists to consider working for groups such as these rather than traditional news organizations. If given the choice, many idealistic journalists who want their work to matter and make a difference in the world might well choose to 'report' for these organizations rather than spending their lives strapped to a computer in anodyne newsrooms knowing that little significant international news is likely to make its way into the newspaper or onto the broadcast.

In their *Foreign Affairs Magazine* article 'The new foreign correspondence', academics Hamilton and Jenner observe:

> Contemporary international news flows are more complex than at any time in history. We cannot assess the health of foreign correspondence the way we have done for so long, merely by counting the number of reporters sent abroad by major news media, or by simply analysing stories covered by The New York Times, Newsweek, and ABC News. To think otherwise is to display what scholars have called a 'fortress journalism syndrome.' (Hamilton and Jenner 2003)

References

Cockburn, P. (2007) War reporting Iraq: Only locals need apply. *Independent*, 26 February.

Gettleman, J. and Schmitt, E. (2008) Airstrike kills key militant in Somalia. *International Herald Tribune*, 1 May.

Hamilton, J. M. and Jenner, E. (2003) The new foreign correspondence. *Foreign Affairs*, September/October, http://www.foreignaffairs.org/20030901faessay82510/john-maxwell-hamilton-eric-jenner/the-new-foreign-correspondence.html.

Speak to senior media executives these days – particularly but not exclusively in print – and the tale of woe is the same: audience is migrating, income is in free-fall, the internet is taking over but to what end? The story from reporters and editors is almost identical, bemoaning the collapse in resources for serious reporting and the shrinking 'news hole' in favour of personality, advertisements and glossy fillers. When even the publisher of the *New York Times* states, perhaps only half seriously, that continuation of a print edition cannot be guaranteed, the media is clearly in crisis.

'The American press has the blues', writes Russell Baker in a recent article in the *New York Review of Books*. '[T]oo many good newspapers are in ruins … owners seem stricken by a failure of the entrepreneurial imagination needed to prosper in the electronic age …. [There is] a melancholy sense that the press is yesteryear's thing, a horse-drawn buggy on an eight-lane interstate' (Baker 2007).

But which media, and what crisis? While the established Western players especially in the United States scramble, refit their broadcasts or their newspapers, and continue to slash budgets and reporting staff, a major transformation is happening in the rest of the world.

'Out there', in emerging markets, in developing regions and even in countries experiencing the most severe of crises and violence, there is a journalistic explosion.

New talent, new institutions, entirely new mentalities of how to communicate within and abroad about countries in transition are transforming the media landscape in Africa, Asia and elsewhere, and even beginning to take up the slack in – if certainly not as yet to replace – international coverage by the established Western media.

Al-Jazeera is only the tip of the iceberg, and given the controversy over the station, perhaps a distraction from a deeper trend of which it is really only a representative. From community radio stations to continent-wide internet news providers, from challenging TV broadcasters to in-depth investigative reporting, local journalism is establishing itself as an increasingly reliable, responsible and indeed creative new force. Even struggling under the worst of circumstances, from bad economies to harsh dictatorships – or in some cases perhaps striving only harder because of them – local media is making a difference. Indeed, because the physical violence is preventing Western media from deploying adequately, Iraq may be the first major conflict whose narrative is largely being told through the reporting, and sometimes even the bylines, of people from the country itself.

Far from a crisis, then, 'international media' in the broadest sense is entering an exciting new era. The emergence of local media as a significant player in the global information environment is potentially one of the most important and indeed positive communications developments of our time.

Independent Voices in the Balkans

The roots of emerging local journalism can be traced globally, and the reasons are political and social, professional and technological, strategic and anecdotal.

But every story needs a beginning, and in a trend as broad and multi-faceted as this one, the choice of where to begin the narrative is inevitably subjective. Journalism, like archaeology, tends to have a historical date-stamp, with conflicts and crises serving as geological layers of experience from which our instincts and connections, our successes and failures – and thus our conclusions about both politics and the profession – are forged.

Like many in the mid-ranking journalistic crop, my formative experi-ence was the Balkans. This is not to denigrate the work of other local journ-alists and emerging media elsewhere, whether in other post-communist countries in Eastern Europe or beyond. But it was in Yugoslavia that I learned the extraordinary ability and energy of local journalists. It was there, too, that local journalists put themselves on the map to help drive a global movement.

Tito's collapsing federation was a perfect place to experiment with the use and abuse of media, and unfortunately it was a communist-turned-populist called Slobodan Milošović who led the way, followed all too readily by other nationalist extremists throughout the region.

For the story, often told, of his infamous visit to the Serbian-controlled southern province of Kosovo was more than anything a media story. There has been considerable research and reporting to suggest that the foundation episode – in which Milošović lent his support to Serbs living in the Albanian-majority province and thus created the central political myth that would drive him and his country through three disastrous wars – was staged. It only took a few well-placed rocks to plot a street scuffle between Albanian police and local Serbs, so that an ambitious Belgrade apparatchik could, on an apparently impromptu walkabout, pledge that 'No one should dare to beat [Serbs]!', and thus become an overnight political sensation (as quoted in Little 2006).

What even Milošović apparently never fully anticipated, however, was the way the episode would take on such power through the media. Filmed and directly aired back in Belgrade, it immediately took on enormous political importance.

The lesson was clear, and he grasped it straightaway. Not only did Milošović ensure that that clip continued to be played repeatedly, and thus establish his pre-eminence, he recognized the imperative of seizing control of the state broadcaster and using it to forge a mentality of hatred and violence towards other nationalities. Through egregious propaganda and lies – skilfully exploiting historic Serbian iconography of fear and victimization – Serbian media laid the groundwork for the coming war crimes in Croatia, Bosnia and Kosovo: what writer Mark Thompson, Balkans programme director of the International Crisis Group, early on referred to as 'forging war'(Thomson 1994).

But in response, another dynamic was unleashed – weak, chaotic, often at odds with itself, but ultimately evolving, strengthening and having an enormous impact within the region and far beyond. It is in the Balkans, as much as anywhere else, that the positive power of local media also became clear.

Compared to today's brutality in many parts of the world, in retrospect, the Milošović era was a golden time for dissidents and alternative voices. There were repression and closures, bogus tax charges and confiscations, arrests and even a few murders. But the regime ran what Serbian commentators called a postmodern dictatorship. As long as the main broadcaster was under total state control, alternative print publications and a few radio stations were allowed – a political zoo of democracy, tolerated in Belgrade as long as it did not have any impact on the country's heartlands from where Milošović drew his real support.

'Dictatorship, *moi*?' Milošović would effectively ask visiting diplomats, with all his awful boozy charm, pointing to the Belgrade press. 'See how they are kicking me?'

Kick him a few media and human rights groups did. Radio B-92, under the visionary but modest leadership of Veran Matić, became most known – emerging as both a medium and a movement and after many years establishing a network of independent radio stations across Serbia which directly contributed to the civic action through which Milošović was ultimately removed. As such, the radio station (in combination with the student movement) served as a model for numerous 'colour revolutions' that would erupt across the former communist countries in the coming decade – and put dictators on notice around the world about the power of civil society.

Yet in the worst days, for me at least, there was nothing like the depth and wit of the weekly Belgrade newsmagazine *Vreme*. Stojan Cerović was the political analyst, Petar Luković the irrepressible 'radical democrat', Dejan Anastasijević the courageous war reporter; 'Cofax' the illustrator whose weekly covers caught – or more likely set – the mood of the (few) Belgrade refuseniks. Here was real professionalism, commitment, a dose of forgivable taking themselves seriously – and a lot of talent.

My closest colleague for much of that time was Miloš Vasić, *Vreme*'s self-styled military analyst, who became intimately involved with our work at the Institute for War & Peace Reporting (IWPR). A former cop with a soft-spoken manner and unbelievable alcoholic capacity, Miloš was as sharp and as dedicated a reporter as it was possible to be, finishing every single night – no matter how late or inebriated the hour – typing the day's newly minted contacts into a computer database. Come the (usually rather rough) morning, everything would be turned into copy.

But the role of B-92 and the *Vreme* intellects was not just to keep the flame alive for Serbian democracy – no small feat though that was. In an extremely complex conflict, the quality, clear-sightedness and general feistiness of *B-H Dani* and *Slobodna Bosna* in Bosnia, *Feral Tribune* in Croatia, and the small but vigorous Belgrade free media scene was invaluable in contributing to international understanding.

While they were not able to reach and influence a mass audience at home, their publications, and their personal efforts at briefing, providing contacts and sometimes couches, and greatly assisting the Western media in every possible way, made a difference. With so much misinformation and confusion – in no small part spread by Western governments, too – the local independent media in the Balkans played a vital role directly and indirectly in helping explain the conflict to the rest of the world. Though some would no doubt disagree (and certainly few in Belgrade of any stripe supported the ultimate Western bombing of Serbia), arguably their role contributed to a major and more or less successful policy shift, effectively from appeasement of Milošović to confrontation, and finally to his overthrow.

Electronic Samizdat

Over this period, at least three key factors evolved to take the 'local media movement' global. Again, it is important to emphasize that different regions will have had different experiences and different players, and all have made a contribution. Much no doubt occurred in parallel. But the most obvious trends and lessons as I and others took them from the Balkans were as follows.

First, of course, was technology. There were flickerings of the internet at the start of the wars, but much of the early years depended on telephones, faxes and – where possible and affordable – expensive satellite technology. It was all but impossible to track freelance contributors in Sarajevo, and even if by a miracle they had actually written their piece, it was a nightmare to get it. By the end of the full decade's cycle of conflict, however, everyone was glued to their email and their mobile phones, websites were everywhere, and the new technologies were making it increasingly possible to cross borders and outwit dictators.

A particular highlight was the closure by the Belgrade regime of B-92 at a moment of particular political tension. The radio station immediately posted its output on the website – a very early use of audio online, and a demonstration that they would not be silenced. The government gave a lame excuse – something about the weather disrupting a connection – and shortly after they were back on the air.

IWPR had its own particular breakthrough – dispensing with a printed publication (which never could be disseminated properly anyway) for a website and playing a key role during the Kosovo campaign in what was deemed the first 'internet war'. We even initiated a comment and feedback section, though had to close it down quickly due to the scale of offensive nationalist diatribe from all sides that it collected.

Over the first two weeks of the bombing, an intrepid Albanian journalist named Gjeriqina Tuhina filed copy about her personal experiences and reactions as she essentially waited to be expelled or worse by the Serbian forces. We published them to considerable attention online and via email listserve – and widely syndicated them in newspapers in Britain, Europe, North America and beyond. We thought it was just a really good eyewitness column, but in many ways it could be said to be the world's first war-time blog.

All of these changes made it far easier and cheaper for any medium to collect, produce and widely disseminate within the region and internationally (and in multiple languages). This is not to say that all of it was very good – Macedonia, at one point, was reputed to have a television station for every village. But the entry level, the dissemination mechanism, and perhaps most importantly of all, as IWPR found, the on-going cost and inconvenience of information gathering, which had been so difficult, fell dramatically. Local and alternative media could proliferate, and in many cases indeed flourish, in the Balkans and of course globally.

A second key factor was 'media development'. Even now, when I explain what my organization does – strengthening local media in conflict areas – most people at first look at me very strangely, as if I have said the most bizarre and incomprehensible thing in the world, an inscrutable and unimaginable specialization.

In fact, the media-development sector is itself a maturing movement now, and the founding meeting of our sector-wide association – the Global Forum for Media Development – held in 2005 in Amman, Jordan, attracted representatives from 400 different groups and media from every continent.

To their credit, a few organizations, such as the International Center for Journalists, started to support free media even before the fall of the Berlin Wall. Others, such as Internews, threw themselves hard into Russia. But if the sector had a crucible, it was definitely the Balkans, where over a decade (and it is still going, although at a much reduced level) millions upon millions of dollars were spent by the full array of international government and private donors to try to build peace, democracy and development through the media.

At first there seemed something a bit cynical about it all – what was the point of sending $5,000 to a magazine in Sarajevo, however excellent, when the real issue was the West's failure to confront the Bosnian Serb gunners on the hills who had turned the city into a veritable shooting gallery?

Mistakes were also made – especially in big 'white elephant' projects which soaked up huge sums: a 'peace boat' in the Adriatic which could not broadcast over the Herzegovinan mountains; a transmitter 'ring around Serbia' which became out of date before it was completed; perhaps most famously 'Biltova TV', the broadcaster established after the conflict in Bosnia (hence named after the first high representative, Swedish politician Carl Bilt), which cost so much for so little result.

But lessons were learned, along the lines of any development guide-book: go gradually and with broad cooperation, work from the ground up and through local partners, eschew quick fixes for long-term engagements.

A great deal of journalistic training and other professional capacity building was also funded throughout the region. Training was held in everything from basic skills to specialist techniques, from human rights and economic reporting to investigative journalism and internet research. Countless Western journalists, glad for the opportunity to 'give something back' to Balkan colleagues who had helped them so much, opted to come to the region for short and longer-term stints to serve as trainers and mentors. Some may have been better than others, but the intentions were earnest. Balkan journalists too were offered exchange programmes to come to the West, to visit broadcasters and newspapers, universities and human rights NGOs.

IWPR's approach emphasizes practical experience, matching training and instruction with apprentice- or on-the-job-type learning in producing journalistic reports with intensive support and active mentoring. One of our most memorable experiences was of a lanky and somewhat wired Bosnian journalist from Mostar, who trained with us in London for four months during the worst of the horrible fighting in that scarred city, and then (as he was supposed to do) took his fresh skills and connections and *went back*. It was hard to fathom, but he continued his reporting throughout the war and long after.

Donors and participants became somewhat tired of constant 'training seminars' with poor results, and the focus has moved on. Indeed, the process of reviewing and assessing this period of investment in the Balkan media sector continues. Despite many accomplishments, there is a sense that sustainable professional improvements were not really achieved, and most of all that the media has failed to solve the underlying political problems.

Yet overall, the Balkan media has a high energy and basic capability, and 'graduates' of many media development programmes and projects have moved on to head up Balkan media, media-development and other organizations and initiatives that should continue to help the region move forward in the coming decade. Even if the results remain patchy, the core task of the media – to contribute to accountability and good governance – is well understood, both within the region and by Western donors.

At the same time, numerous media-development organizations emerged or were strengthened through their activities in the Balkans and elsewhere in the post-communist region, before extending their work in the communist transition countries and then expanding internationally, from Asia and Africa to the current focus region of the Middle East. The lessons learned have been spread, refined and multiplied – arising from different challenges and new creative talents in other areas. There is a palpable momentum.

A third factor in spreading the importance of local media – and perhaps most vital of all – may have been on the level of relationships, and an appreciation of the value of local knowledge and understanding.

Inevitably, any local journalist brings his or her own perspectives and biases to their work. But equally so, a local journalist lives and breathes that society and by definition knows it better. With increasing skills and experience – much of it gained in what may be the best training of all, working as 'fixers' to international media – at least a cadre of Balkan

IWPR Afghan journalist on assignment
PHOTO COURTESY OF IWPR

IWPR African journalists at work

journalists demonstrated that professionalism trumped 'national feelings', thus building increasing confidence across the local/international divide. Anyway, who else was going to put in that much time in all of these places to be able to report on them properly?

Western media still use their own correspondents and stringers for news and analysis, and much of Balkan journalism remains problematic. But professional levels have come closer in some areas. And certainly it is true that a strong op-ed opinion piece from a local source would now be actively welcomed more than ever before.

Everyone's a Blogger

This all still leaves those American media executives in Manhattan sitting at their lunches in Times Square or West 59th Street, wringing their hands. Numerous studies by Poynter and other institutes have demonstrated the fall in resources for foreign correspondents news and the shrinking space for hard news. A single bureau chief for 'Africa' simply cannot do a comprehensive job. As has been much commented on, the demands of 24-hour news to be always in front of the camera mean there is actually no time to report. These developments have further opened up the gap for local media – as well as NGOs, themselves functioning very much as media these days with serious research resources.

Three other developments have contributed to the opportunity for local journalists. The explosion of media and media formats in the West has destroyed the old concept of network news as the country's common hearth. Americans just don't gather around the box any more for the daily dose of news from a trusted Walter Cronkite figure. Those days are over, and are being replaced by partisanship and opinion – the CBS effect morphing into the CNN effect being overtaken by the Fox effect.

With TV becoming more opinionated and partisan – a development that is mostly, but not entirely, by the way, a bad thing – the same is occurring online, through the blogosphere. Now everyone is a commentator, and the internet has itself morphed into the earth's (unedited) letters-to-the-editor page. Some of the content amounts of course to invaluable civic contributions, while some of it (as with our Kosovo feedback section of a decade ago) is offensive drivel.

But in the circumstances, who is now to question the professionalism or supposed 'objectivity' of a local journalist, especially one with unique information or a special personal insight or experience? In the global information free-for-all, they have as much a right as any one to have their say.

Jayson Blair also played a role. The result of the ethical crisis at the *New York Times* – sparked by Blair, a journalist there, fabricating not only facts but also the location of his reporting – compelled the Gray Lady to institute a fresh policy of transparency over sourcing (Barry et al. 2003). Everyone in the profession has always known of the importance of the local fixer and 'researcher', doing much of the legwork for the bureau chief or the big-name presenter or correspondent, who always got the byline.

In the new era, that has had to change (at least a bit). I remember being instructed by an East Coast op-ed editor that they didn't like joint bylines (I was pitching a piece co-written with a Bosnian professor) because it takes up more space. Now, however, even news pieces are regularly followed with an extended list of journalists who 'contributed reporting'. The line between fixer and reporter is further blurred, and increasingly the 'local staff', one way or another, get their names in the paper.

Mess in Mesopotamia

All of these developments converged in Iraq. Whatever one's perspective on the intervention itself, there is little debate that the country has to be helped to move forward, and with the past decade's experience in the media development sector, and a very lively Iraqi professional class ready to engage, Iraqi media is set for a real boom.

In the heady early days after the fall of Saddam Hussein, publications proliferated like mushrooms, radio stations were launched throughout the country, and satellite dishes were huge sellers at the electronics shops in Baghdad and elsewhere. Starved of real information for decades under one of the world's most brutal dictators, Iraq was wired for news, and it was a revelation.

A detailed review of the Iraq media scene is a subject for another discussion. While overall a very positive development, needless to say the explosion in media outlets has not been met by a commensurate rise in professional quality. The biggest single mistake was made by the US government, which with no irony ploughed nearly $200 million into the creation of a public broadcaster called the Iraq Media Network (IMN). Yet Washington chose as its implementer a defence contractor from Virginia more known for disseminating arms than news, with predictable results. And no one knows where a fair proportion of those funds actually ended up.

Indeed, despite all the professions of support for free media and democracy, there has been no strategic investment in independent media in Iraq whatsoever, with 87 per cent of all international media support (according to IWPR research), and fully 96 per cent of US government support, being spent on the IMN, with the balance allocated piecemeal to separate short-term projects as well as an undisclosed amount on PR and military-led propaganda. It was a wasted opportunity on a monumental scale, especially after the lessons which should have been learned from the Balkans.

But in the end, everything in Iraq has come down to security. By August 2007, more than 220 journalists and media workers had lost their lives there; for comparison, 68 journalists died in World War II and 66 in Vietnam. This is according to the Committee to Protect Journalists (2004); other groups, taking different counts or defining 'media professional' differently, come up with even higher figures.

Adding to all of the crises of international media, the simple fact is that nowadays there are places where it is not possible for Western journalists to function. Safety and security have become a much higher priority (in no small part due to the efforts of one of the editors of this volume, John Owen), and episodes like the beheading of Daniel Pearl remove (or ought to) any lingering sense of reckless glory in foreign adventure.[1]

As a result, Western media have been forced to rely on local journalists in Iraq as never before (many of them trained through IWPR programmes), and Iraqis have responded. Tragically, they are giving their lives to the effort – 80 per cent of the Committee to Protect Journalists (CPJ) total are Iraqi nationals.

But they are also distinguishing themselves. The vast majority of media in Iraq have fallen into the partisan or sectarian trap, with every party, businessman and ayatollah launching their own personal media platforms and the public space representing a chaos of argument and polemic.

However, there have been notable exceptions. Within Iraq, Radio Dijla launched a phenomenon – shades of Veran Matić – with talk-radio programming unleashing a torrent of public dialogue and debate (as well as general all-round whinging) that had been stifled for decades. A number of publications, in Baghdad and Erbil, and even some joint ventures from London, found the teams, resources and spark to create credible professional products. The *Guardian* newspaper in London engaged an Iraqi stringer, Ghaith Abdul-Ahad, who emerged as a phenomenal reporter and scooped the prestigious James Cameron Award for Foreign Reporting in 2007 – the first time ever it was won by a local reporter. 'Salam Pax', the so-called Baghdad blogger whose first piece surfaced in the opening moments of the war and amazed readers, emerged as a superb video diarist/documentarist, with incisive and moving insights into the trauma and dynamics of current Iraq, commissioned for one of Britain's main news programmes.[2]

The mix of dedication and skill was driven home to my organization in June with the assassination of our colleague Sahar Hussein al-Haideri on the streets of Mosul, just outside her home. A print and radio reporter who had worked for local publications, an Iraqi news agency and IWPR, Sahar was also the main bread-winner for her family. But she was also deeply conflicted – at moments desperate to leave the country, as when her name surfaced on an Al Qaeda target list, and at other times so keen to continue as a journalist that she returned to Iraq without telling any of her anxious editors.

'Our psychological state is unbalanced because we live and think in fear and worry, and always think about our destiny and that of our family', she said, some months before her death. 'But I never thought about quitting, as journalism is my life, and I really love it.'

Sahar Hussein al-Haideri, IWPR reporter, murdered in Mosul, Iraq,
outside her home in 2007
PHOTO COURTESY OF IWPR

Think Global, Act Local

Pre-1989, the Cold War framework dominated the media as well as politics, and however inequitable, it made a kind of sense that Western, indeed American, news agendas were so dominant. If it didn't make the *New York Times*, it didn't happen, and purported news values – 100 peasants equal 10 priests equal 1 American – were brutally clear. Honourable efforts were made to strengthen coverage from the developing world – *South* magazine, Inter Press Service – but however much many of us may have disliked it, in the context of a bipolar US–USSR conflict, there was a logic to the overall news environment.

The world is completely different now, especially post-9/11. America is the 'hyper-power', but real power is more diffuse, and there is no longer a single overarching political narrative. Local news is more complex than ever before, and potentially – as Osama bin Laden proved – more important. Just when the structure of an overarching news environment is so radically changing, the need for detailed information around the world has never been more urgent.

The explosion of local media should, therefore be welcomed, not feared. Western broadcasters and Western media will find a way to survive, and remain predominant, whatever the changes. The quality and importance of Reuters, for example, remain its best asset, and it will always be needed.

Local media, too, still suffer grave problems. In Zimbabwe, journalism is all but illegal for anyone seeking to operate professionally outside the party line, and in Iran the risks of pursuing critical reporting include imprisonment, beating and public hanging.

IWPR dissents from the 'training fatigue' fashion, as we work with thousands of local journalists and their copy, and see both their abilities and their weaknesses. Basic skills always need to be strengthened and renewed, and specialist subjects are always emerging. And of course the financial concerns of the major media are often nothing compared to the impossibility of creating 'sustainable' local media in countries where there is no functioning economy.

Yet against all these obstacles, a vibrant local media scene is growing. Styles may vary from the US to the UK to the continent, and equally there will be different approaches to presentation around the world. Not everyone has to believe in a 25-word hard lead. But the concept of international standards, and the basic ethical and reporting conventions, can be agreed, and the number of reliable and reputable gatherers and sharers of news and information is spreading fast.

Perhaps the most important result of all of these developments would simply be a change in thinking – a dropping of the concept of an 'international journalist' (read: American or British) vs. 'local journalist' divide. What matters is the information. Who can get it, and the multiple ways to gather, produce and disseminate that information, should be celebrated. Quality and commitment are the key, not the nationality in your passport or that of your proprietor.

Anna Politkovskaya was the most informed and devoted chronicler of the long-standing tragedy which is Chechnya. The quality of her work, the searing nature of her insights, the commitment with which she travelled at such risk to speak to normal people in that disputed territory – this all speaks for itself. No one else could – or, given the risks, *would* – continue to report from there as she did, such that Chechnya was practically an information black hole but for her work. Widely showered with journalistic awards in Europe and the US, the only place she was not appreciated was in Moscow, where she was finally assassinated in autumn 2006.

In the outrage and sorrow following her death, Anna was praised around the world – not as a 'local' reporter, not as an activist, or someone who had become 'too involved'. Rather she was recognized for what she was, one of the greatest reporters of her generation anywhere. Nothing could be a better testimonial.

Notes

1 Daniel Pearl was a reporter for the *Wall Street Journal*, kidnapped and murdered in Pakistan in 2002.
2 'Salam Pax' was a student on City University's MA International Journalism programme in 2007–8.

References

Baker, R. (2007) Goodbye to newspapers? *New York Review of Books*, 54(13), http://www.nybooks.com/articles/20471.

Barry, D., Barstow, D., Glater, J. D. and Liptak, A. (2003) Times reporter who resigned leaves long trail of deception. *New York Times*, 11 May, http://www.nytimes.com/2003/05/11/national/11PAPE.html?ex=1367985600&en=d6f511319c259 463&ei=5007&partner=USERLAND.

Committee to Protect Journalists (2004) Iraq: Journalists in danger. http://www.cpj.org/Briefings/Iraq/Iraq_danger.html.

Little, A. (2006) Slobodan Milosovic's road to ruin. http://news.bbc.co.uk/1/hi/world/europe/4819388.stm.

Thomson, M. (1994) *Forging War: The Media in Serbia, Croatia and Bosnia-Herzegovina*. Article 19, International Center Against Censorship.

Questions for students

1 Is Maggie O'Kane right? Is it time for 'Western' news organizations to stop sending their international correspondents to cover stories in dangerous conflict areas where, for safety or cultural reasons, it is better to use a local correspondent who knows the language and has access that a 'foreigner' wouldn't have? Or is there always the need for a detached outsider perspective from a trained foreign correspondent who brings experience, context and fresh eyes to the story that may not been pursued by local correspondents for many reasons?

2 How have technology and the internet made it more dangerous for local journalists to work for international media groups?

3 What responsibilities do international news organizations have to local stringers or freelancers if something should happen to them?

4 What are the difficulties that local journalists face in their day-to-day journalistic work, especially in pursuit of stories that expose corruption or human rights violations?

5 Can NGO/journalistic organizations such as IWPR, Human Rights Watch or International Crisis Group be truly independent if they depend upon donor contributions and are inclined to be partisan if necessary?

10

Taking the Right Risk

Chris Cramer

Introduction

JOHN OWEN

When 22-year-old Iraqi photographer Namir Noor-Eldeen was killed in July 2007 by a US air-strike in the eastern part of Baghdad, he became the fifth Reuters journalist to lose his life covering the Iraq war. His driver and assistant, Iraqi Saeed Chmagh, a father of four, also was killed in circumstances that may never be fully explained to their families or to the Reuters news agency.

A day later in Iraq, another Iraqi journalist, 23-year-old Khalid W. Hassan, a reporter and interpreter for the *New York Times*, was shot to death on his way to work. According to the Committee to Protect Journalists (CPJ), his normal route was blocked for security reasons, and he was forced to take an alternative route.

Two journalists and a media assistant killed in one week in Iraq in a war that has claimed the lives, as of August 2007, of more than 220 journalists and media workers, more than 80 per cent of whom are Iraqi.

The deaths of these three Iraqis underline one statistic amongst many grim findings in the International News Safety Institute's (INSI) inquiry into the deaths of journalists over a 10-year period: two

Iraqi photographer Namir Noor-Eldeen, 22, became the fifth Reuters journalist to be killed covering the Iraq war, July 2007

PHOTO COURTESY OF ASSOCIATED PRESS/PHOTO-GRAPHER KHALID MOHAMMED

journalists have been killed every week somewhere in the world. The 2007 INSI report, *Killing the Messenger*, examined what was the bloodiest decade in history for journalists – 1996 to 2006. One thousand journalists and media support workers lost their lives during that period, nearly two-thirds of them murdered.

It has been said that murdering a journalist is the ultimate act of censorship. The INSI study reinforces the terrible truth that in far too many countries gunmen or contract killers can murder journalists with what press rights groups term impunity, the near certainty that they will never be arrested or successfully tried and punished.

What the INSI study reminds us is that those paying the greatest price are local journalists whose probing of human rights violations, government corruption and organized crimes make them targets for murder.

It is rare that the international media spotlight the killing of a local journalist but an exception, as mentioned in the previous chapter, was the murder of Russian journalist Anna Politkovskaya in Moscow in October 2006. She had been an outspoken critic – in print and at international conferences – of President Putin. She had also refused to stop reporting on the human rights violations perpetrated by Russian troops in the forgotten war in Chechnya. She was shot dead entering the elevator in her Moscow flat.

Where the international media do pay more attention is when journalists and camera crews working for leading Western networks or newspapers are killed in the line of duty. The best-known example was *Wall Street Journal* correspondent Daniel Pearl, whose grotesque execution was posted on websites.[1] And when a militant Islamic group in Gaza held the BBC's Middle East correspondent Alan Johnston hostage for more than three months in 2007, the BBC made

A man walks past flowers laid down in front of Russian journalist Anna Politkovs-kaya's house in central Moscow, October 2006

PHOTO COURTESY OF THOMSON REUTERS/PHOTOGRAPHER SERGEI KARPUKHIN

certain that he wasn't forgotten. Johnston's ordeal ended when he was released unharmed.

For Reuters and the BBC, two of the world's most conscientious news organizations when it comes to training and protecting their newsgathering teams, it is a stark reminder that their journalists are always at risk in a post-9/11 world.

However seemingly futile are efforts to protect journalists in places like Iraq, there is still a powerful case to be made for ensuring that every member of a news team, whether an international journalist, a local reporter, a freelancer or a media assistant, is provided with a hostile-environment training and first aid course.

The safety training movement began in earnest in the mid-1990s when it became clear that international journalists covering the wars and conflicts that erupted in the Balkans after the collapse of the Soviet

Union and the fall of the Berlin Wall were facing dangers they'd never experienced before. Instead of worrying about being killed because they were in the wrong place at the wrong time, journalists were now being targeted by insurgents and militia groups with little respect for or understanding of international law and the rights of journalists to cover them. And journalists used to wandering wherever they liked without any special protection were losing their lives in increasing numbers. According to the CPJ (who have failed to include in their figures those local journalists who serve as legitimate media assist-ants – local fixers and/or interpreters), 42 journalists were killed in 1992, 57 in 1993, and 66 in 1994 (Committee to Protect Journalists 2007).

And like everything having to do with news, it was the extraordinary that captured our attention. In October 1993 in Mogadishu, three photo-journalists and a news agency soundman were beaten to death by a mob of Somalis, furious because of an American air attack that had killed scores in an unsuccessful raid on what was thought to be the headquarters of the Somali warlord Mohammed Adid. Amongst the dead was Dan Eldon, a charismatic 22-year-old photojournalist working for Reuters. Later his mother Kathy and sister Amy would produce a moving documentary, *Dying to Tell the Story*, about him and the sacrifice made by other journalists who'd lost their lives.

But it was local journalists and media caught up in brutal civil wars and military coups who were at much greater risk, but as usual there wasn't much international attention paid to their plight. At what may have been one of the first conferences devoted to the issue of safety training, held at my European Centre of the Freedom Forum in London in September 1997, the secretary-general of the Paris-based Reporters sans Frontières (RSF), Robert Ménard, deplored the killing of 59 jour-nalists in Algeria between 1993 and 1996. He noted that 58 were Algerian.

Ten years after that major London conference on news safety, the most outspoken advocate of safety training remains Chris Cramer, until recently executive vice-president and managing editor of CNN International. When Cramer spoke at the Freedom Forum, he was the head of BBC Newsgathering, where he had earned a reputation as a boss who evoked both fear and admiration. Stories were legion about

'Cramer' (as he's universally known in the television news business) and his no-nonsense overseeing of correspondents and producers.

For tough guy Cramer to champion safety training as well as trauma counselling gave these initiatives legitimacy inside the BBC and credibility with other news organizations just waking up to their responsibilities to protect and train their own staffs. I was the chief of CBC Foreign Bureaux at the time, and because Cramer and the BBC had purchased armoured cars and outfitted their field teams in Bosnia, I could make a more convincing case with my colleagues in Toronto that we needed to spend the money to do the same.

Cramer has also been instrumental in helping establish and promote the work of the INSI and continues to serve as its honorary president.

Note

1   Daniel Pearl was kidnapped and murdered in Pakistan in 2002.

References

Committee to Protect Journalists (2007) Journalists killed in 2007. http://www.cpj.org/killed/killed07.html.
International News Safety Institute (2007) *Killing the Messenger: Report of the Global Inquiry by the International News Safety Institute into the Protection of Journalists.* INSI.

One of the most depressing parts of safety management is when something happens which undermines all the work we think we have done and all we think we have achieved in the past 20 years with regard to raising the profile of safety and safety awareness in the media industry.

The most recent for me was during the Israeli–Lebanon conflict in August 2006. CNN had deployed its largest contingent of staff to the region for many years; around 120 if you include those already stationed there, correspondents, producers, fixers, camera folk and the like. It was the most serious outbreak of hostilities since the mid-1980s and was clearly deserving of the kind of coverage CNN is famous for.

Adrienne Arsenault, CBC News,
wearing a flak jacket, 2006
PHOTO COURTESY OF CBC NEWS

The safety of our staff was obviously uppermost in our minds as we dispatched people from Europe, the Middle East, Africa, Asia and the United States. Were they battle trained? Were they properly equipped? Did they have the right vehicles and security staff with them?

These questions – and the appropriate answers – are now standard practice for assigning editors and producers at CNN, indeed for most mature news organizations as they cope with the dangers of covering a troubled world. More media people and those who support them have been killed in the last few years than ever before. In 2007, up to the time of writing (28 November), 171 journalists and media staff were killed (INSI 2007c).

The setback I refer to may seem trivial but it represents the principle of two steps forward, one backward, in protecting staff.

The conversation that depressed me was one I had with the assignment desk about a correspondent reporting from the war zone without wearing a flak vest – to my mind, exposing himself unnecessarily to dangers as he provided hourly coverage from one side of the conflict.

'He doesn't really want to wear his vest', I was told. 'He feels as if it's like a new boy at school being told to wear his blazer, though he will put it on if we insist.'

Which, of course, we did.

The reason this exchange is depressing is that it reminded me of exactly the same kind of machismo conversation I experienced when head of newsgathering at the BBC in the early 1990s. There were correspondents and support staff who were resistant to the attempts by management back at base to impose their safety views on the frontline practitioners; wily operators who saw this as, at best, a kind of nanny interference and, at worst, actions designed to reduce the company's legal responsibilities towards those in hostile zones.

The truth, of course, is neither of those.

By and large – despite their apparent intelligence – members of the media believe they are immune from that which they cover. They sally forth in their thousands each year to cover hostilities and disturbances the world over, safe in the belief that they cannot be touched – mentally or physically – by the mayhem around them. Then they return to the safety of their homes and their families and pick up where they left off. For many of them, as Anthony Loyd describes it in his book *My War Gone By, I Miss It So*, it can be like jumping off a speeding train: surreal, frightening, and frequently resulting in acute depression (Loyd 1999).

Much of the media industry is in denial that post-traumatic stress disorder affects reporters, photographers and others in the news business. Only recently have many news organizations even accepted the most basic thinking when it comes to preparedness for what many of them do on a regular basis.

Let us first of all turn to physical safety training.

Until very recently – perhaps only 10 years ago – the media at large believed that journalists simply did what they had to do: get into a war zone or hostile environment, cover whatever story was unfolding, report the story, and get out again. To do so unscathed was mostly a matter of luck rather than judgement. Tell the story, get back home, do your expenses and relax until the next time.

There was no training before you arrived. You learned on the job, kept your feelings and experiences to yourself, and, if you were lucky, got assigned again when the next story went pear-shaped.

Recently things have started to change.

At the BBC, change coincided with some particularly onerous legislation in the early 1990s which made it clear that employers were liable for where they sent their staff, what they asked them to do, and how they asked them to do it.

The wake-up call for me came when BBC newsmen covered the siege of Dubrovnik in October 1991. The team I had assigned there decided the situation was too dangerous to stay. The city was under constant bombardment and their lives were at risk. They told me they were leaving.

I was furious, knowing that our media competitors were going to stay and, as it turned out, produce remarkable coverage which won several broadcast awards.

How could my staff do this to me? How could they leave a story of such magnitude when the world needed to know what it looked like and how it felt to the people who lived there?

Then – my epiphany. How could I react this way? This was not only the wrong emotion; it was, and is, fundamentally bad management. Since I had deployed staff to a war zone or hostile environment, then I was legally – and for that matter, morally – responsible for their safety. Everything else was secondary.

None the less, I was personally still troubled. Media men and women, I thought, did what they did – they always had. Our profession was inherently dangerous.

For years journalists had set out to cover the world at large with nothing but a pen and paper, occasionally a tape recorder or still camera and, more recently, a video camera There were occasions where they would don a steel helmet, sometimes a flak jacket, but for the most part they had only their vocation, and precious little else, to protect them.

A safety officer for BBC's News department, Peter Hunter, convinced other managers and me that appropriate safety training and safety awareness were a prerequisite for a responsible media company. 'Do you think for a moment that fire officers and members of the armed forces go and do what they do without safety awareness and first aid training?' he argued. 'Why should members of the media be any different?' He was right. And the media industry worldwide owes him a huge debt for raising the issue and giving it the recognition it deserved.

For years, journalists from all parts of the business had adopted the principle that you never refused an assignment, no matter how dangerous it might turn out to be; that doing so would run you the risk of losing some professional esteem. For men and for women, it was all a matter of 'balls'. And there was the added hazard many of us felt that if you displayed a lack of courage to your bosses there was a real risk of losing the assignment.

But Peter Hunter's campaigning led to BBC managers like myself wanting to change the system. We wanted to send out a very strident signal that it was perfectly OK to talk about safety and safety training – that it wasn't in any way 'wimpish'.

And change it we did, though it was an uphill and frequently depressing experience.

In 1991 and 1992 the BBC's deputy head of newsgathering, Ray Gowdridge, and I drew up a mantra for reporters, producers and technicians. And then we communicated it to all other staff and freelancers working for the BBC:

No story is worth a life. No picture sequence is worth an injury. No piece of audio is worth endangering our staff.

And we went much further. We committed ourselves to spend all it took to provide the best equipment, the best training, the best vehicles and the best insurance for our staff, including freelancers, in harm's way. We eventually got support from the BBC's Boards of Management and Governors.

We also declared that no staff would be deployed to a war zone without training in battlefield first aid and battlefield knowledge. That policy was painful and meant that some reporters did not go.

But we were rigid: only the most experienced of correspondents and crews were allowed to bypass this policy, and then only if they went on refresher courses. We put these courses out to bids.

Companies sought the business and we adapted their programmes to suit our needs. Senior management also took the training programmes, introduced some of the sessions and endorsed the courses back at headquarters. Veteran correspondents went, listened – and appreciated what they learned.

However, some BBC staff, still in denial, were appalled. They accused us of using this safety policy as an insurance scam to avoid our responsibilities. They refused to wear their flak jackets and ridiculed us as managers. But we persevered.

I've heard all the excuses as to why correspondents and support staff don't wear flak jackets:

'They are too heavy. They get stolen.'

'They become targets.'

'They distinguish us from the local population and render us incapable of doing our job.'

What they were really saying to me was: 'Let me do my job. Let me get killed in the course of my work. Let me be a martyr to my cause.'

Another excuse we frequently heard from bosses and employers was: 'Print is different from broadcasting.' Their theory was that print journalists travel much more safely by themselves, are more experienced, and don't need safety awareness training.

Nonsense. This was, and still is, the worst form of arrogance from employers. My view has always been that print journalists, more likely to operate away from the media 'pack', are probably in more danger than their broadcast colleagues. They tend to be less well equipped, less able to afford armoured or properly protected vehicles, and more likely to be targeted.

And there were other excuses from some media bosses: 'We don't send staff, we send freelancers. We couldn't possibly afford to insure them.'

I find this really dangerous and irresponsible talk from employers. My experience has been that some newspaper bosses are more irresponsible than those in broadcast when it comes to deploying their staff without regard to their safety.

Some news organizations in the United States, for all their sophistication, are frequently the most reluctant to confront the issues I have been talking about. With some notable exceptions – including my own company, CNN, ABC and NBC and the *New York Times* – few American news organizations have any formal safety training schemes for journalists travelling into harm's way.

So who is taking the lead? Where are the guidelines? Where are the best practices?

In Britain, courtesy of the BBC, CNN and some other organizations such as ITN, Reuters and Associated Press Television News (APTN), a new set of safety guidelines was endorsed and agreed to at the Newsworld Conference in Barcelona in November 2000.

They read as follows:

1 The preservation of human life and safety is paramount. Staff and free-lancers should be made aware that unwarranted risks in pursuit of a story are unacceptable and must be strongly discouraged. Assignments to war zones or hostile environments must be voluntary, and should only involve experienced newsgathering practitioners.

2 All staff and freelancers asked to work in hostile environments must have access to appropriate safety training and retraining. Employers are encouraged to make this mandatory.

3 Employers must provide efficient safety equipment to all staff and freelancers assigned to hazardous locations, including personal issue Kevlar vest/jackets, protective headgear, and properly protected vehicles, if necessary.

4 All staff and freelancers should be afforded personal insurance while working in hostile areas, including cover against death and personal injury.

5 Employers are to provide and encourage the use of voluntary and confidential counseling for staff and freelancers returning from hostile areas or after the coverage of distressing events. (This is likely to require some training of media managers in the recognition of the symptoms of Post-Traumatic Stress Disorder.)

6 Media companies and their representatives are neutral observers. No member of the media should carry a firearm in the course of his or her work.

7 Media companies should work together to establish a data bank of safety information, including the exchange of up-to-date safety assessments of hostile and dangerous areas.

These guidelines were just the beginning, but what they were intended to do was to raise the issue of safety to a new level. What they did not address was the large number of indigenous journalists around the world who need to report on the hostilities inside their own countries without the benefit of proper training or safety equipment. This category was and remains the most likely to be at risk.

Greater safety awareness by the media won't stop the profession being targeted or being killed or injured by accident. But the Barcelona safety guidelines were an important start.

Post-Traumatic Stress Disorder

Let me now turn to another, more controversial area of concern: what I have described as 'safety training for the mind'. That is post-traumatic stress disorder or PTSD. This will be described in greater and more eloquent detail in chapter 11 of this book, but I mention it here because it is only in recent years that the issues of safety for the mind and safety for the body have been linked in the thinking. I mention it also because I speak from bitter experience and because, in common parlance, I have a victim's-eye view.

In April 1980, I briefly became a hostage in the Iranian Embassy in London. I was there to take delivery of a visa to visit Teheran for the BBC, where a large number of other hostages had been seized by Iranian revolutionaries inside the US embassy. For me it was a masterpiece of bad timing as, within minutes of my arrival inside the building in London's

Kensington, it was stormed by six terrorists, backed by Iraq and to publicize a disputed region of Iran. Before the siege was broken six days later by Britain's Special Air Services the gunmen had killed one hostage and were threatening to murder another each hour before blowing the building up and all of us with it.

On the second day, after personal intimidation and a pistol-whipping, I faked a heart attack to get out.

Back at the BBC I was offered counselling by my bosses. One person suggested that I go out that night and get drunk and come back to work the following day. I took the latter's advice, mainly because I then belonged to the school of journalism that believed that real men (and women) simply returned to work and shrugged off their memories and anxieties. So I refused any form of psychiatric counselling, and refused two additional offers over the next few years or so.

I know now that I could not have been more wrong. I personally went through many years of hell, for the most part concealing this from all those around me. I couldn't travel in planes, in elevators, on escalators, couldn't go to restaurants, cinemas or theatres. I drank too much, went from one unsatisfactory relationship to another and only avoided drugs because I figured I might enjoy them too much! For years I was, in my mind, persecuted. I looked under my car for bombs each day for a while and, of course, didn't find any.

My problem was typical. I was afraid to admit I had lost my nerve.

These days I am much wiser and better understand that journalists cannot be immune from the stories they cover or are involved in – that the flak jackets they wear and the armoured vehicles they may travel in are not effective protection against mental and emotional stress.

At the BBC in the early 1990s we introduced confidential counselling for staff and training for managers to spot the effects of PTSD. It was very controversial, though more recently many mature news organizations have, thankfully, adopted this practice. But it took far too long for the media industry to realize that it is perfectly natural for journalists, like other folk, to feel the effects of trauma. There is nothing particular about the work they do that keeps them immune from what they experience; to deny it and think otherwise is unnatural at best and dangerous at worst.

These days I have my own personal profile of a media person who is probably suffering from PTSD. He or she will start conversations with phrases like 'This is my thirtieth war, you know'; 'When I get home I go out and get drunk and get laid or whatever – and then I am fine.'

In addition I find it most curious that in the United States of all places, where they invented the notion of grief counsellors, most people in the media haven't until fairly recently given it a moment's thought. There is virtually no acknowledgement at all within the industry, apart from some notable exceptions, that PTSD even exists among their ranks.

The media industry has been in the dark ages for far too long when it comes to understanding the dangers it operates under. News coverage of the world is inherently dangerous and those who continue to travel to challenging regions are more at risk now than ever before. They face more risks from more factions, sometimes governments, than their predecessors ever did.

The first thing we should do is consider the facts.

According to the Committee to Protect Journalists (CPJ), more than 600 members of the media were killed around the world between 1992 and 2006. Most have been murdered rather than killed in combat and, terrifyingly, the statistics show that government and military officials are behind many of the killings. Few killers are ever brought to justice.

When the CPJ figures were released in September 2006 (Committee to Protect Journalists 2006), they showed that an average of three journalists were being killed each month. And this did not include accidents or health-related deaths, except in war zones. Eighty-five per cent of the deaths affected local reporters, editors and photojournalists.

Similar findings by the International News Safety Institute (INSI) in its global safety inquiry of 2007, which show that 1,000 journalists were killed between 1996 and 2006, compound the on-going tragedy facing the profession (International News Safety Institute 2007a). INSI has a policy of including not just journalists and media workers but also those who work with them, such as drivers, translators, fixers and security staff.

And yet, despite these screaming statistics, many parts of the media believe they are somehow immune from all they cover and refuse to confront the obvious. Some of us have been saying this for almost 20 years now. The simple fact is that much of the media industry is in denial when it comes to safety awareness and an awareness that we can be affected mentally as well as physically by what we cover.

The establishment of the INSI has taken the entire issue of media safety and appropriate training to a new level of sophistication, as has the work of the Rory Peck Trust (www.rorypecktrust.org), which was set up after the death in crossfire of distinguished British freelance Rory Peck in Moscow in 1993. The trust relies on public donations to honour the work of freelances around the world as well as sponsoring hostile-environment training for selected freelances.

Both organizations also act as lobby groups to draw public attention to the dangers the media work under. The organizations' work is painstaking and frequently frustrating.

INSI has marshalled the efforts of many broadcasters and print organizations to review and update constantly some of the safety guidelines first drawn up by the BBC in the 1990s and then finessed by UK news organizations at the Newsworld Conference in 2000.

INSI's guidelines now state:

1 The preservation of life and safety is paramount. Staff and freelances equally should be made aware that unwarranted risks in pursuit of a story are unacceptable and strongly discouraged. News organisations are urged to consider safety first, before competitive advantage.

2 Assignments to war and other danger zones must be voluntary and only involve experienced news gatherers and those under their direct supervision. No career should suffer as a result of refusing a dangerous assignment. Editors at base or journalists in the field may decide to terminate a dangerous assignment after proper consultation with one another.

3 All journalists and media staff must receive appropriate hostile environment and risk awareness training before being assigned to a danger zone. Employers are urged to make this mandatory.

4 Employers should ensure before assignment that journalists are fully up to date on the political, physical and social conditions prevailing where they are due to work and are aware of international rules of armed conflict as set out in the Geneva Conventions and other key documents of humanitarian law.

5 Employers must provide efficient safety equipment and medical and health safeguards appropriate to the threat to all staff and freelances assigned to hazardous locations.

6 All journalists should be afforded personal insurance while working in hostile areas, including cover against personal injury and death. There should be no discrimination between staff and freelances.

7 Employers should provide free access to confidential counselling for journalists involved in coverage of distressing events. They should train managers in recognition of post traumatic stress, and provide families of journalists in danger areas with timely advice on the safety of their loved-ones.

8 Journalists are neutral observers. No member of the media should carry a firearm in the course of their work.

9   Governments and all military and security forces are urged to respect the safety of journalists in their areas of operation, whether or not accompanying their own forces. They must not restrict unnecessarily freedom of movement or compromise the right of the news media to gather and disseminate information.

10   Security forces must never harass, intimidate or physically attack journalists going about their lawful business. (INSI 2007b)

At the same time the INSI's members debated the value of media workers wearing or displaying an internationally recognized insignia such as 'Press' or 'Media' or 'TV/radio', before deciding that this was far more likely to make its bearers a target than give them immunity from violent acts. That controversial debate is still very much on-going.

Media in Iraq

Probably the most challenging story the media has ever covered has been the on-going conflict in Iraq – unquestionably the most dangerous since World War II. As of October 2007, 163 media workers and those who supported them had died since the US invasion of that country in 2003. In the first few months of the conflict, I calculate the chances of dying for international media were 1 in 100, compared to 1 in 1,000 if you were a serving US or Coalition soldier. Ten times higher!

For those international media organizations that have chosen to stay and cover the story, the safety of their staff far outweighs any other consideration. The costs in terms of staff attrition and the rising price of security and safety requirements have caused many organizations to pull out of the country.

The local Iraqi media, of course, have no such luxury, and the death toll among indigenous reporters, photographers and camera staff is grim evidence of that.

The most safety-conscious of news organizations, such as BBC, Reuters, Associated Press (AP), CNN and other US broadcasters, now deploy only their most experienced staff to Iraq. Some media, like CNN, have banned novice staff from entering the country without the most stringent of hostile-environment training or additional security to accompany them.

A popular saying with news executives such as myself is:

> Working in Iraq is akin to a frog sitting in a pan of boiling water. The water is heating up the whole time and the dilemma for us is knowing quite when to order the frog to jump – knowing when is the right time to abandon the story. Our nightmare is that when we give that instruction it will be too late. The frog will have boiled to death.

What the executives mean by these remarks is that the danger to media workers in Iraq has transcended any experience thus far in the history of news coverage. There are no safety textbooks available to news managers, no 'best practice' guidelines to determine how to operate. In short, we make it up as we go.

Who could possibly have predicted the level of safety precautions now standard for those who want to keep staff inside the country: dozens of armed guards, concrete gun emplacements, armoured vehicles for travelling even the shortest of distances, the real need for security consultants carrying heavy weapons as journalists and crews carry out their basic reporting?

Most news organizations operate from purpose-built 'fortresses' situated in and around Baghdad and elsewhere with 24-hour guards, vehicle inspection points and multiple roadblocks. The cost for most media companies has soared into the millions of dollars each year. And all of this before a single story is covered.

The assignment is certainly not for the faint-hearted in the profession.

Merely getting into Iraq requires steel nerves and a passion to cover the most dangerous story in the world.

CNN's senior vice-president of newsgathering and operations, Tony Maddox, who has succeeded me as the head of CNN International, described for me his visit to the country in 2005.

> Talk to people who have been in the news business for a long time and they will agree there has never been an assignment quite like covering the conflict in Iraq.
>
> In a sustained and focused manner we have not seen before, on this dateline journalists are prime targets.
>
> Add to the usual horrors of being caught up in a war the feeling that you are seen as a more valuable prize than the enemy.
>
> And the usual horrors of this war should be re-stated. There are attacks on civilian populations with sickening regularity. Massacres are commonplace. With each week come details of another atrocity more wretched than the last.

And news teams have to live amongst this. Sustained by hugely courageous local staff our reporters, crews, producers and engineers live in complexes which house the bureau, their living quarters, and an ever present security force.

CNN's property in Baghdad is what was once a fine house in an upscale neighborhood. Now it resembles a fortress.

And I was due for a visit.

CNN employees are some of the most courageous news professionals in the business. That description would certainly not apply to me, but I do manage many of them, and it was time to see what life was like in this operation which eats so much of our budget, and so much of my time.

On hearing of my plans to visit I got plenty of unsolicited guidance that the journey in and out was probably the most frightening part of the assignment. I realize international news is an unlikely career choice for a nervous flyer, but believe me, I am not the only one. That said the expensive once a day flight from Amman to Baghdad would test the enthusiasm of the most eager fly-boy. I suspect you have heard about the corkscrew landing, where the plane spirals to the ground to avoid any 'incoming'? The only good thing I can say about it is that it is marginally less terrifying than the return flight, where a fully loaded passenger jet tries to gain altitude while flying in ascending circles, with one wing pointing at the ground.

And the plane journey is as good as it is going to get, because it is followed by the drive to the bureau.

This is along a 12 km road known as the BIAP (Baghdad International Airport). The military call it Route Irish, and others call it the Road Of Death, due to the staggering number of attacks that take place on it. During the time of my visit, in September of 2005, the mayhem was at its height, with roadside bombs, mines, armed ambushes and countless other sorts of badness.

The least bad option for traveling down it is in a two car convoy. Like most media organizations we use armor plated vehicles, driven by our security advisors, who are in constant radio contact with each other, and with an operator at our base.

In a Kevlar vest and helmet I was in the back of an SUV, affectionately known as the 'bomb magnet', and in full 'eyes on' mode – looking for any sign of mischief. I had been advised by the driver to stay alert and not to doze off after the long journey from Atlanta. I am not even sure he was joking.

For the world's most terrifying stretch of highway it is rather barren looking terrain, with the bulk of the journey going through not much of anything, with worryingly long grass on either side of the road.

'Makes perfect cover for attackers. You would think the Yanky would get someone to mow the bloody lawn,' said one of the security guys. A very good point, I thought, although probably the world's least desirable gardening assignment.

It says something about a drive that arriving in the shambles that is downtown Baghdad is something of a relief, and the bureau felt like sanctuary.

Strange how we are able to recalibrate our expectations. Sitting in Atlanta I would not say that working in the Baghdad bureau is a relaxed environment, but compared to the rest of that city it is a relative oasis of calm and control.

CNN ex-pats do tours of varying length, but most are there for at least a few weeks. Before anyone goes for the first time we always push back. We need to make sure people have thought it through. It is not just the obvious risk – many of our folks are more intrepid than I – it is also the grinding nature of the work.

Obviously all work travel outside of the bureau is challenging and requires a lot of preparation and planning. There is no social life beyond the bureau; you cannot even go outside for a decent walk.

Our facilities and catering are decent, for many Iraqis they would be considered real luxury, but in reality you are stuck with the same folks in the same place eating the same food for a long time.

There is not much else to do but work, and there is plenty of that. Every day. It's a grind.

Yet here is the odd thing. There are very few complaints. It is as though the nature of the story and the circumstances of covering it bring their own sense of perspective. The sort of things that would annoy or frustrate the best of us in our regular jobs have to take their place alongside far more important issues.

For many of our people, certainly those in the earlier parts of their career, it can be a life changing experience.

I was reflecting on this as I sat in a pub in London, before undertaking the final leg of my journey back to Atlanta.

For those of us who oversee this kind of assignment there is a much needed heightened sense of awareness about the damage that our people can suffer in covering one story of suffering and inhumanity after another. We employ trained professionals to help individuals work through such issues, and our managers are tasked with looking for signs that people may be struggling.

Along with the focus on safety I would identify our willingness to tackle issues such as Post Traumatic Stress Disorder as one of the most important developments in the news business in the past ten years.

But we also need to recognize that people will always be willing to do assignments like the war in Iraq, and that if properly managed, such experiences can be a huge benefit to their development.

I know that my brief visit certainly had a positive impact on me.

I got an improved understanding of the pressure on our operation and its people, and a far better insight into the story.

And I was not nervous on the BA flight from London to Atlanta. Well, not as nervous as I used to be.

Maddox's description of the journey in and out of Iraq and his brief experience of life there, almost under siege, explains precisely why reporting events there is so difficult. And why it is hardly surprising that most members of the media think twice before venturing out of their compounds into the city.

Those that do, only do so after a detailed risk assessment of the trip's purpose and the story or information to be gained.

It is called 'risk versus reward'.

For many news organizations, certainly the more mature ones that place the welfare of their staff ahead of the story, the mechanics of covering the war in Iraq are completely overshadowed by safety considerations. CNN has a series of strict protocols which determine whether a story or assignment even begins. The Baghdad bureau chief, or his nominee, is required to provide a detailed risk assessment of what is planned, which is then discussed with one of the resident security consultants permanently housed in the CNN bureau. They need details of the trip, the chosen route from the bureau, time spent on the ground, and the expected return time to the bureau. The CNN crew must maintain constant communication with the bureau, including check calls, and alternative routes to be taken in case of emergency.

And the risk assessment is then discussed with senior managers back at CNN's Atlanta headquarters, who must sign off on the assignment. Each time the question is asked: 'What is the risk, what is the reward?'

A bureaucracy such as this was unheard of in any media organization until recent years but has been forced upon newsmen because of the harsh realities of covering such a conflict. CNN, in common with many other media organizations, has had staff murdered, injured and taken hostage in Iraq and now takes every step it can – short of leaving the country – to protect its employees.

Armed Security

Unbelievable though it may sound to veteran journalists and media practitioners used to safer times, it is now not unusual for broadcasters and print workers in Iraq and elsewhere to be accompanied by security personnel – and sometimes they are authorized to carry weapons.

There is a very big distinction here between journalists carrying weapons and those who are paid to protect them, though the distinction, to be candid, is not appreciated by some purists.

Under no circumstances have the senior management of companies such as the BBC and CNN authorized their staff to arm themselves. To do so would destroy both the practice and the principle that journalists should never be seen as combatants. Which is why those few in our profession – like Geraldo Rivera of Fox News in the United States – who say they would carry guns – ill-serve the entire profession. Not that the notion of journalists carrying guns is particularly new. Perhaps the most famous was Winston Churchill, when he travelled for *The Times* as both a soldier and a journalist. And he has been emulated by many others down the years.

But Iraq and Afghanistan and Somalia are different.

In those countries the dangers to members of the media are so heightened that only irresponsible managers would choose to ignore the obvious. Our staff can be targets. Some people want to harm or kill us. And we gain nothing by being martyrs.

This controversial issue – the subject of much pontificating on subsequent media discussion panels around the globe – came to a head in the first few weeks of the Iraq War in 2003 when a CNN crew found themselves driving through Saddam Hussein's home town of Tikrit in Iraq.

One of CNN's most experienced and accomplished correspondents, Brent Sadler, had already been the subject of attention by extremists who seemed bent on attacking a high-profile Western media team. For that reason he was travelling through Iraq with armed security, locally hired staff and British Army-trained personnel when their car came under attack.

This is what happened, in Brent's own words.

We were able, during the hours of light, to get into the center of Tikrit – but not before penetrating the outer layers of the ancestral home of Saddam Hussein.

The CNN team got there even as the coalition forces, the U.S. Marines, were heading north toward Tikrit to start a battle to really crush the last [holdout] of Saddam Hussein.

We were able to get into two very major Iraqi military complexes. One was a regular Iraqi army tank unit, a vast area. In this complex, [we found] bunkers of abandoned armored personnel carriers, abandoned tanks. The hatches were open on some of these fighting machines, the soldiers apparently having fled in haste.

There was also a lot of destruction, quite clearly from allied air strikes over the past days. We certainly heard more air activity when we were on the outskirts of Tikrit.

We also went to a Republican Guard tank regiment. Their fighting machines were not in place, suggesting they may have moved to defend the inner core of Tikrit.

That [presumption] figures with what we're hearing from the latest reports of the U.S. Marine Corps, that five Republican Guard tanks were destroyed by helicopter gunships in the past few hours.

Now when we got into the very center of Tikrit, a [person at a] checkpoint waved us through. It wasn't particularly hostile, nor was it particularly friendly.

We went through, started speaking to some people, then after just a few moments we came under gunfire and had to drive at speed out of Tikrit, running a gauntlet of fire from many, many machine guns. (CNN 2003)

It was just a few months later, in January 2004, that a second CNN team was attacked with much more tragic consequences.

The employees were returning to Baghdad in a two-car convoy from an assignment in the southern city of Hillah, when they were ambushed on the outskirts of Baghdad.

Translator and producer Duraid Isa Mohammed, 27, and driver Yasser Khatab, 25, died from multiple gunshot wounds. Cameraman Scott McWhinnie, traveling in another vehicle, was grazed in the head by a bullet.

The CNN vehicles were headed north toward Baghdad when a rust-colored Opel approached from behind. A single gunman with an AK-47, standing through the sunroof, opened fire on one of the vehicles.

That lead CNN vehicle, hit at least five times, managed to escape from the gunman as the CNN security adviser returned fire.

'There is no doubt in my mind, that if our security adviser had not returned fire, everyone in our vehicle would have been killed', said correspondent Michael Holmes. 'This was not an attempted robbery, they were clearly trying to take us out.'

Holmes, producer Shirley Hung, a security adviser and a second driver were traveling with McWhinnie and were not hurt.

The Opel spun around on the median as the second CNN car, with Mohammed and Khatab inside, drove off the highway, according to CNN crewmembers.

The CNN crew in McWhinnie's vehicle drove to an Iraqi police station and asked officers to go back to the scene to help Mohammed and Khatab.

The crew then drove to a forward operations base of the U.S. 82nd Airborne, where McWhinnie was treated, and the U.S. military sent a team to find the missing CNN employees. (CNN 2004)

So once again armed and professional security managed to protect at least some of the CNN staff, while others in the industry realized that the die had been cast when it came to the level of care and protection required in war zones.

Conclusion

So what next for the media as they continue to cover this challenging world?

Certainly a complete awareness that we are no longer a protected species, even if we ever were.

There are those out there who wish us harm and wish to disrupt our mission.

The best protection, as I see it, is to ensure that every journalist and media worker has a complete appreciation of the inherent risks we face.

People entering the profession must realize that risk assessment is as much a necessity as skills in shorthand or an appreciation of the law or the ability to conduct an interview and shoot a story on video or for the stills camera. Media students need to be taught about safety for the body and for the mind at school or university.

They also need a forensic understanding that exemplary journalism might actually be a protection against violence and intimidation. If we conduct our job with care and precision and a sense of fairness then maybe there will be fewer reasons to attack us as we work.

Appendix: Surviving the Story – Staying Safe in a Hostile World

In its 26-year history CNN – covering the world as it does – has had hundreds of staff in harm's way. Fortunately, most have come away from dangerous assignments unscathed. Tragically, some have not. In the course of the network's history, personnel in the field have encountered serious illness, injury, detention, kidnapping and even death. Each searing incident served to underscore the fact that proper survival training and preparation are essential to any assignment into a zone of hostility.

CNN policy requires staff deployed to an active war zone to have previously completed a five-day 'hostile regions' course. AKE Limited – a UK-based company which specializes in field safety for journalists – provides the instruction. The course, officially known as 'Surviving Hostile Regions' (SHR), covers a broad range of life-saving skills including intensive first aid and situational awareness. Since inception, over 600 CNN personnel have completed the SHR course.

SHR provides a framework of how to deal with dangers lurking in not only areas of combat but countries where the risk to life isn't bombs and bullets, but the setting itself. Indeed, common, everyday accidents or illnesses encountered in the developed world mean a quick trip to the emergency room for a suture or a dose of medicine. Take that same set of circumstances, put it in a location where the closest hospital is 100 kilometres away via unmarked roads, and the injured person dies due to lack of immediate care. AKE training provides techniques on how to survive on your own or with the help of a colleague with the same training.

CNN is not alone in its approach to safety adherence or training; many other networks in the US and internationally have similar programmes. AKE is one of at least three companies in the world which offer such a survival course aimed specifically at journalists.

The AKE course was established in 1993 – and was the first of its kind. Founded by former British Special Air Service commando Andrew Kain (the 'AK' in AKE), the training draws upon military knowledge used in high-risk settings, but adopts that know-how to what is required to do newsgathering in the field – be it for newspapers or broadcast.

The SHR course falls into four categories: awareness; medical; self-sufficiency; planning (AKE Group 2008).

The training is delivered in a blend of classroom lectures and, more dramatically, practical outdoor scenarios. These scenarios drive home what is learned in class by having the course participants react to very real, unrehearsed exercises on the training ground. Using role players to take the part of combatants, the journalists are put into circumstances they may have never imagined themselves in, but perhaps know can happen on assignment.

Let's look at one survival training example called the 'roadblock'. SHR participants having had at least two days of lectured course material are 'put into the field' (adjacent to one of AKE's three regional training facilities). An AKE team leader informs the journalists they are about to set out on a story – and one of their fellow journalists has arranged for a just-hired fixer to drive them to a rendezvous where they will meet the person they wish to interview. Nothing unusual here; most journalists are familiar with such a routine.

The students are allowed to discuss amongst themselves what they should do before embarking on the journey. The group is then driven off and after a series of confusing turns they come upon a wooded area. A road barricade is pulled in front of the van and it is suddenly surrounded by masked men banishing guns.

For the next 30 minutes the course participants face a jarring episode which has played out all-too-really for many colleagues – armed men with automatic weapons have stopped your van. What do you do? 'Get out! Exit the vehicle now!' a gunman yells. The menacing, camouflaged belligerents yank at the doors and point AK-47s at the faces of the occupants. Doors are opened and the journalists are manhandled to the side of the road.

Wallets and passports are demanded. 'Keep your head down! Do not look around. If you do not obey you will be shot!' The fighters are unrelenting in their hostility.

The SHR participants by now have had little time to think. The scenario is so realistic many are visibly shaking. It's unnerving to all. The 'commander' then walks behind the now lined-up and bowed-down travelling journalists.

'Where are you going? This road is *controlled*! You must all be spies for the CIA!'

It is at this point that whatever SHR framework was learned in the classroom comes to the surface. Some protest the interrogation. Others stay quiet. One perhaps considers making a run for it. The rest aren't sure what to do. This is as close to real as it gets.

The scene continues to play out and even escalates – including a moment where one of the female journalists is dragged away by a couple of the militiamen. In some course scenarios there's a muffled scream and gunfire is heard. But the action takes place out of sight of those being held at the van, who must then wonder – *am I next?*

Each class may end the action play a different way. Some outcomes could be benign – someone takes charge and artfully finesses the release of everyone. Other times the conclusion may be violent – a result of an ill-advised action by one of the well-intentioned but wrongheaded course students. What's said and what's done prove one thing: nothing is certain. Each class reviews its roadblock scenario, and AKE instructors discuss the merits of how individuals handled their situation. The field episode shows there are no absolute 'rights' or 'wrongs'. You as a journalist can only do so much – but what you can do is be as prepared as possible. The AKE SHR training gives participants a skill set of how to *optimize survival* if caught in an actual life-threatening confrontation.

The roadblock session is one of at least three field exercises experienced during the five days' training. Additional course material covers how to recognize weapon types, including artillery, mines and booby-traps. If one questions the need to have knowledge of weapons, consider the value of understanding whether the 'trigger safety' is on or off on that AK-47 being pointed at your head. Faced with likely execution – and a split-second chance to escape – knowing that bit of assault weaponry trivia becomes glaringly important.

From the dramatic to a bit more mundane, the other elements of the training give the participant further confidence. They include how to size up conventional and non-conventional military. If it's a conventional army, what is their level of professionalism and abilities? Who's in charge? How do you lower your profile – and not look threatening? When and when not to wear body armour?

As mentioned earlier, surviving a hostile region isn't by any means limited to avoiding gunfire, mines or kidnapping. Keeping healthy in the settings journalists often work in is equally important. Disease and injury can take a life just as a bullet or a bomb can. To that end, the AKE SHR course puts a big emphasis on medical aspects. Going far beyond a standard Red-Cross-type 'first aid' lesson, the session covers:

- assessment of injury, airway management;
- controlling major bleeding, wounds;
- fractures;
- cardiopulmonary resuscitation (CPR);
- climatic conditions – heat/cold, altitude sickness;
- venomous animals;
- common diseases, how to avoid;
- travel medicine.

Self-sufficiency also plays a big role reducing risk in the field. The course provides a good overview on how to maximize flexibility and resilience on hardship assignments. Highlights of this include:

- food intake, exercise and proper clothing;
- maintaining mental equilibrium and psychological strength;
- navigation skills;
- hostage avoidance skills.

One of the most important aspects of the SHR course is an emphasis on planning – simply thinking ahead. AKE stresses the following in this regard:

- Define the aim and the risk.
- Do the homework – who's involved, climate, geography.
- Essential gear – what's needed?
- Contingencies – what if?
- Teamwork, responsibility – work out in advance?
- What to do upon arrival – fine-tune plans.

It is important to make clear that working as a journalist in a 'hostile region' is risky no matter the training. While taking the five-day SHR course gives a reporter, producer or photographer a new sense of confidence, as well as a life-saving skill set, it does not make them bullet-proof. Thoroughly adhered to in the field, knowledge from the course is all about building the odds in your favour. Even if those positive gains come in single-digit percentages, the added sum can be critical – the factor between sickness or health, between being injured or being wound-free – and indeed the difference between death and life.

References

AKE Group (2008) Surviving hostile regions. http://www.akegroup.com/shr.htm.

CNN (2003) Sadler: Shots fired at CNN crew in Tikrit. Cable News Network. http://www.cnn.com/2003/WORLD/meast/04/13/otsc.irq.sadler.

CNN (2004) 2 CNN employees killed in attack. Cable News Network, http://www.cnn.com/2004/WORLD/meast/01/27/sprj.nirq.cnn.casualties/index.html.

Committee to Protect Journalists (2006) http://www.cpj.org/deadly/index.html.

Committee to Protect Journalists (2007) Journalists killed in 2007. http://www.cpj.org/killed/killed07.html.

Cramer, C. (2002). We have a long way to go. In *Sharing the Front Line and the Back Hills: International Protectors and Providers, Peacekeepers, Humanitarian Aid Workers and the Media in the Midst of Crisis*, ed. Danieli, Y. Baywood for the UN.

International News Safety Institute (2007a) *Killing the Messenger: Report of the Global Inquiry by the International News Safety Institute into the Protection of Journalists.* INSI.

International News Safety Institute (2007b) *The INSI Safety Code*, http://www.newssafety.com/safety/index.htm.

International News Safety Institute (2007c) News deaths hit all-time high. INSI Brussels, 28 November,http://www.newssafety.com/stories/insi/insideaths281107.htm.

Loyd, A. (1999) *My War Gone By, I Miss It So.* Atlantic Monthly Press.

Acknowledgements

I should like to thank the following for their contributions to this chapter: Will King, CNN International, the BBC, Tony Maddox and Brent Saddler.

Part of this chapter was published previously as Cramer (2002). The editors would like to thank the publishers for their permission to reproduce this.

Questions for students

1   Is Chris Cramer (and are others who share this view) right that 'No story is worth the life of a journalist'?
2   Has the used of armed guards to protect journalists in war zones such as Iraq and elsewhere undermined the role of journalists as neutral observers?

3 Is it morally right for a journalist wearing a flak jacket and helmet to interview civilians in war zones who do not have similar protection?

4 Discuss the following questions with a news organization of your choice.

  (a) What is their policy on paying for hostile-environment training courses for any of their staff members who may be assigned to conflict zones or any potentially dangerous assignment?

  (b) What is their policy on paying for training for local journalists and freelancers they deploy and on the provision of safety equipment for them?

  (c) Do they have any programme in place that tells them what to do if one of their journalists is taken hostage? Would they pay a ransom? How closely would they work with their government? Would they make a similar effort for any local fixers who were also taken hostage?

11

Emotions, Trauma and Good Journalism

Mark Brayne

Introduction

JOHN OWEN

He was a good snapper, but it didn't take much for Charlie to persuade him to, as he put it, go into motion pictures. From then on, they were insepara-ble; Slovenia, summer 1991; Novska and Pakrac, October 1991; and Sarajevo, Christmas 1992, Mostar, summer 1993, and on and on: Mogadishu, Luanda and Huamabo, Kabul, all the assignments lined up in his mind like so many rows of tape. They were holidays from hell every one of them, and Jacek seemed to survive them by keeping everything contained within the black frame of his viewfinder. (Michael Ignatieff, Charlie Johnson in the Flames)

Killing comes quickly enough and most people can do it when certain influ-ences are either removed or exerted. Instead, it was the sight of the bereaved, which chilled my core. I had seen them in every war I had visited, thousands of people who had to deal with a sudden shell, bomb, or sniper's bullet that in an instant had torn them from one or several of their greatest loves. And they had managed to absorb that pain and carry on. How did they do it? (Anthony Loyd, Another Bloody Love Letter)

A standard line in a Chris Cramer speech to journalist groups was that news teams who'd been covering dangerous and disturbing stories when they arrived home needed to do their head laundry as well as getting their dirty clothes washed and cleaned. As Cramer noted, in the past, the tendency was for journalists returning after seeing and experiencing terrible things to find re-entry a difficult process. Most couldn't bring themselves to tell their families and friends about what horrors they'd seen in Bosnia, Rwanda or Chechnya. Instead they often turned to other journalists who'd both understand and accept what they were going through, often lubricated by heavy drinking.

Some of these returning war correspondents found themselves engaging in bizarre behaviour that concerned, even alarmed, their loved ones. Allan Little, the BBC's veteran correspondent, recalls being at a dinner party that included the young children of his host, after he'd just come back from an assignment that had exposed him to the death and suffering of young children. Little says that at some point he said how nice it was to be around children who weren't dead or dying. That remark stopped the usual innocuous dinner-party chatter and raised many questions around the table about his state of mind. Little eventually did seek help.

In the past, there was little recognition in news organizations of just how serious the problem was for those being dispatched to dangerous places and troubling assignments. Many news organizations did have in place formal counselling programmes for all kinds of mental health problems, but nothing specifically aimed at supporting their journalists who found themselves emotionally destabilized by what they were experiencing in far-flung places.

There was also a dominant male culture that pervaded all news organizations. In the late 1970s and early 1980s it was rare for news organizations to employ women correspondents and producers, let alone women video journalists. The macho approach to anything that cut across things psychological or emotional was to take a tough guy stance and deal with whatever was troubling you in whatever way seemed to work outside the workplace.

Once, on assignment as a field producer for CBC News in El Salvador in the early 1980s when death squads, supported by the American-backed Salvadorian military, were executing rebels or those thought to be sympathetic to them, I had to deal with a problem I had no idea how to solve. Our young Salvadorian fixer had guided us to the scene of a massacre, a family – mother and father and their 20-something-year-old sons – shot dead, floating in a pool of blood. After we recorded those ghastly images and gathered what information we could from Salvadorians living close by, we retreated to a café. I became aware that our soundman hadn't said a single word. In fact, he had become catatonic, so traumatized by what he had witnessed that he was unable to utter a word. About all we could do was put him on a plane back to Toronto and what we hoped would be a full recovery away from this menacing place, chilling enough to give most of us sleepless nights.

If I were field producing today for CBC or another enlightened major news organization, I would have been prepared to deal with most safety and trauma crises. I certainly know whom I would have called immediately for guidance.

It would have been to Dr Anthony Feinstein, a professor of psychiatry at the University of Toronto and the world's foremost authority on the 'psychological hazards' of covering war and conflict.

I got to know Anthony in the course of collaborating on what became a groundbreaking study that documented the full extent of war journalists' susceptibility to what is called post-traumatic stress disorder or PTSD (Feinstein et al. 2002).

Anthony's findings, that close to a third of all those who took part in this study (more than 80 per cent of the best-known names in internationalism responded) suffered symptoms associated with PTSD, shocked the news industry and jolted many, including BBC, CNN and other big broadcasters, into action.

CNN and Chris Cramer turned to Anthony Feinstein to help with counselling journalists who'd struggled after disturbing and dangerous assignments.

Shortly after Anthony's study became a talking point about trauma and journalism, Mark Brayne, a long-time correspondent and editor, first with Reuters and then the BBC World Service, became an outspoken voice about the need for news organizations to practise a far greater duty of care.

Brayne himself had been on a personal journey from journalism to studying psychotherapy. For him there was a direct link between one's state of mind and the quality of one's journalism. He'd considered himself a burnt-out case after risky and exhausting reporting of the turbulent events of 1989, including the Tiananmen Square massacre in Beijing and the bloody Romanian revolution in Bucharest. Brayne felt that after witnessing so much violence and suffering he'd lost his ability to maintain his detachment and his impartiality. He thought that it was time to come off the road and practise his journalism in the more sheltered role of a senior inside editor.

Mark Brayne the journalist and Mark Brayne the practising psycho-therapist found the perfect organization for his duel identity: the Dart Center for Journalism & Trauma. Founded by Dr Frank Ochberg, an American psychiatrist who'd done seminal work in PTSD, the Dart programme began challenging journalists and the media to improve their coverage of violent events in the United States. Then Dart expanded overseas, and Mark Brayne became its founding European director.

Like safety training, trauma support has more than its share of detractors in the news industry. Many working journalists abhor the idea of reporters worrying too much about their psychological state and too little about honing their craft skills. But enlightened heads of news organizations have recognized what Mark Brayne has referred to as 'emotions, trauma and good journalism'. It is this linkage that Brayne discusses in his chapter.

References

Feinstein, A., Owen. J. and Blair, N. (2002) A hazardous profession: War, journalists and psychopathology. *American Journal of Psychiatry* 159: 1570–5.
Ignatieff, M. (2003) *Charlie Johnson in the Flames*. Grove Press.
Loyd, A. (2007) *Another Bloody Love Letter*. Headline Review.

Imagine you've just qualified in journalism studies and are preparing for your first job interview.

The post advertised is for an economics and finance reporter, working in New York. You're not an economist yourself. You studied history at university before you did a journalism course. But you're keen to learn.

How might you prepare for the interview?

Would you want to find out, for example, about Futures markets and how they work? Would you want to know more about the Dow Jones,

FTSE, the NASDAQ or the DAX? Perhaps you might want to learn the basics of how to read a company's annual report?

Or let's say you're going for a job as a sports reporter. You love sport but aren't too sure about some of the disciplines you may be asked to cover.

Before going before the selection panel, might you consider, for example, checking on what sports constitute the pentathlon? Would you be confident of explaining the rules of baseball? Would you at least want to know the difference between American and British football?

Here's another question, bringing us closer to the subject of this chapter.

How much of the standard Western news agenda – reflected in television bulletins, newspaper front pages, radio headlines or indeed online – deals at some level with trauma; trauma, that is, as in the experience of extreme human distress, whether aftermath, experience in the moment, or anticipation?

The usual answer we get in training, regardless of nationality or culture, is somewhere around two thirds.

So, thinking of the sports analogy – that knowledge of the game is a prerequisite for intelligent reporting – and considering at the same time that trauma is the mainstay of the daily news agenda in most news cultures, how much training do you think journalists either get, or ought to get, in understanding the rules of trauma (for there are rules of trauma, and it is a subject which can be quite easily understood)?

The answer to the first question – how much training is done? – is not a pretty one. Traditionally, and until very recently, journalists have had no training in trauma, either at journalism school or in entry-level training on the job or in what in other walks of working life is called continuing professional development, or CPD.

I was a journalist for 30 years with Reuters and the BBC, and the only introduction I had in emotional awareness was when I stepped to one side in the 1990s, got myself some therapy, trained as a psychotherapist, and then brought those ideas back into journalism to campaign for a new approach to trauma.

Let's be fair. Journalists and their employers should not be condemned for not doing something they didn't know should be done.

After all, it was only relatively recently, in 1980, that the diagnosis of PTSD – post-traumatic stress disorder – was first formally defined, and it's also taken a while for other First Responder professions that deal with disaster and tragedy, such as the police, emergency workers and fire fighters, to acknowledge that psychological trauma is a key dimension of their work.

The argument of this chapter, however, is that ignorance and lack of training in trauma in the field of journalism are no longer defensible.

So the answer to the second question – how much training do journalists need? – is an emphatic 'a great deal more than the nothing they've had so far'.

And while it won't be possible to turn you into a trauma expert in 7,000 words, I do hope that by the time you've got to the end of this chapter you'll be convinced that this agenda matters.

Why Do I Need to Know about Trauma?

Understanding trauma isn't about becoming all touchy-feely, weeping over the screen or your copy or reporting only good news. Nor is it about sending journalists off to a shrink the minute they have to cover the trauma of a cat stuck up a tree.

Trauma knowledge matters in journalism because trauma and emotions are far and away the most important drivers of human behaviour.

Whether they're choosing a partner for life, a political party or a brand of toothpaste, human beings operate far more from their gut than from their reason and their head. The difference between humans and animals is that people have the illusion that they're making rational choices.

So a basic knowledge of emotions and trauma is one of the most important tools we have to be better journalists.

In particular that knowledge helps us:

- understand how and why human beings do the things they do, especially when they're affected by extreme distress (which is often how we find them on a big story);
- do the best possible interviews and practise the best journalism;
- tell the story of tragedy and disaster well – authentically, accurately and with respect;
- have, as vulnerable individuals and human beings, the tools to keep on track and functioning as well as we can, both professionally and emotionally (something you will do well to bear in mind if you do find yourself covering extreme trauma).

In short, this is about emotions, trauma and good journalism, and how they all relate to each other.

What is Trauma?

As products of evolution, we are programmed as human beings to be both fascinated and affected by violence and tragedy. Well before the advent of news and journalism, our response as human beings to traumatic experience helped determine how we've survived and prospered as a species.

The experience of trauma is as old as the human race and has been well described in literature from the Bible and the Ancient Greeks (indeed, the very word 'trauma' itself is Greek, meaning a piercing or a wounding), to Shakespeare and the English poets of World War I.

The science of trauma, however, is much more recent, developing from the late nineteenth century through the two world wars to the formulation of the PTSD diagnosis in 1980.

Before going into the implications for journalism and self-care, let's consider the basics of what might be considered traumatic as opposed to simply stressful.

Judith Lewis Herman, a leading American psychologist, talks usefully in her influential book *Trauma and Recovery* of psychological trauma as an affliction of the powerless. 'At the moment of trauma', she writes, 'the victim is rendered helpless by overwhelming force. When the force is that of nature, we speak of disasters. When the force is that of other human beings, we speak of atrocities. Traumatic events overwhelm the ordinary systems of care that give people a sense of control, connection and meaning' (Herman 2001: 33).

It doesn't need to be major, like war or catastrophe. It might be something bad that's happened to a friend. It might be something which to an observer might seem pretty minor, but in the individual's universe is big. Nor does the person experiencing a traumatic response need actually to have been there; they might just have had a connection.

What counts is how something was experienced personally. It's not for outsiders to say to someone who's feeling traumatized that it wasn't that bad really and that they should pull themselves together.

That can help explain when you're covering a story why some people are much more dramatically affected than others by the bad things that are happening to them.

If you realize that as a journalist, there's a much better chance that you can understand them and retell their story with authenticity and compassion.

More narrowly, PTSD as a *clinical diagnosis* as currently defined by the American Psychiatric Association is understood as the distress that can follow from:

> Direct personal experience or the witnessing of an event involving actual or threatened death or serious injury, or other threat to a person's physical integrity; or learning about unexpected or violent death, serious harm, or threat of death or injury experienced by a family member or other close associate. (American Psychiatric Association 2000: 463)

In this definition, the person will have experienced intense fear, helplessness or horror. To summarize the diagnostic criteria from the American Psychiatric Association (2000), the symptoms on which a diagnosis of PTSD can be based, if they continue for more than a month, can include:

- recurrent and intrusive recollections, including for example flashbacks or nightmares;
- emotional numbing and avoidance of people and places that are reminders of the event;
- persistent physiological arousal, which may include irritability, poor concentration, sleep disturbances, physical symptoms such as stomach cramps or sweating, and an exaggerated startle response.

That's a much tighter definition of trauma, but shouldn't be understood as meaning that if someone doesn't collect the right number of points on a trauma scorecard, they're absolutely fine.

Psychiatrists across the world are in fact currently (at the time of writing) working on a new diagnosis expected to be included in the next 'cookbook' of psychiatric disorders due around 2012, and likely to be termed 'complex PTSD' or similar. This will capture experiences of debilitating emotional distress that have their roots in more broadly defined trauma such as childhood abuse, divorce or bullying.

That said, when you're reporting or dealing with trauma and extreme human distress, be aware (and we'll come back to this) that most people, most of the time, recover pretty well from trauma, and especially so if they have good social support from friends, family and work colleagues.

That was true of New York after the 9/11 attacks on the World Trade Centre in 2001. It was true of Londoners and Berliners during the bombing of World War II. It is true most surprisingly, perhaps, for survivors of rape, which research shows is the single most psychologically traumatic experience any human being can go through.

People are changed by trauma, and bad experiences are not forgotten, but human beings, in all cultures and at all times of history, are astonishingly resilient.

It is therefore important not to pathologize trauma, nor to see it as a massive clinical problem. Remember also when covering or experiencing trauma yourself that even among those who find themselves wounded in the longer term, full-blown PTSD as such is a less likely outcome than depression and anxiety, relationship breakdown, alcoholism or substance abuse.

Taking this positive assessment to its extreme, there are those who argue that PTSD is just a Western political construct, invented in the 1970s by left-wing, anti-Vietnam-War American feminists.

As a journalist and psychotherapist who's worked as a hack or a shrink with people from most global cultures, I disagree.

True, the majority of people in most cases of trauma won't go on to develop PTSD, but a significant minority will. Why should they continue to suffer, sometimes for decades, when simple education, support, recognition and, for some, treatment could transform their lives?

Data from the 1990s suggests that the incidence of PTSD shown in table 11.1 can be expected in an American or European population after these events.

Table 11.1   Expected incidence of PTSD in an American or European population

Event	Expected incidence of PTSD (%)	
	Male	Female
Witnessing death/injury	6	8
Life-threatening accident	6	9
Physical attack	2	21
Combat	38	–
Natural disaster	4	5
Rape	65	46

Note: No figures are available for the incidence in women resulting from combat.
Source: Kessler (1995).

Note that men and women respond differently to trauma.

Research studies consistently indicate that women are roughly twice as likely as men, on the whole, to go on to develop PTSD.

Note also that natural disasters are less likely to cause PTSD than violence or attack at the hands of other human beings. If human beings aren't to blame, then, however tough, it does seem easier to come to terms with loss.

True, different cultures handle trauma differently, and putting a Tibetan herdsman, a Sudanese refugee or a Bosnian rape survivor into Freudian psychoanalysis would be a very bad idea. Many would argue now that that kind of therapy isn't the best course of action for a Western trauma sufferer either.

Most trauma specialists in most countries do now, however, recognize that human beings are much more similar in their emotional responses to trauma than they are distinct and that social support, attachment and connection can make a profound difference in how any human being comes to terms with tragedy and loss.

Reporting Trauma: The Journalism

At its most immediate level, trauma and the profound physiological survival responses set off by the witnessing or fear of injury or death can do extraordinary things to an individual's perception and judgement, whether they're a victim, survivor, eyewitness or reporter.

One example from the London newspaper the *Guardian* illustrates the point: a young Shanghai-based reporter for the *Guardian* found himself in October 2005 reporting the apparent beating to death of a civil rights activist at the hands of rural vigilantes in a southern Chinese village. The reporter and the activist had driven into the village together, against the reporter's better judgement, as the village was known to be a violent place and he feared they would be attacked. The activist was indeed set upon violently. In terror for his own life, the reporter locked himself in his car and watched with horror through its windows as he saw his friend being beaten, he thought, to a pulp – one eye out of its socket, his neck ligaments exposed, his body twisted and broken – in short, dead. The reporter rushed back to his hotel and filed a long and emotional account of what he had seen. It led the front page of next day's edition. The reporter had indeed reported the interpretation his traumatized brain had put on what he was witnessing. The only problem was that the activist had not been killed at all, but turned up a couple of days later, black and blue from the beating but very much alive.

Once it was clear what had happened, the aftermath was well handled by the *Guardian's* editorial team, which realized, a little late, that the reporter had had a major traumatic experience and unconsciously over-interpreted what he had seen.

Apologies were made to the authorities in Beijing, corrections printed,[1] and a great deal of compassion and understanding shown to the reporter. But with a little more training in trauma awareness, both on the ground and at head office, this could have been avoided

So, what happened?

The reporter's experience was unfortunate in a journalistic sense but makes complete sense in terms of brain science.

It's the brain's job to filter, interpret and make personal sense of the mass of information it's getting from the five senses. That's true even at the quietest of times.

But faced with traumatic stress – and depending on a host of other factors – the brain codes and interprets the signals it's getting in particular ways. The system switches rapidly into alarm and survival mode and people can suddenly feel and behave very differently from their normal selves.

That's why eyewitnesses to traumatic events are notoriously unreliable and why even seasoned journalists at moments of high emotion can sometimes get it wrong, as did the *Guardian* reporter (and possibly many more journalists, sometimes highly experienced, whose mistakes may never be known).

Getting the Story

Approximately half of the journalists who conducted these interviews acted professionally and with incredible empathy and understanding. It worked both ways and in return I gave them a much better story … Likewise I had a lot of bad interviews. In every case a bad experience triggered re-traumatisation and I identified two common threads. I believe the two most important factors in triggering re-traumatisation during a trauma victim / survivor interview are loss of trust and loss of control. (Dr Mary Self, whose story of recovery from terminal cancer was international front page news in 1999)

Good journalism – and above all being accurate and fair – matters whatever the story, and when it comes to the journalism of trauma and extreme human distress, the principles matter even more.

Observing them will both give you a better story and help ensure that your reporting does not make things unnecessarily worse for those whose story you are telling.

Traumatic events often bring with them very tight deadlines and intense competitive pressure. In your determination to interview survivors and victims and get the story, don't forget that you're dealing with vulnerable human beings who may be going through the worst experience of their lives.

Here are some suggestions, as valid for covering crime or tragedy in the local community as for reporting on war or global-scale catastrophe.

- Victims and survivors, people who've been violently bereaved and also, often, people who have 'merely' witnessed such events or dealt with the aftermath, can experience a sometimes sudden loss of feeling safe in the world. It's not just about what they've physically been through. Remember the opening definition in this chapter about what can constitute trauma – what counts is the meaning it has for the person affected.
- Reactions differ, and can surprise and even shock. People may seem supercool, rational and calm. They may show dignity and sometimes astonishing composure. On the other hand, people may be intensely emotional. They may be overcome with grief and despair. They may be angry and bitter. They may be confused and distracted. They may be frozen and unable to talk. All are part of normal, predictable trauma reactions.
- Victims, survivors, families and friends will often be struggling to regain control after their world has been turned upside down. An interview with such people is very different from interviewing a politician or an expert, so do what you can to give them a sense of control of the conversation.
- Allow them to set the pace; to take breaks; to end the interview. If you sense they're worried about what they've said and there's time, you might read them back some of the quotes you've recorded or noted and check you've got their story right.
- However urgent your deadline or impatient your editors back at base, take things slowly. Be confident and clear, respectful and kind. Be aware that people you speak to may not be able to remember later either what you asked or what they said.
- As a journalist, there can be no excuse for gratuitously making things worse for the people whose stories you report. Being treated or reported

badly by the media can be experienced by victims and survivors as even more traumatic than the original event.

One important thought: the moment that someone hears of the death of a loved one can be experienced as the most traumatic moment of their life. Before you make an approach for an interview, find out if possible whether they have already been told of what has happened by the appropriate authorities. If you can, avoid being the first person to break such news to relatives or close friends.

Interviewing

Good and sensitive interviewing is central to all good journalism but when you're dealing with trauma victims and survivors, these skills are especially important.

It's about more than asking good questions. It's about creating, however briefly, rapport and a relationship – one that allows both you and your interviewee to give of your and their best.

- Be clear before you approach anyone or begin an interview what you want from it. What information do you need? How does this person's experience potentially fit into the bigger narrative that you are exploring? It's important to have done your preparation and your research, but remember that the expertise will come from the interviewee.
- You may yourself be feeling nervous, fearful, even angry about the story you're reporting. It's important to acknowledge and be aware of your own feelings, but try to let your emotions inform rather than cloud your understanding. Take it slowly and remember to breathe.
- Check whether it's OK to ask a tough question. Then listen! The worst mistake a reporter can make is to talk too much.
- Use active listening skills such as appropriate eye contact, non-verbal signalling of interest and engagement, mirroring the movements of your interviewee. Remember that much more communication takes place through body language and tone of voice than through the actual words you use.
- Simple, open questions work best. (Almost) always avoid anything that can be answered just yes or no. Don't ask more than one question at a time.
- Reflect back. Paraphrase, summarize, check understanding. Try prefacing questions with: 'I wonder ….' Allow silences and pauses.

- Never ask that most overused and least effective of journalistic questions: 'How do you feel?' You may get tears in response, but you're far less likely to get a coherent, useful and meaningful answer. Indeed, 'How do you feel?' is the one question survivors and victims consistently say they find the most distressing and inappropriate. Instead, how about 'How did you experience that?' or, 'How are you now?'

Get it right, and people are much more likely to tell you their story clearly and powerfully, which is good for you, good for them, and good for the journalism.

So, What Is the Story?

In the immediate aftermath of a traumatic event or experience, many of those involved will experience PTSD-like symptoms, including intrusive recollections, numbing, avoidance and hyper-arousal.

Just like bleeding after being injured or the pain of bruising or a broken bone, symptoms of psychological as well as physical distress are entirely natural and the beginning of what the body intends to be a process of healing.

Just as flesh wounds take a couple of weeks to heal and bones a couple of months, there's a natural cycle to recovery from emotional trauma, and generally most people will feel quite a lot better within four to six weeks.

What they need in the first instance is practical support, human warmth, reassurance and education about normal responses to trauma.

Similarly, the classic disaster story will move through a cycle, and it's good as a journalist to know which part of that cycle has been reached. It can help you keep perspective at a time of especially high emotion:

- As the impact sinks in of what has happened, there will often be at first a mixture of initial shock, confusion and bewilderment. People will be literally at times at a loss for words.
- At the same time, there can be the dramatic early rumours – inflated death tolls, fear of contamination and disease, reports of social breakdown. Some of this may be true. More often, however, first rumours and reports turn out to be exaggerated.
- Very quickly, as rescue operations get into gear and the news machine settles in, there can follow a period of heroism and stoicism: brave

BBC correspondent Jeremy Bowen – moments after his fixer Abed Takkoush was killed in southern Lebanon in 2000 when an Israeli tank shell hit the car he was sitting in

… and as the impact sinks in …

survivors; heroic rescue workers; resilient city, etc. This too is a phase which, while sometimes helpful and appropriate, can be associated with some denial of the enormity of what has happened.

- After this initial, perhaps adrenalin-fuelled phase (usually not much more than a few days), both survivors/victims and the media can shift into blame mode. Criticisms are made; of slow rescue services; chaotic government response; poor construction of buildings that collapse in an earthquake; architects at fault, etc.
- After a few days or weeks, depending on the dimensions of what happened, the caravan begins to move on. The media find new headlines. People are left to get on with their lives. By the wider public at least, the story is forgotten.
- For individuals going through their own emotional response to what has happened, most will be getting back to their normal selves within a few weeks, but some will still be raw and hurting long, sometimes years, after the media caravan has moved on. Everyone recovers – or not – in their own way.

Remember this cycle as you report the story.

Writing the Story

I believe we ought to invest equal energy to finding out what happens after the cameras have left. To provide this diet of raw emotion is only half the story. We capture the grief, the anger, the tears but there are many more human emotions and a range of feelings which are excluded from our obsession with the immediate. To truly reflect our world we need to report those more discreet human responses as people seek to rebuild their lives and reconcile themselves to what happened to them. (Burdin 2006)

If the 'Act I' of journalism is the immediate reporting of what happened and how people were impacted – the blood and pain, the violence and the despair – 'Act II' is the often unreported narrative of what happened next.

Sometimes that involves healing, recovery and confronting the past, allowing communities, families and individuals to move through their trauma to a new sense of meaning. Sometimes that doesn't happen, and the bitterness remains.

Whatever the aftermath, journalists owe it to their readers, listeners and viewers to report Act II as well as Act I.

After a disaster or major tragedy, stories do not need to be sensationalized or embellished. Rely on good, solid, factual journalism and a healthy dose of sensitivity.

- Even more than in other forms of journalism, make sure you don't take liberties with facts, quotes or details. This is a story you must tell or write with accuracy, insight, sensitivity and kindness.
- People who've been through trauma can be deeply distressed by the simplest mistakes. Thoroughly check and re-check facts, names, times, places.
- Be careful and respectful with what people have told you. In print, try to use the exact words your interviewee gave you with as little tidying up as grammatically necessary.
- When you're reporting trauma, think especially carefully about the phrases and words you use. Does your language add to the listener/viewer/reader's understanding? Is the phrasing respectful without being maudlin? Don't say, for example:
  - 'This shocked community mourns the death ...' This is superficial and obvious. Just describe what has happened and how people are responding.
  - 'The villagers are still trying to come to terms with the tragedy ...' Of course they are. Again, focus your reporting on what people are doing and saying.
  - 'Even today this community is in mourning' or 'The parents/brothers/sisters are already missing their son/brother ...' This can imply that grieving has a defined time period, starts only at a given point, needs to be quickly concluded, and extending that period is unusual or unnatural.
  - 'Trained counsellors are on hand ...' If they were untrained, that might be newsworthy. In any case, those brought in to support the survivors and victims probably aren't actually offering counselling but more practical help or simply listening.
  - 'So-and-so is receiving counselling ...' Check with professionals what kind of emotional support is being given. It's unlikely to be formal counselling. That is recommended only for those who are unable naturally to recover from a traumatic experience, which isn't usually evident until a few weeks have passed.
  - 'This community/school/family will never get over this ...' Most individuals and communities do recover, and sometimes astonishingly

quickly. What is more relevant is that they will have been changed by the experience – and that's the story.

- Consider above all: if this was being written about you and your own experience, would you consider it to be a fair representation? If your instinct as a journalist tells you that the answer is no, even in a small way, then your story needs rewriting.

Reporting Trauma: The Journalist

If those are the implications for the journalism of trauma, what does this knowledge mean for you as a journalist? Probably more than you think, or may want to admit even to yourself. If you're a journalism student wondering how to get a job and make your name, be very aware of the reality of the profession you're choosing.

Details and names have been changed in the following stories.

- John was a picture-desk editor at a television station when images began coming in of the 9/11 attacks in New York in 2001. For 24 hours he absorbed sequence after sequence of mayhem, death, falling bodies. Some weeks later, John fell apart emotionally, with distress he couldn't understand. What had happened is that old and unprocessed memories from a war zone a decade earlier had been ripped open and overwhelmed him with post-traumatic distress.
- Carolyn was a local court reporter and found herself covering the trial of three men who had beaten another young man to death with sledgehammers. The details were so gruesome that network news decided not to report the trial at all. Carolyn was left alone with the information she'd had to hear, and began to have nightmares and be unable to sleep. It was only when a friend explained the connection with what she'd had to witness that she began to feel better.
- Yevgenia's job in journalism was to monitor radio broadcasts in Russian. She'd grown up in Chechnya, but was already living in England when the war there began. For years she listened to and reported the stories of atrocity and death from Grozny. Without understanding what was happening, she gradually developed full-blown PTSD. When she and her managers realized what was happening, she had to take nearly a year off work to get well.

- Andrew had only recently joined his local newspaper straight from journalism school when he was asked to report a particularly nasty car crash just outside his home town. Two young men on a Saturday night had gone off the road at high speed and smashed into a tree. Andrew had never seen a dead body before and was profoundly shocked by the state of the two men, whose bodies were mangled beyond recognition. For years afterwards, he would wake at night bathed in sweat with pictures of the crash burning in his brain and was terrified of telling anyone for fear of being labelled unable to cope.
- For David it was a reporting trip on famine in Africa. He had travelled before to the region, and thought he was coping well. A mother's distress and David's powerlessness to help her dying child tipped him over the edge for a time when he came back to base.

Everyone experiences trauma in their own personal way and that's true also of journalists. It depends on the kind of person you are, the things you've been through in the past and how you personally took on board what you were reporting and witnessing.

Journalists who deal with extreme human distress often find their work profoundly rewarding both personally and professionally. To get the job done – like doctors or police dealing with illness or crime – they need to some extent to build a professional wall between themselves and the survivors and witnesses whose stories they tell.

But even the most seasoned and professional journalists can be affected and possibly distressed by exposure to tragedy.

We are, after all and to stress this point yet again, human beings first and journalists second. That means that we too can hurt, whatever our belief in journalistic 'objectivity' and distance.

Bear in mind that photographers and camera operators seem to be particularly vulnerable to accumulated trauma.

It may be because, unlike writing journalists, they don't sit down every day and construct a narrative of what they witness, with the beginning, middle and end, which helps the brain make some sense of what happened. It may be that their craft requires them to dissociate as they witness events through a viewfinder, their bodies clearly there but their mind on the photographic product.

Team and collegial support are key to the maintenance of emotional balance and health. If someone isn't coping so well, however, or if a new experience of trauma is bringing old distressing material to the surface, or if someone is finding it difficult to handle everyday life, it's important that journalists should not be afraid to turn in confidence to a professional counsellor or to suggest that their colleagues consider doing the same.

And as you consider all of this, remember that being open to emotional experience can make you a better reporter. After all, if you can't empathize with those whose story you're reporting, you won't be able truly to reflect their experience.

Tips for Dealing with Potentially Traumatic Events

The most important ways of keeping yourself on an even keel emotionally are also what you should sensibly do for your physical health.

- Those who deal professionally with trauma need, of course, at times to be tough and get the job done. There's a place for the stiff upper lip. But acknowledging your feelings and choosing to talk about emotions is not a sign of weakness. On the contrary, when done well, an appropriate and informed post-event or post-assignment discussion with peers and – where the trust is sufficient – with caring managers and editors is an expression of resilience.
- Establish a standard routine of healthful habits. There's good research to show that even small amounts of gentle exercise are the most effective anti-depressant. A 30-minute walk does you as much good as a 30-minute run, so it doesn't have to be heavy. Bad eating habits and dehydration have an instant effect on mood. So, eat healthily and drink lots of water.
- The British military have a phrase for a key part of self-care: 'Three Hots and a Cot'. In other words, try to eat well and healthily three times a day and – especially – get enough sleep. Surviving on too little sleep is nothing to boast about. It affects your physical and emotional well-being and your journalistic judgement.
- Take breaks and encourage others to do so. A few minutes or a few hours – or on a longer project, a day or two – away from the story or the material helps the body and the brain to process and assimilate more healthily what it's experiencing.
- Know your limits. If you've been asked to undertake a difficult or dangerous assignment that you'd rather not do, don't be afraid to say so.
- Find a hobby, exercise, take time out for reflection, spend time with your family or with close friends – or all four.

- Try deep breathing. Take a long, slow, deep breath to the count of five, and then exhale slowly to the count of five. Imagine this as a circular movement, breathing out excess tension and breathing in relaxation.
- You can also use your imagination to take yourself to what in trauma therapy is sometimes called an internal 'safe place' – somewhere warm and nurturing and relaxed, like a beach or a beautiful mountainside or somewhere in nature.
- Find things that make you laugh. Take care with alcohol. It's fine in moderation, but if you find you are using it to help block out memories or as a way of getting to sleep then you need to think carefully about your situation and consider asking for help.
- Keep an eye out for delayed reactions. Journalists who feel they have managed well for years covering difficult stories might find that something relatively small suddenly tips them over the edge. If that happens, don't bottle it up but talk to colleagues and perhaps seek professional support.
- If you find yourself becoming negative about your job or yourself after covering traumatic events, internal self-talk such as 'I'm useless' or 'What a wimp' needs to be challenged and replaced with a more positive and appropriate assessment. If this is hard to do, then talk with someone to help you shift your thinking.

Seeing traumatic events as challenges and opportunities to do something good in the face of tragedy can strengthen your resolve and keep you focused on the value and meaning of your work.

The Management of Trauma: Before, During and After

Dealing with trauma isn't a problem to be exaggerated or feared. It's part of what journalism is about. Good trauma management is, in essence, good management. It is time for an end to be put to the stigma and ignorance that have long characterized the way journalism deals with the issue.

It is important to know about trauma before you head off on stories that deal with extreme human distress. You need good support when you're on the story and you need good support afterwards in practical and social terms.

Journalists entering the profession or joining a new team should learn as early as possible that trauma is taken seriously. You need to know how trauma is handled in the culture of the organization you work for, either as staff or freelance.

There's a place for leaflets, brochures and online information, but it's most important that leaders and managers talk naturally and openly about trauma and convey confidence that the organization and its teams can handle whatever happens.

If the culture is trauma-aware, then it's much easier and more natural for managers and editors to sit down with someone going on a potentially difficult assignment and recall what's been already discussed in training and general briefings.

In very practical and simple terms, the things to bear in mind include the following.

Before

- Thank, acknowledge and appreciate, even before the assignment. Feeling valued helps keep people emotionally balanced and well. It's important that people feel they're being sent not just because there is no one else to go but because their manager knows they are up to the task.
- Name explicitly what might be involved, emotionally as well as the challenges of staying physically safe. Don't be embarrassed or frightened to talk of the impact that trauma might have, for it's in these ordinary conversations that the most valuable work of culture change can be done.
- Connection with other human beings helps balance and reinforce the brain chemicals and hormones that allow us to process and survive emotional distress. Make reliable arrangements to keep in touch regularly and stick to what you've agreed.
- Encourage self-care. Remind those who are going out on assignment how looking after physical needs for sleep, water, food and exercise can make a big difference.
- Reassure once again that distress isn't unusual when dealing with trauma but that it's not mandatory either. What matters is how it's dealt with and that it's good to talk.

During

- Keep in regular touch. It soothes the anxious brain.
- Leaders – both in the field and on base – should set an example, with sleep for instance. We know from the experience of the military that if the commander of a unit doesn't go to bed, neither will their subordinates.

There should be no place in journalism for point-scoring with colleagues about how little sleep one needs.

- Be careful with the timing and pitch of any criticism. When people are dealing with stories of extreme emotional distress, their own defences will be down and their sensitivities high.
- Make sure that the home team is on side. When someone's already emotionally stretched to the limit – whether covering a murder trial or a war – a thoughtless, badly timed or inconsiderately worded request from a programme or department (including Finance!) can depress, enrage or even traumatize, leaving scars that can hurt for years.
- Before individuals return to base from a stressful assignment, they might be encouraged where appropriate to spend a day or two in a good hotel on the way back, 'decompressing' before being tipped back into their normal home environment. Many journalistic marriages have been destroyed by difficult transitions between assignments that deal with life and death and the mundane responsibilities of running a home and family.

After

- Remember that social and practical support is the best psychology and that small things make a big difference – appreciation, hero-grams, emails, meeting at the airport, parties, public acknowledgement and so on.
- Information reassures, so make sure it's shared generously. If something big or bad has happened to a journalist or camera operator, it's important that everyone is kept up to date with as much detail as possible of what's being done and how people are. If they're not briefed and informed, destructive rumours will proliferate.
- In planning how to respond to traumatic events that may have taken place, it's not just the stars and the big names that need to be considered. Remember the fixers and translators, the technical staff, the picture editors, the bureau chiefs – and yourself, whatever your role.
- Make sure that individuals who've been through a traumatic time have the opportunity to talk about it. They need time and gentle encouragement to tell their story, which needs to be more than a one-off, brief, 'How you doing, mate?', to which the usual answer is 'Fine' and they're off on the next assignment.

There's a useful way to structure these informal conversations, using the term 'FINE' in a more imaginative way. It's an approach which you'll find works surprisingly well in ordinary, daily journalism.

- F for FACTS. Ask them what happened – the usual journalistic When, Where, Who, What and How. Don't climb straight in by exploring their feelings about what happened. Keep it factual and cool, but don't interrogate.
- I for IMPACT. This begins to focus on someone's personal experience. How did you experience that *then*? How did that affect you *then*? What were you thinking and feeling *then*?
- N for NOW. How are you doing *now*? How have you been since then? Discuss the simple checklists below and assess together how you both think the individual is doing.
- E for EDUCATION. The conversation can be used to reassure that, while different people will respond differently, symptoms of distress are not unusual. It's OK to be human as well as a journalist or programme-maker and, while most people, most of the time, will feel better after a few weeks, it's not unusual either for recovery to take longer.

Don't forget to arrange a time for a follow-up conversation in about a month to see how things are settling down. If they're not, or if matters are getting worse, then it's important that good trauma counselling and support are readily available and viewed without stigma.

So, What Should I Watch Out For?

In the first hours and days after a significant story, assignment or project involving trauma, emotions and adrenalin can run very high. Feeling strange – distressed, elated, confused, numb, somewhat 'hyper' – is not at all unusual. Nor is feeling very flat once the adrenalin has stopped pumping.

How might you know if someone is having difficulties if they insist that everything's fine? Here are some things you can watch out for.

- Post-traumatic distress shows itself above all in a change in behaviour and even personality. Someone may no longer seem to be, or feel, themselves. They and their team-mates sense that something is out of balance, but it isn't always easy to link it immediately to a specific event, especially as these changes will usually show themselves starkly weeks or even months later.
- Someone who's experiencing post-traumatic stress might shut themselves away or, conversely, they might begin to talk obsessively and constantly about what happened.

- They may become uncharacteristically angry or irritable.
- They may talk of feeling guilty or confused. Trauma can also make people be more accident-prone and lose their ability to concentrate or be interested in their work, hobbies or relationships.
- They may start falling sick a lot. Emotional distress that's repressed can often express itself in physical symptoms such as back or stomach pain.
- Uncharacteristically, someone may start coming in late for work or missing deadlines, or the opposite – they may be unable to leave the office in the evening and fear being on their own.
- They may show signs of drinking more alcohol than usual.

Most people will get through trauma, especially if they are well supported by colleagues, friends and family. After a few days, it's good to find time for a measured, reflective discussion – and keep an eye out for each other over the following weeks too.

Britain's Royal Marines have a simple method of checking how team members are coping after an experience of trauma, using a 10-point checklist, also known as the TSQ or trauma screen questionnaire, for symptoms of trauma-related distress (Brewin et al. 2002).

1   You experience upsetting thoughts or memories about a traumatic event that have come into your mind against your will;
2   You're having upsetting dreams about what happened;
3   You sometimes act or feel as if bad things were happening again;
4   You feel upset by reminders;
5   You're having bodily reactions (such as fast heartbeat, stomach-churning, sweatiness, dizziness) when you're reminded of what happened;
6   You're finding it difficult to fall or stay asleep;
7   You're uncharacteristically irritable or angry;
8   You find difficulty concentrating;
9   You're overly aware of potential dangers to yourself and others;
10   You're jumpy or easily startled at something unexpected.

People will quite often tick several of the boxes in the days immediately after a major story, but it's equally normal for distress to diminish during the coming days and weeks.

However, if someone is still scoring high after a month or so – and remember how important it is to check – it could be that some distress is getting stuck in the system and that professional advice or trauma counselling with a specialist could help.

There are also clear risk factors associated with a likely distress response to a traumatic experience – relevant for dealing with trauma survivors and victims and not just for journalistic support. These can include the following:

- The person feared for his or her life.
- The person felt that he or she lost control of their emotions in a moment of panic or was overwhelmed by the experience.
- The person is experiencing persistent shame about their own behaviour or response or blaming others inappropriately.
- The person has experienced previous serious traumas and the memory of distress is coming back.
- The person doesn't have, or isn't accessing, good social support in the shape of friends, colleagues and / or family.
- The person is using alcohol or non-prescription drugs to suppress symptoms of distress.

Personal issues outside work can exacerbate an individual's reaction. For example, someone who is going through a divorce, or who has small children, may be distressed more by events than others.

What if Someone Is Hurting?

In the 1990s, it was fashionable in America and Europe to recommend that pretty much everyone exposed to something seriously and psychologically nasty could expect to develop traumatic stress symptoms and therefore need counselling.

For a while, the expectation was that survivors, victims, witnesses and those involved professionally in dealing with the aftermath should sit down in a group as quickly as possible, talk about the worst aspects of what had happened, get it all out in the open in a two- or three-hour-long cathartic session, and that would avoid PTSD.

It sounded sensible, but ignored the basic fact that most people recover of their own accord, and that forcing disclosure in a group in this way, however much it might be appreciated by those involved, could in fact consolidate the memories, interrupt natural healing and unnecessarily traumatize those who'd coped well with the actual experience.

It's now advised that one-off sessions of what used to be called psychological debriefing should not be used routinely with individuals exposed to trauma. Nor are drugs and medication recommended as a first-line treatment for PTSD, although they do have their place in the treatment of other conditions.

This isn't an argument for doing nothing, but it *is* clear advice not to rush in with ineffective, unproven or possibly even counterproductive responses. It's essential for journalists to understand this, both in reporting the psychological impact of and response to disaster and tragedy, and in knowing what works and doesn't work for themselves.

What is recommended by Britain's National Institute for Clinical Excellence (NICE) is what's termed 'Watchful Waiting' – checking with individuals who've been through trauma how they are in the days, weeks and months afterwards, helping them to understand the impact of what they have been through, keeping an eye out for symptoms of traumatic distress and helping them, if they need it, to get the professional support that might be useful if they do get stuck with the experience (NICE 2007).

That's the purpose also of the approach advocated here.

Rather than farming out responsibility for trauma response to outsiders and trauma professionals, managers, editors and colleagues should themselves take organizational ownership of managing the impact of trauma.

Finally, journalists and managers or colleagues who would like to find a therapist to deal with the impact of trauma are encouraged to ensure that whoever they choose is experienced specifically in dealing with trauma and, if possible, has experience of working with journalists and the media.

And Finally

Reporting trauma can be one of the most rewarding experiences that are open to a journalist. You're living at the edge, dealing with existential matters of life and death.

It's important – for those you are reporting, for those to whom you are reporting, and for yourself – that the job is done well.

In the coverage of extreme human distress and psychological trauma, it is time for change in the culture of twenty-first-century journalism.

That change is happening – and you're part of it. Good luck.

Note

1 The original report was in the *Guardian* on 10 October 2005; the *Guardian* corrected its report on 12 October and the reader's editor wrote about this in his Column on 17 October.

References

American Psychiatric Association (2000) *Diagnostic and Statistical Manual of Mental Disorder* (DSM-IV-R). American Psychiatric Association.

Brewin, C., Rose, S., Andrews, B., Green, J., McEvedy, C., Turner, S. and Foa, E. (2002) Brief screening instrument. *British Journal of Psychiatry* 181: 158-62, http://bjp. rcpsych.org/cgi/content/full/181/2/158.

Burdin, P. (2006) Journalism of Act II. Discussion at the Radio Dart Award Presentation and Discussion at the Frontline Club London, 5 June, http://www.dartcenter. org/articles/dart_center_events/act_II.html.

Herman, J. L. (2001) *Trauma and Recovery*. Rivers Oram Press.

Kessler, R. C. (1995) Epidemiology of psychiatric comorbidity. In *Textbook in Psychiatric Epidemiology*, eds. Tsuang, M., Tohen, M., and Zahner, G.. Wiley-Liss.

NICE (2007) CG26 Post-traumatic stress disorder (PTSD): Full guideline (including appendices 1-13). http://guidance.nice.org.uk/CG26/guidance/pdf/English.

Self, M. (1999) *Tomorrow's Fish-and-Chips Paper: A View from the Survivor's Side*. Dart Center for Journalism & Trauma, http://www.dartcenter.org/articles/personal_ stories/self_mary.html.

Recommended Further Reading

American Psychiatric Association (2003) *Diagnostic and Statistical Manual of Mental Disorders* (v. IV-TR). American Psychiatric Association.

Feinstein, A. (2003) *Dangerous Lives: War, and the Men and Women Who Report It*. Thomas Allen.

Frei, C. (2002) *War Photographer*. DVD documentary film. Christian Frei Film Productions.

Furedi, F. (2004) *Therapy Culture: Cultivating Vulnerability in an Uncertain Age*. Routledge.

Goleman, D. (1997) *Emotional Intelligence*. Bloomsbury.

Heinl, P. (2001) *Splintered Innocence: An Intuitive Approach to Treating War Trauma*. Brunner Routledge

Herman, J. L. (1993) *Trauma and Recovery: From Domestic Abuse to Political Terror*. Basic Books.

Hodgkinson, P. and Stewart, M. (1991) *Coping with Catastrophe*. Routledge.

Knightley, P. (2003) *The First Casualty: The War Correspondent as Hero, Propagandist, and Myth-Maker from the Crimea to the Gulf War II*. Andre Deutsch.

Lloyd, J. (2004) *What the Media Are Doing to Our Politics*. Constable and Robinson.

Lynch, J. and McGoldrick, A. (2005) *Peace Journalism*. Hawthorne Press.

Shay, J. (1994) *Achilles in Vietnam*. Touchstone.

Simpson, R. and Cote, W. (2000) *Covering Violence: A Guide to Ethical Reporting About Victims and Trauma*. 2nd edition. Columbia University Press.

Steele, J. (2003) *War Junkie*. Corgi.

Tehrani, N. (2004) *Workplace Trauma*. Brunner Routledge.

Van der Kolk, B., McFarlane, A. C. and Weisaeth, L. (1996) *Traumatic Stress: The Effects of Overwhelming Experience on Mind, Body and Society*. Guildford Press.

Online Resources

Committee to Protect Journalists, www.cpj.org.

Crimes of War Project, www.crimesofwar.org.

Dart Center for Journalism & Trauma, www.dartcenter.org.

David Baldwin's Trauma Information Pages, http://www.trauma-pages.com.

EMDR Institute, http://www.emdr.com.

European Society for Traumatic Stress Studies, www.estss.org.

Frontline Club, www.thefrontlineclub.com.

International News Safety Institute, www.newssafety.com.

International Society for Traumatic Stress Studies, www.istss.org; http://www.istss. org/terrorism/media.htm; http://www.istss.org/publications/stresspoints.htm.

National Institute for Clinical Excellence (on PTSD treatment guidelines), http://www.nice.org.uk/page.aspx?o=57890.

Poynter Institute, www.poynter.org.

Project for Excellence in Journalism, www.journalism.org.

Traumatic Stress Clinic, http://www.cimhscaretrust.nhs.uk/pages/go.asp?pageID=5 11&Path=4&Parent=287.072&instance=451.

UK Trauma Group, http://www.uktrauma.org.uk/ukservcs.html.

Questions for students

1 What are the defining characteristics of PTSD?

2 Discuss why your emotional state of mind can have an impact on your impartiality as a journalist.

3 From your reading, what are the most salient arguments for and against taking on what might be a high-risk assignment?

4 Ask a news organization of your choice what their policy is on providing trauma counselling for journalists who return from assignments and are experiencing problems in their personal and work lives.

12

Citizen Journalism

Richard Sambrook

Introduction

JOHN OWEN

The debate rages across journalism about the legitimacy of those who are now called citizen journalists and contribute their blogs and mobile photo videos to websites, broadcasts and newspapers.

The mainstream media may have misgivings about the quality of citizen journalism but that hasn't stopped them from using their websites, news holes and airtime to showcase the outpouring of user-generated content (UGC). Usually, it's the latest home video or mobile phone pictures of floods, tornados, hurricanes, and forest fires that dominate websites such as CNN's iReport, which asks you to 'Send, Share, and See Your Stories.' Yet as Richard Sambrook, director of BBC Global News, argues in the following chapter on citizen journalism, 'There is nothing new about members of the public reporting what they've seen to their fellow citizens.'

Sambrook is, of course, recounting the history of Britain and the United States, rich in illustrious examples of non-mainstream daily journalists who battled their way into the public sphere along with amateurs who had the presence of mind and state-of-the-art equipment to record historic moments and events.

The modern-day citizen journalism movement is rooted in the politics of an Asian country – South Korea. There, a frustrated magazine journalist named Oh Yeon-ho was unprepared to accept the stranglehold that the conservative-dominated establishment press had on Korean politics. His breakthrough moment came during the final moments of the presidential campaign of 2002. As Oh tells the story, his fledgling two-year-old organization, called OhmyNews, rallied South Korean support for the reform candidate Roh Moo Hyun when on the last day he was hit with a political bombshell – the withdrawal of his vice-presidential running mate. OhmyNews, realizing that the conservative media allied with the conservative candidate were suddenly poised to snatch victory away from Roh, went on an internet offensive. More than 720,000 hits later, Roh prevailed, and Oh wrote 'The power of media has shifted from conservative mainstream newspapers to netizens and Internet media' (Oh 2002).

There was no turning back for OhmyNews, and this breakthrough election became a springboard for galvanizing his readers and users to report on all aspects of South Korean life. From an initial 727 contributors, Oh built OhmyNews into a juggernaut of 35,000 citizen journalists. He said that they ranged from elementary students to professors. Today they are paid an equivalent of about $20 per story. Their contributions constitute about 70 per cent of the content on OhmyNews.

Oh argues that he didn't 'invent the concept that every citizen is a reporter' but 'I just restored a long-forgotten concept. Just think back to a time when face-to-face communication was the only way to deliver news. Before newspapers and professional journalists, every citizen was a reporter. There was true interactivity. OhmyNews restored that' (Oh 2004).

Going from jolting South Korean politics and journalism to being heralded as a force for democratizing global newsgathering is an astonishing achievement for citizen journalism and those who practise it.

We have yet to grasp just how powerful this movement is in terms of its longer-term effects on governments and politics in closed societies. It's one thing to be Matt Drudge and publish titillating and embarrassing information about celebrities and those holding high office in the United States, or a 'Justice Jimmy' roaming the streets of New York

City recording NYPD cops abusing their privileges to park their cars. The prolific blogger and new media champion Jeff Jarvis calls his work 'vigilante journalism'.

Both Drudge and Justice Jimmy know that they can practise their unconventional journalism in a country protected by a First Amendment and rule of law. Try this approach in China, Burma (Myanmar), Zimbabwe or Iran and you are likely to wind up in prison or worse. A Ukraine new media journalist, Gyorgy Gongadze, was murdered in 2000 because of his outspoken criticism on his website of what he charged were the corrupt practices of the Kuchma government. (The International Federation of Journalists believes – as do other press rights groups – that those at the highest levels of government had him killed.)

In today's 50 million plus blogosphere, very few are putting their lives on the line and posing serious threats to their governments. But there are increasing numbers of engaged activists who, in the words of Global Voices Online founder Ethan Zuckerman (2007), 'perform acts of journalism from time to time'. They are facing threats and censorship. Zuckerman notes that in a number of countries, authorities have put troublesome bloggers under surveillance with the intent of intimidating them. Others find they are experiencing technical problems that government-run service providers are creating for those bloggers deemed 'unfriendly'.

Then there is a new issue confronting mainstream journalism: whether the private blogs of ordinary citizens are legitimate source material during breaking news coverage of stories such as the massacre that took place on the campus of Virginia Polytechnic Institute and State University on 16 April 2007. Did the media have the right to grab the emotional ramblings/blogs of students posted during and after the campus crisis on such popular blogsites as MySpace and LiveJournal? Was this the first real example of what critics called 'digital doorstepping', meaning that instead of the traditional gathering of information by knocking on doors and speaking with eyewitnesses, the media simply found the information that they wanted online? For BBC College of Journalism editor Kevin Marsh, this posed serious questions of 'taste and decency'. Was it not the same as reading someone's private diaries without their permission, Marsh asked during a debate at the London-based Frontline Club (2007)?

What makes Richard Sambrook's views on new media, citizen journalism and peer sharing so important is that he writes from the perspective of a senior journalist working for the largest and most influential news organization in the world. Sambrook has embraced with great enthusiasm new media and blogging after years of heading up all of BBC newsgathering and BBC broadcast news operations.

But as Sambrook makes clear in this chapter, 'the media and journalism are going through a radical transformation, and not all the answers are clear'.

References

Marsh, K. (2007) Blogging: Self-exposure or self-expression? Media talk marking World Press Freedom Day, 3 May, http://www.frontlineclub.com/club_videoevents.php.

Oh, Y. (2002) OhmyNews. 19 December, http://translate.google.com/translate?hl=en&sl=ko&u=http://www.ohmynews.com/NWS_Web/View/old_pg.aspx%3Fcntn_gb%3DA%26at_code%3D226016%26no%3D%26rel_no%3D&sa=X&oi=translate&resnum=2&ct=result&prev=/search%3Fq%3DOhmynews%2BThe%2Bpower%2Bof%2Bmedia%2Bhas%2Bshifted%2Bfrom%2Bconservative%2Bnewspapers%2Bto%2B%25E2%2580%2598netizens%25E2%2580%2599%2Band%2BInternet%2Bmedia%26hl%3Den.

Oh, Y (2004) Speech at the Berkman Center for Internet and Society conference 'Votes, Bits and Bytes' , Harvard University, 11 December.

Zuckerman, E. (2007) Speech at the Al-Jazeera media conference, Doha.

Context

When Abraham Zapruder took his Bell & Howell movie camera to Dealey Plaza in Dallas, Texas, on 22 November 1963 he had no idea he would capture one of the most famous examples of citizen journalism. Balancing on a concrete pedestal, steadied by his secretary to get a shot over the crowds, he captured less than 30 seconds of film – the assassination of President Kennedy. Three copies of the film were made that day. Two were handed over to the investigating authorities. The original was sold by Zapruder to *Life Magazine* for $150,000 three days later. He had no doubt about the importance and value of what he had filmed.

Eyewitnesses to momentous events have always sought to share their experience.

Edward Grim, a clerk from Cambridge, was visiting Canterbury Cathedral in December 1170 and witnessed the murder of the archbishop, Thomas Becket. His first-hand account – 1,500 words long – remains the most authoritative version of what happened (Grim 1875–85).

And, at the other end of the scale, when I started as a reporter on a small weekly newspaper in South Wales, many of the reports of sporting and community events were sent in by the readers – the achievements of the local rugby team or the details of a school fete or charity evening.

There is nothing new about members of the public reporting what they've seen to their fellow citizens either through established channels or, when possible, more directly. Nor is there anything new about citizens expressing their views about events outside of whatever passes at the time for 'mainstream media'. It's often said that if Thomas Paine were alive today he would be a blogger, rather than a pamphleteer, arguing for the independence of America from the United Kingdom. Certainly the invention of the printing press and movable type facilitated an explosion of views and debate – similar to today's blogs – which fed the Age of Enlightenment of the eighteenth century.

The parallel is clear from this passage by George Orwell, in an introduction to *British Pamphleteers* (1948: 15):

> The pamphlet is a one-man show. One has complete freedom of expression, including, if one chooses, the freedom to be scurrilous, abusive, and seditious; or, on the other hand, to be more detailed, serious and 'high-brow' than is ever possible in a newspaper or in most kinds of periodicals. At the same time, since the pamphlet is always short and unbound, it can be produced much more quickly than a book, and in principle, at any rate, can reach a bigger public. Above all, the pamphlet does not have to follow any prescribed pattern. It can be in prose or in verse, it can consist largely of maps or statistics or quotations, it can take the form of a story, a fable, a letter, an essay, a dialogue, or a piece of 'reportage.' All that is required of it is that it shall be topical, polemical, and short.

It could be a guide to modern blogging.

The spirit of today's blogs can, more recently, be seen in independent journalists like I. F. Stone,[1] whose polemical writing was based on close scrutiny of public documents which would otherwise go ignored. Or in *Private Eye* magazine, which publishes what other news organizations won't, based often on tips and information sent in to them. It's a small step from them to Matt Drudge, one of the first of the bloggers to have an impact on the news agenda with his revelation of President Clinton's affair with an intern, and from him to the plethora of blogs and social networks we now enjoy.

So why is there so much discussion of citizen journalism today? Simply, it's the impact of the internet and the opportunities it offers for widespread forms of communication unimaginable just a decade ago. Those opportunities are producing social changes as profound as the invention of the printing press some 300 years ago.

For over 75 years the BBC World Service has broadcast radio programmes around the globe with highly technical studios, lines, transmitters and radio towers worth millions of pounds. Today anyone with a laptop computer and an internet connection can effectively broadcast just as widely.

For more than 100 years, news – journalism – has been based on a model of restricted access. Only a few organizations could afford to send reporters to places where important events were happening or find information of interest to others. Even fewer had the resources to distribute that information – either through newsprint or by access to limited, usually regulated, radio or TV bandwidth. The model was one of central control, top-down, one-to-many.

Today those limitations have gone. Information is increasingly commoditized and widely available on the internet. Distribution of that information can be achieved at almost zero cost with a blog or podcast. The internet model is bottom-up (or edges-in), networked, peer-to-peer with everything from one-to-one to many-to-many.

Now, information has become democratized.

When, in 1991, Tim Berners-Lee invented the hypertext technology which became the World Wide Web, it was to be able to share and edit information. In other words, the social functionality of the web was at its heart when it was invented. It's that functionality – social networking as it's now called – which is driving the huge changes in communication we are currently seeing, including citizen journalism.

As the authors of *The Cluetrain Manifesto* wrote in 1999: 'A powerful global conversation has begun. Through the internet, people are discovering and inventing new ways to share relevant knowledge with blinding speed. As a direct result, markets are getting smarter – and getting smarter faster than most companies' (Levine et al. 1999).

This has certainly been true in the media and in journalism in particular. But although the impact of the internet has been profoundly disruptive and challenging for news organizations it has also, I believe, been a force for good: improving standards and quality, enforcing transparency and accountability, enabling the wide dissemination of free information, and reconnecting the public with the importance of free expression and debate. Citizen journalism can improve the media and strengthen democracy.

Dan Gillmor, in his seminal book *We the Media* (2006: 10), suggests the rise of citizen journalism can spark a renaissance of the notion of a truly informed citizenry. 'Self government demands no less, and we'll all benefit if we do it right.'

He traces the moment when blogging took hold in the USA in the hours after September 11:

> Journalists did some of their finest work and made me proud to be one of them … But something else, something profound, was happening this time around: news was being produced by regular people who had something to say and show, and not solely by the 'official' news organisations that had traditionally decided how the first draft of history would look … Another kind of reporting emerged during those appalling hours and days. Via emails, mailing lists, chat groups, personal web journals – all non-standard news sources – we received valuable context that the major American media couldn't, or wouldn't, provide. We were witnessing – and in many cases were part of – the future of news. (ibid.: 2)

So there is no question that 'citizen journalism', or the opportunity provided by the internet and technology to allow the public to express their views and share their experiences, is having a profound effect on journalism. It is undermining business models, throwing into stark relief a traditional lack of openness and transparency in parts of the news media, and forcing up quality and standards as the army of bloggers 'fact-check your ass', as it was described after they identified a series of mainstream media failings in the USA in 2003–5.

It is also providing enormous opportunities to develop a 'new journalism' through sharing information across networks, tagging, commenting, open source research and more.

As Rebecca MacKinnon, a former CNN producer and now blogger who describes herself as a 'recovering journalist', has said: 'What matters is that journalism survives, not the platform or media on which it exists' (2006).

One new environment journalism is having to adapt to is the social network – sites like MySpace, Facebook, Flickr or YouTube, which allow a collective experience. They are modern online communities with many of the characteristics you would find in a physical community – gossip, information, discussion, argument – and as such are fertile places for journalistic research and for syndication of news. As the newspaper design guru Mario Garcia told the World Association of Newspapers (2007), 'Social networks are the new cities. If people choose to gather there we must be there too.'

When we speak about citizen journalism, we are really talking about a range of different activities – which have different motivations, different purposes and different effects.

Four Kinds of Sharing

Citizen journalism can broadly be grouped into four different kinds of activity – or sharing.

First, there's eyewitness reporting – the sharing of experience. This includes the mobile phone pictures sent to news organizations, email descriptions of what people have seen and, increasingly, video. News organizations have always interviewed witnesses and used their pictures when available. Now witnesses to an event can send their material directly to the newsdesk – and do so in their thousands.

Second, there's the sharing of opinion, usually through blogs. For decades, radio broadcasters have used radio phone-ins to reflect the views of their audience and to encourage debate. Today, on the internet, the same thing can be achieved with blogs linked from a news site or news pages linked from blogs. Citizen journalism sites like Digg.com or Netscape.com, which include recommendation and voting for best items as well, reflect the views of the readers as well as conveying the core story.

Third, there is original, investigative reporting on the web – the sharing of discovery. This is sometimes achieved through conventional means of investigative reporting where an individual uncovers something newsworthy, or occasionally it happens as a group activity – sometimes called a swarm – where a number of bloggers descend on an issue and pick it apart until the bones are revealed.

Finally, there is what some call networked journalism – the sharing of knowledge. This is founded on the idea that, whatever you write or broadcast about, someone out there will know more about it than you. How can you find that expertise and use it to improve the quality, accuracy, insight of your journalism? How can you tap into the collective wisdom, knowledge and experience of the public to report what would otherwise have been unreportable?

And what is journalism's place in the 'new cities' of social networks where the collective views and expertise of the public can be found?

Let's take each in turn.

Michael Hughes, citizen journalist, took this picture at Tavistock Square, London, after one of the four suicide bombings which killed 52 people in London on 7 July 2005

PHOTO COURTESY OF MICHAEL HUGHES

The sharing of experience

Two thousand and five was the year a number of major news events occurred just as mobile technology had become widespread. Cameraphones and small digital video recorders captured the effects of the Asian tsunami in January, the aftermath of the Asian earthquake, and in the UK the 7 July London bombings and the Buncefield fuel depot explosion to an extent few news events had been filmed before.

Take these two examples from the 7/7 bombings.

Adam Stacey was caught up in the Piccadilly Line blast between King's Cross and Russell Square, but was not in the bombed carriage.

After being trapped for about 40 minutes in a smoky carriage and amid increasing alarm, he and his fellow commuters were let off the train and told to walk back down the track.

Seeing others taking out mobile phone cameras, and not knowing there had been a bomb attack, he asked his friend Elliot to take a picture to show his colleagues at work.

Before he knew it the image was being used all over the world and he was being asked to do interviews for all kinds of media, including Japanese TV and American radio …

Having heard that some news sites were using pictures taken by members of the public, Adam first sent his image to the *Sun* newspaper.

It was picked up by a weblog site, Moblog UK, and once on there the image attracted scores of postings from around the world.

The comments later led to Moblog's Alfie Dennen establishing the website We're Not Afraid, which received images and messages of support from across the globe after the bombings.

Mr. Dennen contacted Mr. Stacey on 7 July to ask if he would agree to a Creative Commons Licence on the image, which is a way to distribute information free.

'I said that was fine. I didn't think of the image as my property. It would have seemed so mercenary to make money from it.'

The resulting media attention was 'exciting' for a time admits Mr. Stacey, whose image was selected as one of the best of 2005 by *Time Magazine*. (Dear 2006)

Rachel North was in the bombed carriage of the train travelling from Kings Cross to Russell Square. In the days that followed she wrote a diary for the BBC, which subsequently became her own blog.

> I was in the first carriage, behind the driver's carriage, standing by the doors – it was absolutely packed.
>
> Even more people got on at Kings Cross. It felt like the most crowded train ever. Then, as we left Kings Cross, at about 8.55am, there was an almighty bang.
>
> Everything went totally black and clouds of choking smoke filled the Tube carriage and I thought I had been blinded.
>
> It was so dark that nobody could see anything.
>
> I thought I was about to die, or was dead. I was choking from the smoke and felt like I was drowning.
>
> Air started to flood in through the smashed glass and the emergency lighting helped us see a bit. We were OK.
>
> A terrible screaming followed the initial silence. (North 2005)

The motivation of those sharing these kinds of direct experience varies – but few currently see themselves as journalists. They are simply individuals caught up in extraordinary events who wish to share what they have seen or heard. Some agencies have grown up with the intention of representing members of the public who wish to sell their material to news organizations. As yet, however, these have had only marginal impact due to the volume of material available and the primary motivation on the part of these 'citizen journalists' being sharing or participation rather than money. That's not to say, of course, that anyone capturing a moment of history or an exclusive image in the way Zapruder did would not be entitled or able to profit substantially from it. But the usual market forces apply and thanks to mobile technology, the supply of images of most events is plentiful.

There are risks. At the Buncefield oil explosion and fire in 2005, the BBC was approached by a number of people, including children, who offered to return to the scene and capture 'better pictures' – putting themselves potentially at risk. There are issues of liability here for news organizations that need to advise the public to behave responsibly and safely in capturing their experiences, and that must avoid appearing to commission anything which might involve a risk of injury or worse.

Sharing experience in this way has taken place for as long as mass media has existed. Technology has transformed the volume of material now available and that, in turn, has had a major impact on news organizations. As the BBC's news editor, Jon Williams, said on the BBC Editors Blog:

> I was the home news editor on July 7th last year. We received 20,000 emails, more than 1,000 mobile phone pictures and dozens of bits of video; it was your phone-calls that alerted us to what was going on when the authorities weren't quite sure what to make of the 'power-outage' on the underground. It transformed our coverage – and our view of the role you can play in our output.
>
> Now, whenever there's a story, our readers, viewers and listeners send in pictures from the scene – whether it's the explosion at the Buncefield oil terminal, or the attacks on trains in Mumbai in India. For news – as news editor – it's a magnificent resource to draw on. It's not often we're on the scene when something is happening – our cameras usually get there after the event; we film the aftermath. Very often, you are in the thick of it. It's been called citizen journalism – I prefer to think of it as citizen newsgathering. (Williams 2006)

The sharing of opinion

For decades now, the combination of radio and the telephone has allowed members of the public to share their opinions through mass media. Phone-in shows have become a staple format for talk radio and many of them have developed into communities with regular callers, extended discussions and themes – in much the way that bulletin boards and some blog communities work.

For the media, the ability to tap into their audience for views and opinion has enabled them to produce content, relatively cheaply, which is by definition of interest to, and closely aligned with, their audience. And, although there are good and bad examples, as ever, phone-in shows are a popular format for that reason.

The broadcaster acts as host and the audience is clear what is a caller's opinion and how it may be differentiated from the broadcaster's views or position.

Now, with blogs in particular but also podcasts and video blogs, the ability of the public to express opinion in public has exploded. They no longer need to be 'hosted' by a broadcaster. This explosion of opinion in the public space has had a number of effects. It has put pressure on the traditional framework of impartiality and objectivity for some news organizations. There is clearly a great appetite for opinion. It has undermined the value of the columnist or op-ed writer – there is excellent commentary available for free on the web. But it has also provided a challenge (and therefore an opportunity) for news organizations to integrate the opinions of their readers, listeners and viewers in new ways. The quantity of views, and the means by which they are expressed, have grown hugely. So, too, have the benefits of being seen to embrace and support public discussion.

Where many traditional media organizations have been slow or struggled to integrate this new explosion in public opinion, some start-ups have been quick to see the opportunity.

In 2004, Calvin Tang and Mike Davidson (working for Disney, ESPN) were discussing a number of ideas about what was happening on the web at the time. In an interview with me, Tang said:

> With the rise of personal publishing and the emergence of the blogosphere on the media landscape, our thoughts circled around a model that blended together the best elements of traditional media with those we identified as the hallmarks of new media. In specific, the traditional media companies provided quality content with integrity and accuracy. Yet, bloggers and casual web surfers were increasingly able to offer valuable accounts of and opinions on important events in a manner that was representative of large swathes of society (unfiltered perspectives if you will). In aggregate, these consumers-turned-producers of content were becoming more and more influential and leaders were emerging from the pack.

In their view many traditional media companies had been slow to adapt to a rapidly changing technical and social environment and most did little to truly tap into the resource of their readers. 'What the big media companies lacked in agility and efficiency, we saw bloggers as a whole lacked in focus, purpose and organization.'

So they decided to develop a site which collected, organized and syndicated the huge, growing pool of content on the web in as automated a way as possible. They wanted to leverage those who had a story to tell but who lacked the means to produce and publish content, and to give people ways to interact meaningfully on topics of shared interest and – as a result – discover new material and authors.

Newsvine.com was launched as a discussion site, but built around a conventional news feed from the Associated Press (AP). It allows users to comment on news reports, chat live to each other about them, generate their own content, recommend content, build their own network of users and authors, and 'seed' the site with items of interest from elsewhere on the web. As such it combines blogging, tagging, recommendation, social bookmarking, chat and news.

At its heart is comment on the news and the building of a community around user opinion. 'We encourage our users to turn anything and everything into a conversation. The most important aspect of Newsvine is the composition of our users. They are generally thoughtful, articulate and passionate about being a part of the Newsvine community.'

The site has developed significantly since launch. They originally imagined that the wire (AP) feed would be the bulk of content initially with an increasing amount of user content taking its place over time. In fact, however, they have an even 50–50 distribution of content from both sources in terms of quantity, traffic and distribution of discussion. The wire content serves as an anchor keeping users focused on topics related to the news.

They have since introduced groups – or private discussion threads – rather than have all discussion taking place in a common area. This allows smaller communities to seed themselves within the original community. And they discovered that 'good–bad' percentage-based reputation systems, as used in other social sites like eBay, didn't work for their users, so they introduced 'vineacity', a multi-dimensional measure of a user's productivity and trustworthiness. This allows a transparency about the quality and trustworthiness of contributions as determined by the users.

What is striking about Newsvine is the way it combines traditional news output with user comment and opinion and the multiple social functions it encourages. You can find out what has happened, but also read or engage in a wide range of opinion and discussion about the news you are particularly interested in.

Like a phone-in, it combines traditional media with public views but with the weight very much on the other foot. The users are in charge.

To share opinion and views, of course, doesn't require the functionality of a site like Newsvine. The simplest blogging platforms, some available for free like Blogger.com, enable people to share their views and experiences widely.

One of the earliest and perhaps best-known examples was that of 'Salam Pax' during the Iraq War in 2003. Blogging at dear_raed.blogspot.com, he wrote of life in Baghdad in the run-up to war and during the bombing. He had contempt for the regime, but strikingly appeared to have much in common with his young readers in the West. He wrote in perfect English, quoted David Bowie lyrics and talked of his latest CD purchases. And he was funny. When a BBC reporter spoke of Iraqis maintaining an air of normality, he wrote: 'What are we supposed to do? Run around the streets wailing?' Once the bombs started to fall he wrote tersely about what it was like to sit in your room, door locked, and hoping one didn't fall on you.

His posts were picked up by the *Guardian*, the *New York Times* and the BBC. Crucially he conveyed, more authentically than any Western reporter could do, what it was like to live in the city under attack and in the final days of the Baathist regime.

No surprise, then, that he subsequently made the move from blogger. com to a regular newspaper column – albeit with some reluctance: 'I sold my soul to the devil,' he wrote.

His first column began:

> My name is Salam Pax and I am addicted to blogs. Some people watch daytime soaps, I follow blogs. I follow the hyperlinks on the blogs I read. I travel through the web guided by bloggers. I get wrapped up in the plots narrated by them. I was reading so many blogs I had to assign weekdays for each bunch, plus the ones I was reading daily. It is slightly voyeuristic, especially those really personal blogs: day-to-day, mundane stuff which is actually fascinating; glimpses of lives so different, and so much amazing writing. No politics, just people's lives. How they deal with pain or grief, how they share their happy moments with anybody who cares to read. (Pax 2003)

This is what blogs can bring to the public sphere – the real lives and concerns of ordinary people. That's what 'Salam's' blog reflected during the Iraq war – in a way traditional journalists could not.

However, the sharing of experience and opinion is not all that blogs can achieve.

The sharing of discovery

Mark Kraft is a Californian blogger who got his start in blogging by help-ing run LiveJournal.com – a site which offers discussion forums and com-munities as well as supporting blogs.

After the invasion of Iraq he created a community for non-governmen-tal organization (NGO) workers, overseas contractors and others working in Iraq – including some US soldiers, with whom he built up an online relationship. They would tell him what they were doing – including, some-times, things which weren't being reported.

On 12 November 2004 he posted about phosphorus shells being used on Iraqis:

Fallujah: Many, many Iraqis dead, phosphorus shells being used on Iraqis, anonymous corpses with horrible burns, possible use of cluster bombs. Over 18 US soldiers killed so far, hundreds wounded, over 227 severely – evac'ed to Germany. Nominal control of the roads, but no real control of the city. Elections more distant than ever. House-to-house searches still to come, possible enemies and boobytraps behind every door, a starving city as big as Pittsburgh. Angry Iraqis. Hopeless Iraqis. Iraqis with nothing left to lose. The wholescale slaughter of Iraqi police departments. Massive defections in both Iraqi police and military. Uprisings in major Iraqi cities. Months of progress in some regions destroyed overnight. Bombed mosques. The widescale stench of death. Iraqi men not allowed to leave. Boats, packed and fleeing, sunk by gunfire. Bodies floating down the Euphrates. Winning the battle and losing the war.

He went on to report the personal stories of soldiers, sharing their posts and other news from inside Iraq ignored by the traditional press. 'Some of the stories from inside Fallujah were just awful', he says. 'It was a horrible bloodbath for all sides concerned.' He also released pictures leaked to him by soldiers. Eventually, news media in the UK and the US picked up on the use of white phosphorus shells in Fallujah. However, without Kraft's use of an online community and contacts it might never have been reported. In an interview with me, he said:

It's not enough for journalists to create a weblog and hope people will come to them with the big story ... They need to do more to seek out the weblogs of those involved firsthand and to interact with them, and build up a discussion amongst equals. It's not enough to occasionally monitor a flood of RSS feeds with a newsreader because that does nothing to build either communication or trust.

What I've built up may not be official sources, but I would argue that as sources go they are far better, far closer to firsthand, and generally more detailed and nuanced, providing a more meaningful perspective on what is happening.

In this, he sounds remarkably like a traditional investigative reporter, building trust and working sources. However, in Mark Kraft's case, it's built around the internet, online search, blogs and online communities rather than the neighbourhood bar.

The internet can provide a powerful platform for investigative journalism. Swedish blogger Magnus Ljungkvist ended the short career of Sweden's trade minister Maria Borelius after only eight days in office. Using the Freedom of Information Act to examine her tax returns and business affairs, he revealed tax evasion by the minister, including not paying the payroll tax on a cleaning woman she hired in the 1990s.

Ljungkvist, press spokesman for Sweden's Social Democrat party, pitched the story to *Aftonbladet*, which declined to run it. So he blogged. Another paper, *Expressen*, reported the story, without credit to Ljungkvist, a day after his post, and Borelius quickly resigned.

This case led the Poynter Institute to reach five conclusions:

1 Partisanship is not always bad. Good citizen journalism often relies on some sort of partisanship as a motivator to continue researching a story ....
2 Everyone needs access to information. A well-oiled democratic process requires open access to information – even for people with an axe to grind, whether they are journalists, political activists, or citizens.
3 Journalists aren't always objective. The fact that the mainstream media were not looking where Ljungkvist looked could be a symptom of a lack of personal interest from journalists, or a lack of available resources to investigate. Or it could be related to admissions published in a 2000 book that several journalists were paying their houseworkers under the table. This seems to be a widespread problem in Sweden.
4 Bloggers: constructive nudging. It sometimes takes a committed blogger to force journalists to address issues they'd rather ignore.
5 Giving credit. Only later did some news organizations give Ljungkvist credit for his investigation. This reluctance to give credit indicates an unnecessary degree of embarrassment on the part of the traditional media – perhaps stemming from us-vs.-them paranoia perpetuated by both citizen and traditional journalists. (Maher 2006)

Perhaps the best-known example of 'discovery' on the net is what's become known as 'Rather-gate': the discovery of major inaccuracies in a report on *CBS 60 Minutes*, presented by Dan Rather. In September 2004, the programme reported on criticisms of George W. Bush's record in the US National Guard allegedly made in documents belonging to his commanding officer, Jerry B. Killian.

The authenticity of the documents was challenged within hours on internet forums and blogs. They pointed to anachronisms in the documents' typography which suggested they were fake. CBS initially defended the story, but a two-week period of analysis by bloggers and then rival news organizations forced a retraction from them. Rather said, 'if I knew then what I know now – I would not have gone ahead with the story as it was aired, and I certainly would not have used the documents in question'(2005). CBS News president Andrew Heyward said, 'Based on what we now know, CBS News cannot prove that the documents are authentic, which is the only acceptable journalistic standard to justify using them in the report. We should not have used them. That was a mistake, which we deeply regret' (Heyward 2004).

The item producer, Mary Mapes, was sacked and Rather was forced to announce his retirement early.

Part of the interest of this incident is in the bloggers holding a major news organization to account, and proving to be more thorough and accurate than the professional journalists. However, it also illustrates the power of combined wisdom. The anachronisms came to light through a number of different (right-wing) bloggers pooling their observations and expertise to undermine the accuracy and authority of the report. It was, in some sense, an early example of what's now called networked journalism.

The sharing of expertise

Dan Gillmor describes in *We the Media* how he recognized, when he began his IT column for the *San Jose Mercury*, that many of his readers working in Silicon Valley would know more about his subject than he would. Clearly, this would make it hard for him to write with authority. However, he then had the insight to recognize that if he could harness the expertise in his readership his could be the best informed and most expert IT column in the country. And so through his blog and by inviting comments he allowed his readers to steer his journalism. Using the expertise of the public in this way has now been called 'networked journalism'.

Jeff Jarvis, blogger and professor at the City University of New York, coined the phrase:

> Journalism must become collaborative at many levels. News organizations should come to rely on citizens to help report stories on a large-scale level …, at an individual level (citizens contributing reports to news organizations' efforts), and as a network (news organizations supporting citizens' own efforts with content, promotion, education, and revenue).

Journalism will become collaborative not only on this pro-am level but also pro-to-pro (we need not and cannot afford to send our own reporters to some stories just for the sake of byline ego but we can link to and bring our readers – and help support – the best reporting from other outlets). (Jarvis 2006)

Jarvis foresees a number of consequences from this approach. He believes the role of journalists, and their relationship with the public, will change from 'owner' of the story to moderators, editors and enablers. He sees a broadening of the scope of journalism and news, and a raising of the quality of journalism, as, with the help of the public, there are more ways to get stories and to ensure they are right.

These were some of the principles behind the launch of NewAssignment.Net – a project run by his colleague at New York University, Prof. Jay Rosen. It's a non-profit site that attempted to pioneer 'Open Source' reporting.

At New Assignment, pros and amateurs cooperate to produce work that neither could manage alone. The site uses open source methods to develop good assignments and helps bring them to completion. It pays professional journalists to carry the project home and set high standards; they work closely with users who have something to contribute. The betting is that (some) people will donate to stories they can see are going to be great because the open methods allow for that glimpse ahead. (Rosen 2006a)

As yet unproven, it builds on the idea of tapping into the experience and expertise of the public and using it as a form of widely distributed research. Rosen then sees that raw information being pulled together and developed by professional journalists before 'the story' is disseminated again.

I just think journalism without the media is at this point a practical idea, worth testing … NewAssignment.Net makes it possible for the **people formerly known as the audience** … to originate outstanding work. The design assumes no antagonism at all between 'citizen' users and 'professional' journalists. The assumption is we need both, and ways for them to work in tandem. A journalist who can't work with people *and* tell them the truth isn't right for New Assignment. (Rosen 2006b)

The idea of using the expertise of the public is not limited to journalism on the internet. Minnesota Public Radio has launched what it calls Public Insight Journalism – with a database of expert contributors to help give reporters a more informed view of issues.

The network allows their producers and reporters to learn from people with first-hand experience of the subjects they are covering. The Public Insight web page invites people to join their network:

> Share what you know: become a source for Minnesota Public Radio.
>
> Education. Health care. Community. War. Whatever the issue, Minnesota Public Radio needs your knowledge and your experience to make our news coverage an even stronger public service. (Minnesota Public Radio 2007)

Michael Skoler, the managing director of news, explained the motivation behind the project:

> If 'establishment' media organizations can plug into the energy and wisdom of the collective brain of the public, we'll bring the strength of traditional journalism – editorial judgment, fact-checking, truth-seeking – into a new age of better, more trusted news coverage. If we don't do this, I think the unfiltered, weblog-type model of journalism will overtake traditional media with its sheer energy and we will lose a powerful way of informing the public about critical issues in our democracy. (Skoler 2004)

It's another way of saying that what's important is the survival of good journalism – not the media or platform on which it rests.

So what is the role of journalism in social networking sites like Facebook, Flickr or Twitter? There are at least three kinds of relationship between these platforms and traditional journalism.

First, they provide a source of information. On many of these sites there are specialist groups where people with a particular interest or expertise post their thoughts and engage in discussion about new developments. If you are interested in technology, for example, the discussion of the latest software developments in a specialist group of this kind is likely to be at the leading edge of information available. Others may focus on celebrity gossip, or simply be a place to post photos or videos – but whatever kind of journalism you are interested in, social networks provide as much information or as many tip-offs as any other gathering place. As one example, in Facebook, the BBC's *Newsnight* has a group called 'So You Want To Be on Newsnight' as a way to encourage followers of the programme to contribute ideas, examples and interviewees to the reports being put together.

Second, social networks provide a way for news organizations to reach new audiences. Many of those subscribing to these sites are not consumers of traditional news. We know from numerous academic studies that the under-thirties are using the internet more than TV, radio or newspapers for their information (Pew Research Center 2000; Ahlers 2006; Ofcom 2007). By syndicating news feeds into the online communities younger people choose to use, news organizations can extend the reach of their services. In early 2007 the BBC reported the situation in Turkey with bespoke videos for YouTube and photographs on Flickr.

Finally, for the same reason – they are places people choose to gather – these sites offer new marketing opportunities. So Reuters has a bureau in Second Life, Sky News offers headlines on Twitter. These are much more about raising awareness of the news brand than providing a news service.

And so news organizations are learning how to use the technology and sites that encourage citizen journalism to support their traditional purposes of providing professional journalism as widely as possible. If good journalism is to survive it's essential they adapt in this way.

In this first part of the twenty-first century, as traditional news operations are disrupted by the internet, there is much concern about viable business models for news. With so much information apparently available for free on the internet, are the public losing the habit of paying for news and information? What might that mean for some of the great, long-established media organizations of the last century?

The media, and journalism, are going through a radical transformation and not all the answers are yet clear. However, there is no question that citizen journalism, the ability of the public to contribute to and steer public news and information, will be one of the defining characteristics of journalism in the future. And, in parallel, news organizations are adapting to a new relationship with the public and to new ways of distributing their journalism. In years to come I suspect people will look back at the debate about citizen journalism, and whether it is real journalism, whether it is in opposition to mainstream media, with some bewilderment. The fundamental purposes, principles and values of good journalism are unchanged by the internet. But the opportunities for sharing experience, opinion, discovery and expertise are greatly increased and can enrich and improve journalism in the years ahead.

Note

1   American journalist Stone began a newsletter, *I.F. Stone's Weekly*, in 1953.

References

Ahlers, D. (2006) News consumption and the new electronic media. *Harvard International Journal of Press/Politics* 11(1): 29–52, http://www.ksg.harvard.edu/presspol/research_publications/papers/research_papers/R26.pdf.

Dear, P. (2006) Images of 7 July: Tunnel horror. BBC Online, http://news.bbc.co.uk/1/hi/uk/5102860.stm.

Garcia, M. (2007) Speech at the WAN/WEF conference, Cape Town, June.

Gillmor, D. (2006) *We the Media: Grassroots Journalism by the People, for the People.* O'Reilly Media, http://wethemedia.oreilly.com.

Grim, E. (1875–85) Vita S. Thomae, Cantuariensis archepiscopi et martyris. In *Materials for the Life of Thomas Becket*, vol. II, ed. Robertson, J. Rolls Series.

Heyward, A. (2004) CBS statement on Bush memos. CBS Broadcasting, http://www.cbsnews.com/stories/2004/09/20/politics/main644539.shtml.

Jarvis, J. (2006) The definition of networked news. http://www.buzzmachine.com/2006/09/08/the-definition-of-networked-news.

Levine, R., Locke, C., Searls, D. and Weinberger, D. (1999) *The Cluetrain Manifesto.* Perseus, http://www.cluetrain.com.

MacKinnon, R. (2006) Speech at the 'We Media' conference, May, Reuters London.

Maher, V. J. (2006) Bloggers investigation ousts Swedish minister for foreign trade. http://www.poynter.org/column.asp?id=31&aid=112322.

Minnesota Public Radio (2007) Public insight network. http://minnesota.publicradio.org/publicinsightjournalism.

North, R. (2005) Coming together as a city. 7 July, http://news.bbc.co.uk/1/hi/uk/4670099.stm#thursday.

Ofcom (2007) *New News, Future News.* Ofcom.

Orwell, G. (1948) Introduction. In *British Pamphleteers*, vol. 1, eds. Orwell, G. and Reynolds, R. Allan Wingate.

Pax, S. (2003) I became the profane pervert Arab blogger. Guardian Unlimited, 9 September, http://www.guardian.co.uk/Iraq/Story/0,2763,1038253,00.html.

Pew Research Center (2000) *Internet Sapping Broadcast News Audience.* Pew Research Center.

Rather, D. (2005) Dan Rather statement on memos. 20 September, http://www.cbsnews.com/stories/2004/09/20/politics/main644546.shtml.

Rosen, J. (2006a) Welcome to NewAssignment.Net? 19 August http://newassignment.wordpress.com.

Rosen. J. (2006b) Introducing NewAssignment.Net. Department of Journalism, New York University, http://journalism.nyu.edu/pubzone/weblogs/pressthink/2006/07/25/nadn_qa.html

Skoler, M. (2004) Interview with Leonard Witt. Public Journalism Network PJnet.org, http://pjnet.org/post/111.

Williams, J. (2006) Citizen newsgathering. 20 October, http://www.bbc.co.uk/blogs/theeditors/jon_williams.

Questions for students

1 Discuss how citizen journalism has influenced mainstream journalism. Are the mainstream news media genuinely changing the way they gather and disseminate news?
2 Is there a danger that traditional newsgathering will suffer as newspapers and broadcasters turn to citizen journalists to provide inexpensive video and material?
3 Discuss the impact of bloggers and citizen journalists on the coverage of recent international stories such as the clash between Buddhist monks and the military government in Burma (Myanmar).
4 Is it necessary for citizen journalists and bloggers to strive to achieve fairness, accuracy and impartiality?
5 What do you think is the longer-term impact of this new wave of citizen journalism on politics?

13

Working at the Coalface of New Media

Ben Hammersley

Introduction

JOHN OWEN

It is one thing for the heads of news organizations and news agencies to embrace with near-religious fervour citizen journalism, user-generated content (UGC) and peer sharing. It's another thing for the journalists who are already feeling the pressures of meeting the never-ending deadlines of 24-hour news cycles and website filings to have to post blogs and incorporate UGC into their reporting.

But news organizations may have no choice but to move swiftly to exploit these phenomenally popular trends or risk becoming irrelevant to their readers, listeners and viewers.

In the past, news organizations have been slow to change their news practices. Few broadcast news networks deploy 'one-man-band' video journalists (vjs) who record their own pictures as well as report and write their stories. Yet the steadily evolving miniaturization of camera equipment has made this practice possible for decades, and a few networks such as my old one, CBC, have been in the forefront of sending out vjs to produce features and back-stories. But for many reasons – the richer networks had no financial imperative to reduce the size of their newsgathering teams; union resistance; the culture of resistance to change in most newsrooms; and no commitment to training prospective vjs – there's been no large-scale support for video journalism and smaller newsgathering teams, especially in the American networks.

But ABC News in the United States has recently announced that it plans to open seven mini bureaus, which represents a major reversal of its retreat from international newsgathering. As ABC News president David Westin told the *Hollywood Reporter*:

> 'Technology now makes it possible for us to have bureaus without a receptionist, three edit suites and studio cameras and so on ... The essence of what we do is reporting, it's not production. Production is the way you get it on the air and to people, but reporting is the essence.'
>
> Each of the seven reporters will work from home and travel around their region carrying a small DV camera and editing-enabled laptop. They'll report, write, shoot and edit their pieces, though they also will have support from others at ABC News. Most of the work will be uploaded via broadband to New York, though they will carry a portable satellite dish for the field where broadband isn't available. (Gough 2007)

In the chapter that follows, Ben Hammersley, one of Britain's leading new media reporters who came out of a print background and lately has filed reports across all media platforms for the BBC World Service, reflects on what lessons he's learned trying to do it all.

Reference

Gough, P. (2007) One-man show at ABC o'seas bureaus. *Hollywood Reporter*, 3 October, http://www.hollywoodreporter.com/hr/content_display/news/e3i47e6403b3602038866ba096cb9fcdc29.

Search the internet, read any blogs, pick up any journalism tome, or attend any lectures on the state of our industry and you're likely to come across the same few topics: citizen journalism, online communities, convergence, and, if you're really unlucky, Web 2.0. I have no doubt that you will have already read in this book, no matter which order you're reading the chapters in, mentions of blogging, podcasting and perhaps Facebook.

Ben Hammersley in Turkey, where he covered the Turkish election for the BBC as part of his social media experiment in June 2007

PHOTO COURTESY OF BEN HAMMERSLEY

If there's a single thing that puts the willies up working journalists at the time of writing (the end of 2007), it is the impact of the internet on our jobs. Just what is going on?

I don't know. No one does. However, I have been trying to work it out, and make it up, for many years. In this chapter I'll try and pass on some things I've learnt or thought about digital reporting. I'll be doing so from the point of view of someone who has been working online for long enough to remember the first time around: having been a huge fan of the ideas, and noisy proponent of experimenting with new forms of reporting, I now suspect some of my views are too cynical, and liable to induce claims that I just don't get it. At 31, I am, in internet years, effectively senile. Maybe so, but – and here's my first point – the internet's biggest export has always been punditry, and punditry from non-practitioners at that. Journalism is not an exception, and although many of the things we're told we're now supposed to be doing sound very good, in practice it's not so easy. It's this experience I'll try to sum up.

First, citizen journalism: I'm going to ignore it. It has its place, but, as you are reading this book, presumably you want to be a reporter every day, and not just on those when you and your cameraphone happen on a major incident. (Or when you happen upon an opinion that must be shared with the rest of the world, as is more often the case.)

It's also not a threat to what you do, unless your output is on a par with that of random bystanders. Yes, all of the major broadcasters have had success using amateur footage from major incidents, and the prime examples of citizen journalism can be remarkable. But the very fact that the only citizen journalism you see used in mainstream media is remarkable somewhat gives the game away. There has never been a citizen journalist covering a dull story, or one that requires more reporting than just being there and pointing the camera in the general direction. If there's any competition from citizen journalists at all, it will only push us towards deeper investigation, better shooting, and finer reporting of the why and the how, not just the what. On that note, the very acceptance of 'citizen journalism' as a phrase seems to me to be deeply demeaning to our own profession: I can't imagine lawyers referring to people who had once seen an episode of *Quincy* as citizen barristers, and nor do we have citizen surgeons, or citizen plumbers. Can we reclaim some pride in our hard-learnt skills, please?

We are, though, in a world that invites participation. User-generated content (UGC) is here to stay. Outside of journalism, UGC is redefining culture to the very core: that anyone's brain-work can be placed online, for virtually no cost, and made available and searchable to the entire world, is, I think, a cultural shift more far-reaching than the Renaissance.

But UGC in the news world is not quite that. Where it stands alone, as on YouTube or Flickr, UGC is just another form of citizen journalism: if it's a threat to you, you've either found a new colleague to recruit – give them a job and get on with it – or you should move on.

Where UGC touches mainstream journalism is another thing: comments underneath stories. Bloggers started this, and bloggers can, in my now scarred opinion, keep it. But let's look at what it is, in the first place.

The pro-commenting camp gives various reasons to have comments underneath stories. They allow for reader participation, and there will be a reader, almost by the law of averages, who will know the subject matter of the story better than you do. Allowing this person to comment underneath the story will give the other readers some added value; comments allow a community to build up around stories, which hopefully will foster brand loyalty and more visits to the website; comments keep the writers on their toes, by fostering debate; comments remove any unsightly appearance of elitism.

The anti-commenting camp would have it differently. First of all, they say, the quality of the debate is not as high as you might hope. (Reference must be made here to Godwin's Law (1990), which states that 'As an online discussion grows longer, the probability of a comparison involving Nazis or Hitler approaches one', and which is, sadly, almost universally true.) Second, there are few pieces of reporting on which discussion is actually worthwhile. Opinion pieces and editorials are written to be debated – the *Guardian's* Comment is Free (http://commentisfree.guardian.co.uk/index.html) site is a good example of this – but there's little to be said for debating factual reporting unless the person doing so is in a position actually to debate the facts.

That sounds obvious, but having comments underneath your factual reporting in practice means getting into debates about your perceived bias, and not about the matters in hand. A quick review of comments left under reporting from anywhere in the Middle East shows this in action. Indeed, the act of minutely picking apart factual reporting for signs of bias has a name on the internet. It's called Fisking, after Robert Fisk's reports from the region.[1]

At the moment, my personal opinion is that opening comments underneath your reporting is at best pointless, at worst actively dangerous and off-putting to other readers. But for me this is mostly an aesthetic decision based on having read too many comments seemingly written in green ink. For others the prospect of online commenting carries a legal risk too far. By allowing people to publish comments on your site, you're setting yourself up with a serious risk of libel, and with that potentially a great deal of cost.

You will need to have a facility to moderate, edit and if necessary remove any comments, and this takes time and money, and it's not certain that the additional traffic to your site from people writing comments and then returning to read the resulting thread is ever enough to make up for the cost of having the comments there in the first place. To date there has not been any data available to judge whether financially it's even worth doing.

I suspect that UGC for the smaller, single-topic, highly specialized blogs might be a perfectly good way to run a site and make a living for one or two people. Scale it up to generalist pages on newspaper sites, say, and the returns diminish greatly.

For all that I'm trashing the UGC buzz, UGC is also the greatest thing to happen to journalism since the invention of the notepad. It's not the content that users generate that we should be happy about, but the tools they do it with. This is the real revolution. Ten years ago, content management systems cost hundreds of thousands of pounds, now they're free; server space and bandwidth were hugely expensive, now they're almost free; video hosting was next to impossible, and now we have YouTube; and so on and so on. Your local high street retailer will sell you an HD camera for less than a grand and you can edit that video on a consumer-level laptop.

Digital cameras, digital audio gear, even high-bandwidth mobile data connections are so common as for it to be weird to point them out as special, but they're capable of doing jobs that a decade ago would have required a second mortgage to pay for, and a van to carry the equipment around. It's not journalism that has driven innovation in the tools we use, but regular people wanting to film their kids' birthday parties, or take pictures and share them with their friends.

So, if we dismiss the C that the U-s are G-ing, we can still take advantage of the tools they're using. It's here that we can make all the difference. I won't go into the different types of blogging tool or photo-hosting site available (I'd be out of date by tomorrow morning for one thing), but there is a general principle to be noted. In the past, software was split into two divisions. Enterprise software would be huge and expensive and would work, whereas home-user software would be small, cheap and poor quality. Since the web, and especially with the Web 2.0 era, enterprise software is still huge and expensive but has gained the poor-quality crown. Home-user software, however, is increasingly free, hugely powerful and good. Chances are that whatever enterprise-level tool you're using in your office, it has a consumer equivalent that is free, better, and designed to be used by 10-year-olds. Video bloggers are so prolific because of, not despite, their cheap editing software; teenagers have massively sophisticated blogs and MySpaces precisely because they're not using the sort of content management system that a newspaper would buy, or did in the 1990s.

The new new-media reporter, then, should use only consumer-level services to get their stories out. These services are both better and cheaper, and they're quicker to set up, and much easier to take down or improve as you go.

Working with the new internet tools also invites working in the new internet way. Look at any successful internet company and you'll see they work in many of the same ways: small teams, rapidly prototyping new products with the cheapest possible tools, launching them as soon as possible, and then rapidly iterating them as they go, making improvements to the product as the product is consumed and they get feedback. Compare this to most mainstream media launches: large teams using expensive tools, launching something late, and being loath to change it after the fact. This is a shame, because innovation requires us to try lots of new things. Many of them will fail, which is a good and positive thing, and one happily mitigated by the use of cheap tools and rapid development techniques. You can then just move on and try something else: a mindset that is hard to find in, say, television.

The equipment needed to create, edit and publish video, stills photography, audio and text is so cheap and so easy to use that the modern reporter is now able to work across all of the media: the barriers to entry created by, say, TV cameras costing more than a family car have completely gone. Now is the time for experimentation.

My personal interest, and one that has excited newsgathering operations for years, is the idea that because the gear is so small and cheap, a single reporter, or a two-person crew, could get to places with only a backpack or two, and produce output previously impossible to get without a satellite truck and a full production team. For conflict and foreign reporting this is especially exciting, as it opens up whole swathes of the world where previously it would have been too hard, too dangerous or just too expensive to operate.

Sending TV back via a satellite phone isn't new, of course, but now the necessary gear is the size of a hardback book. It fits into the side pocket of a backpack. Cameras can be even smaller, and an entire edit suite, albeit a slow one, can fit onto a mini-laptop. I've worked alone in Afghanistan in this way, and filed video daily, with consumer-grade equipment that could fit into a small flight case, and which cost altogether less than ten grand.

This revolution alone, allowing for so many more journalists to be out in the field, and further out than before too, is world changing enough.

With the sort of giddiness that the options that the new storytelling technology can give us, we are liable to try even more things. One experiment I tried was for the BBC in June 2007, when I went to Turkey to make a documentary on the upcoming general elections.

Apart from the television – for which I had the shot/edit producer Keith Morris with me – I planned to share the experience of reporting the story itself online. I was writing to a blog, posting pictures to Flickr, sending a running commentary to Twitter, and uploading behind-the-scenes footage to YouTube. I explained why like this:

> From broadcasting live from an Afghan hillside, and delivering news almost as it breaks, to getting reporters and crew to the most remote, most dangerous, most important areas on the planet, all in time to send news home in time for tea. It's not just magical. It's plentiful as well: there's never been so much reporting available. There has never been a time where so much information is available to those who want it. Whether online, on television, or on the radio, news comes to you faster, deeper, and in more flavours than ever before. But while there's more news available to you, you're much less likely to know how it was made. The days of newspapermen meeting someone in the pub, scribbling some notes on the back of a beer mat, then rolling into the office to type it up are long gone. The modern journalist is a multi-media creature, feeding the beasts of television, radio and the web. The demands on our time are much greater, the prospect of going down the pub in the middle of the day much less and the number of educated eyes looking at our work far beyond anything any media professional has ever had to deal with. And as any conjuror will tell you, producing magic under so many eyes is incredibly hard if you want to keep your methods secret. Many do want to preserve the mystique, but frankly, I think it's easier, and more productive in the end, to do what my maths teacher was always forlornly begging me to do, and show my working. (Hammersley 2007)

We learnt a lot of lessons from this. First of all, it's not physically sustainable. Live reporting, by which I mean filing reports while you're still in-country, is arduous enough work in one medium, but add in a couple more – radio and the web on top of TV, for example – and you're going to fade very quickly if you're out on your own. Live, multimedia, solo: pick two.

Second, the self-referential blogging style, although very popular on the internet, is dangerous. How great stories were reported may well be interesting, but writing the history as you go presupposes a success that you can't guarantee. Live blogging a foreign reporting trip, for example, opens you up to a great risk of public anticlimax. This wasn't the case in Turkey, but I, and others, have made the mistake elsewhere of promising some cracking action to come, only to arrive at the story to find everything quiet. With documentary subjects like a general election, you are at less risk of this, but the more you trail the forthcoming feature, the more likely it is that you'll turn up during a war's first ceasefire, or the day after a crisis has blown over.

Producing your multimedia reports after the event, and then publishing them as diary-like serial, is one alternative that gets you out of this risk.

It's safer, and stylistically more useful, to publish in instalments from the comfort of your home office, once you know you've got the story, rather than do it live and hoping for the best.

This also gets you out of the time pressure of producing the cut stories on a daily basis. Quite apart from needing to carry editing gear – even if it's just a laptop, it's still a pain – it radically cuts into your time in the field. Of course, producing edited pieces from the field is the bread and butter of a single-media reporter, but if you're planning on producing reports in all media, and you don't have to file from the field, then very seriously do not. The new tools will enable you to capture masses of raw material in all forms of media, but this still takes time and concentration and a huge skill-set: forcing editing on top of that makes life very hard indeed.

It's not impossible, in the short term at least, but to be able to produce such a massive amount of output across all media eventually calls for an aesthetic to your pieces for which demand just isn't there at the moment. In other words, as you get more tired, your stuff will get weird, and then get spiked.

Innovations in journalism come in two forms, the stylistic and the technological, and it's important not to get these two things mixed up.

One may follow the other, in the way that lightweight cameras provided for the handheld documentary style of video, but just as you can't always detect the one by the presence of the other, having the new gear doesn't mandate making your reports wackily stylized.

We can make huge technological advances in the way we can produce and deliver news, but still have the end product stylistically identical to the things we made before. Or we can use old technology in new ways, and break new ground stylistically: witness the New Journalism of the early sixties, or the constant innovation in radio today. But trying to do both, especially within the confines of a changing organization, can sometimes be pushing it.

In short, the new technologies do offer a great many advantages: stuff is smaller, and cheaper, and easier to use, and offers the potential for reporting from places, and for prices, previously unreachable. But digital storytelling does not deliver everything at once. As well as a skill, journalism is a craft, and one that takes time to produce the best work, and it's this craft that makes a professional reporter worth their pay over a citizen journalist. Digital journalism makes this all the more true.

Note

1 Robert Fisk is the Middle East correspondent for the UK's *Independent* newspaper.

References

Godwin, M. (1990) Quoted in 'Meme, counter-meme'. *Wired*, http://www.wired.com/wired/archive/2.10/godwin.if_pr.html.
Hammersley, B. (2007) New frontiers in journalism. 27 June, http://news.bbc.co.uk/1/hi/in_depth/europe/2007/webreporter_turkey.

Questions for students

1 Is Ben Hammersley right in worrying about how making so many demands on journalists working across all platforms may dilute the quality of reporting?
2 What are the journalistic and professional practice arguments for and against asking journalists to work across all platforms?
3 Discuss with your local newspaper or broadcaster what their views are about asking reporters to work across all media platforms.

14

Reporting Humanitarian Crises

Peter Apps

Introduction

JOHN OWEN

Our final chapter is devoted to reporting on humanitarian disasters around the world. Ask foreign correspondents or network news teams about the most troubling stories that they have ever covered, and the chances are that they will recall the haunting images of the victims of an earthquake or mudslide. It is one thing to chronicle wars and conflicts where man's inhumanity to man is often beyond comprehension; it is another thing to see how the force of nature can wipe out communities on an unimaginable scale and create unbearable suffering for the old and vulnerable, usually in developing-world countries that are already impoverished.

As I write, one of the poorest countries in the world, Bangladesh, is experiencing its latest humanitarian crisis caused by both flooding and a cyclone that caused an estimated 3,500 deaths and displaced millions.

This grim reading is available on the Reuters Foundation's AlertNet web page (http://www.alertnet.org), the most comprehensive tracker of humanitarian crises around the world.

Along with the latest information about Bangladesh, AlertNet aggregates international information about natural disasters and provides tips about looming crises large and small. There is even now a 'global warming watch' that aims to explain the link between climate change and disasters. It says that the number of weather-related disasters has increased by a factor of four in the last 20 years (Reuters AlertNet 2007).

So there is no absence of information about natural disasters. But will the international media care enough, be willing to spend its shrinking newsgathering budgets on stories where the victims are usually not affluent North Americans or Europeans on holiday, as they were during the tsunami of 2004, but instead the world's downtrodden, faceless millions living in desperate poverty, as many do in Africa or Asia?

For certain, the news agencies, as discussed in earlier chapters, will have their cameras and reporters at the scene, whether it is racing to the site of an earthquake in a remote part of the world or trying to find a way to get to an area where there are reports, usually from aid agencies, about widespread hunger and a possible famine.

A reporter who for the past year has been part of the Reuters AlertNet team based in London writes this final chapter about how to report on natural disasters. It isn't an assignment that Peter Apps had planned to have at this stage in his career.

After all, in the summer of 2006, it was foreign corresponding that was Peter Apps's life at Reuters. He was then posted to Sri Lanka, where he was assigned to cover the vicious civil war that has raged there between the government and the Tamil Tigers since 1983. More than 70,000 have been killed, and there is an on-going humanitarian disaster caused by the displacement of an estimated 500,000 people.

On 5 September 2006, Peter Apps was in a rented minibus, en route to a place where child soldiers were being recruited by the rebels, when his own disaster struck – a terrible road accident after his bus collided with a tractor. Apps was aware instantly that he'd broken his neck, as he couldn't feel anything below it.

It was a miracle that he survived, saved probably because an American landmine clearance team happened to come along shortly after the accident.

But Peter Apps was and is paralysed from the waist down, confined to a wheelchair.

Yet he refused to accept that fate had taken away his life as a journalist. Five months later, he wrote on the Reuters website about how 'I have learnt to drive a wheelchair with my head' and 'I have taken up painting with a brush held in my teeth' (Apps 2007a).

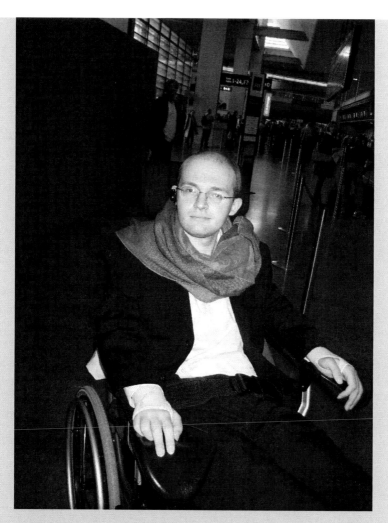

Peter Apps at Stockholm Airport, 2007
PHOTO COURTESY OF THOMSON REUTERS

Nine months after his accident, Peter Apps wrote about how 'I was wheeled up to my new desk in London to get back to work.' He had achieved this. Yet as he wrote, the recovery had been painful and he had often felt isolated:

> I was stranded in agonising limbo in hospital far west of London, far from people I know with little to do, simply clinging to hope of a more useful life – brutally aware that in many countries I would already be dead from lack of care …

I require 24-hour care, cannot feed or wash myself, use my mobile phone or make handwritten notes. There have been a handful of disabled and wheelchair-bound foreign correspondents before. But all have had largely working arms and much more independence. (Apps 2007b)

Amazingly, 14 months after his accident, Peter Apps was – with the support of two care workers – boarding a plane and flying off to Stockholm to represent AlertNet. He was back doing what he loved, being a correspondent, maybe not yet in the developing world but writing about what mattered to him. As he had foretold it: 'But for me, I will know I have bounced back when I'm back in a minibus in my wheelchair, heading out somewhere in the developing world to talk to people who are usually ignored about problems the world barely cares about' (Apps 2007a).

References

Apps, P (2007a) Witness: Getting used to life with no working limbs. http://www.reuters.com/article/reutersEdge/idUSL0973827520070212?sp=true.
Apps P. (2007b) Witness: Still paralyzed, but back reporting overseas. http://www.reuters.com/article/businessEditorsPick/idUSL2471118920071025?pageNumber=2&virtualBrandChannel=0.
Reuters AlertNet (2007) http://www.alertnet.org.

Wailing children, the stench of death, shattered buildings and traumatized survivors. Covering humanitarian disasters can seem at once both clichéd and overwhelming.

It brings with it its own unique challenges – technological and logistical as well as psychological. And yet at the same time, many of the same rules apply as in other forms of reporting from fluffy celebrity news to hard-news business and market reporting.

For a reporter at a wire agency such as Reuters – and perhaps for most reporters – it is always worth thinking through in advance. At the risk of stating the blatantly obvious, disasters can often strike without warning. In the developing or the developed world, you might only be minutes away from racing to pin down the details of an earthquake or explosion – and

Peter Apps, 2007
PHOTO COURTESY OF THOMSON REUTERS

not much longer from having to pick through the rubble yourself search-
ing down the story.

Sometimes, you can see a humanitarian disaster coming months in
advance. In 2005 in southern Africa, largely because I was covering the
South African grain futures market, I ran the first stories on rains failing
across much of the region in February or early March. But because farm-
ers harvested at least some food the shortages themselves only really
began to bite much later in the year, and global media attention didn't
begin to turn until September or October.

Many creeping crises take longer still, evolving over the years or decades. They bring with them their own unique reporting challenges – not
least the challenge of making them into a news story at all.

Some suddenly burst into existence out of a pre-existing story – perhaps a war that suddenly sparks a refugee crisis, further stretching already
possibly overcommitted journalistic resources.

Some blast into existence without notice or warning, wreaking havoc
and leaving journalists – like aid workers and government officials –
scrambling to catch up. They can strike in the middle of the night – or, like
the 2004 tsunami, in the middle of a holiday.

Particularly in the world's poorer and under-covered corners, I would
argue it is a singularly important form of reporting. If you miss an unnoticed crisis, it is quite possible no one else will pick up on it either. Media

attention is one way – sometimes the only way – of attracting the notice of donor nations or politicians. Handled right, few doubt it can save lives. Handled badly, it can exacerbate political tensions and even make delivery of aid harder.

And on top of everything else there is the never-ending challenge of simply producing fresh and interesting reporting that will actually hold a reader's or editor's attention in a world that can seem increasingly tired of and overwhelmed by an unceasing tide of bad news.

Initial Reports

For agencies such as Reuters or the Associated Press – as well as for broadcasters and daily newspapers – the main business is breaking news. Reports of an earthquake or tidal wave spur a bureau into frenetic action much in the same way as a bomb blast or seismic political event.

As with any breaking story, the priority is to pin down exactly what has happened – where, when, how serious, what will happen next? Gauging the scale of the body count and infrastructure damage is at the heart of working out how serious a story it is. But that can be a mammoth task.

Trainee Reuters journalists are run through the process again and again in the training room so that – hopefully – if something happens on their watch they will be ready.

First warning can come from a variety of sources. An earthquake may jolt the bureau – as happened with the Pakistani earthquake in 2005, felt by reporters in a string of South Asian cities and capitals. Or it may be picked up by the United States Geological Service, and the first 100-character news alert may be issued from Washington before the country bureau involved is even aware it has happened.

It may be reported first by local press, newswires, television or radio – although as a matter of pride international news agencies would still try to be faster. There might be a torrent of text messages or phone calls, particularly from local staff with much better roots in the community.

Polishing off a story late at night in our bureau in the Sri Lankan capital Colombo, I was once tipped off to a bomb attack by a telephone call from a stockbroker who had heard the blast go off near him and wanted to know what was going on. I'm ashamed to admit I didn't believe him and told him so – but it tipped me off to the story and I did call him back later to admit he had been right all along. The same thing can happen with earthquakes and tsunamis.

Invariably, communications collapse almost immediately. Once-reliable mobile phone networks may be overwhelmed or simply too badly damaged. That means it is always worth having as thorough a contacts list as possible – including landline numbers. But landlines too may be knocked out or people may simply not answer their phones, perhaps because they have fled – or because they are dead or injured.

Officials are invariably the first port of call for journalists desperate to pin down details. Police, military or civilian administration figures may be able at least to give the scale of the damage. Hospitals may be able to give an idea of the types of injuries. Sometimes they may be able to give a guide to the number of dead.

But if things are really bad, the priority will invariably be helping the living, and the dead may be left where they fall.

In August 2006, as tens of thousands of people fled new fighting in eastern Sri Lanka, the closest I could get to a rough death toll was through simply asking people how many dead bodies they had seen. With so many people desperate to flee the conflict area and many injured by shell and mortar fire, removing corpses on the battlefield was hardly a priority. As a result, there were reports of massacres we never managed to pin down and any body count was by necessity rough and incomplete.

Images of a disaster are key if people are going to use the story. Local victims and holidaymakers – as in the tsunami – may already have the still and video images that will ultimately define the story. But in the short term, with mobile phone networks down, they may simply be unable to transmit them and the first images are likely to come from local television stations and possibly newspaper websites. An agency like Reuters will pick up local television footage and send it on to clients around the world. In the tsunami, local Sri Lankan television footage of water rushing through the bus station in the town of Galle offered some of the first real pictures of how bad the disaster was.

A news agency will also start looking to rush its own television crews and photographers to the scene. On a big story, they may well be flown in from overseas. Aid agencies may also send in photographers and video crews and make the material available to raise awareness.

Writing the Story

Sometimes, it is literally possible to write the story from the scene. I once spent a night at the top of an earthquake-hit gold-mine shaft in South Africa with a laptop connecting to the internet through my mobile phone every couple of hours to update the story as the rescue crews brought in the dead and wounded mineworkers. I've sat in the front seat of a minibus pulled into the side of the road with a satellite phone on the roof filing text stories as fleeing Sri Lankans choked the roads in front of me.

Then, you can sometimes find a story almost writes itself. Sometimes, you may be trying to write a story from an air-conditioned office dozens, hundreds or even thousands of miles away while still giving it that feeling of immediacy.

As always in journalism, there are no hard and fast rules about what makes a good story. The line between cliché and good writing can sometimes seem dangerously thin.

Ultimately, whether you are there or not, the basic requirements of the story are the same. You want scale, context, colour, quotes and impact. You want powerful individual stories without losing track of the bigger picture.

If you can't get on the ground yourself – often the case – then the most important thing is to track down people who are. The world wants to know how many people are dead but it also wants to know what it looks like at the sharp end. Ask witnesses what they can see. Text reporters can write descriptions of the scene from reliable photographs or television footage.

In trying to describe such a visual story, I sometimes try to think of the story almost like a television package, putting in a mixture of hard facts (death tolls, times, dates, figures), talking-head quotes (ideally mainly real people and victims, perhaps followed by more officials or aid workers giving context) and visual images (women sitting by the road crying, soldiers holding towels to their faces against the stench of dead bodies, insects buzzing and children coughing inside an overcrowded school room).

Strong personal stories can make entire sidebars on their own – but with a little thought and effort can also be distilled down to little more than a quote or paragraph in the middle of the main story, bringing a big picture piece down to a human level often with a simple, concentrated example of human suffering – much the same as a single shot in a television news report.

For example ...

'I go to a home and they tell me there are 10 children,' said Sam Kaijuka, a Ugandan aid worker with the US religious agency Samaritan's Purse, WFP's [World Food Programme's] partner organisation (in this corner of southern Mozambique in August 2005). 'There is only money from WFP to feed three. I tell them to give me the three that are most deserving. That makes people very hostile. Sometimes we are chased away, but we always find another community that will take the food.'[1]

Sometimes, getting that kind of input from the ground is impossible. Sometimes all you may have to work with is a few sentences or quotes from a stringer or official or a dry wire report. If possible, it is always worth trying to give some colour or human detail – but it is not always doable.

Reuters East Africa deputy chief correspondent C. Bryson Hull may find himself doing several such crises a day from a desk in the Kenyan capital.

Putting together a story about a crisis from afar is the stock-in-trade of wire services. The reasons are many – the locations are too remote to reach in time to get the news or are too dangerous for foreigners. Such is the case for us across the east and central African regions. When floods hit in remote parts of Ethiopia, violence breaks out in the Great Lakes region or drought strikes in distant parts of Kenya where roads barely reach, we have to rely on our local reporters.

They themselves may be distant but can put their local contacts and knowledge to use in reaching witnesses. We try as often as we can to get out to the scene of the news so that when we write from the desk, we have some practical experience of a place – invaluable for reporting an accurate picture. But most of the time, we work by remote control.

The most difficult case for us is Somalia, which we write out of Nairobi based on the work of our extremely brave reporters in Mogadishu and elsewhere. Language, remoteness and the ability to blend in – which foreigners never can – all make Somali reporters the best-suited people to report accurately and safely.

During the height of fighting between Somali troops, their Ethiopian allies and insurgents in March and April 2007, we in the bureau listened as the thunder of artillery and gunfire crackled across the phone lines. Our colleagues reported calmly and professionally despite the fact they were on the firing line and under enormous physical and mental pressure.

It can be frustrating to sit at a desk far away while the action is going on at the end of a phone. It is, in a sense, like working with a blindfold, lacking the input of all the senses you would have if you were there – the food that feeds your instincts. But the trick is to visualise being there and how you would operate safely – knowing what details you would look for, how you would describe the action to create a picture for the reader. The most difficult decisions we have to make – from the safety of our desks – involve advising our field reporters to cover the story while minimising physical risk. That requires knowing your people in the field, staying in constant touch and trusting them and their own instincts to stay safe and get the news right.

Feature Writing

Writing a feature, particularly on a humanitarian issue, is a different art to writing a breaking news story. Whereas one of the key priorities on a breaking disaster story is speed, with a feature there is more of a premium on quality.

A feature can give you the chance to get really into underlying issues – but written badly it can do little more than state the spectacularly obvious, failing completely to capture the reader.

A couple of months into my assignment in Johannesburg in 2004, I found myself in the highlands of the mountainous southern African kingdom of Lesotho covering a range of stories from agricultural decline to mining. On a swift trip to a village organized by one of the aid agencies, I asked how many people in the village had died of AIDS in the last year. One of the village headmen told me it was some 200.

I was flabbergasted – there were only a handful of huts around me. How many people were in the village to begin with, I asked. He said there were around 600.

I wrote up a feature on precisely those lines, filled with concerned quotes from aid workers and government officials. The village headman was the only character in the story who could realistically be classed as a normal person. The feature never saw the light of day – an editor told me there was simply nothing new about it.

With hindsight – and I probably realized this at the time – I had probably simply been too scared to go digging to talk to someone living with HIV who might have given me a powerful enough personal story to carry the feature beyond simple figures. The figures were shocking – even in a country where a third of adults were said to be HIV-positive – but not enough on their own. And several years later, I cannot help but wonder if they were exaggerated – something again that could have been relatively easily checked.

Reuters features editor Sara Ledwith suggests seven tips for writing features from crisis areas – many of which are equally applicable to writing hard news stories.

> Contrast with what people expect to read – for example, accentuate the positive of an individual or individuals in miserable circumstances by finding something innovative they have done to survive. Give a sense of how their day pans out.

> Excellent photos – particularly of the people you are quoting in the story – bring it to life in a way no words can.

> Give a sense of any fallout of the crisis in rich countries.

> Speak to 10 people and expect to quote at least four. Think round as many perspectives as you can.

> Don't shy away from asking hard to answer questions in your copy.

> Remember you are competing for the attention of people who read headlines about Paris Hilton.

Working with Aid Agencies

In many developing countries, aid agencies may already have a presence on the ground when a disaster strikes. They will also be rushing to conduct what they describe as 'needs assessments'. Again, it helps to have as many pre-existing contacts as possible, but otherwise central aid agency headquarters in Europe or the United States may quickly be able to put you in touch with experts on the ground. This is often in their interest as media exposure can attract donations.

The Reuters Foundation website AlertNet (www.alertnet.org) offers a 'who works where' function allowing users to find which aid agencies work in which crisis areas and countries, and providing contact details. Access is free and no password is required. It also provides an 'aid agency newswire' of the latest press releases from groups, which in any breaking emergency may include contact details for staff on the ground.

From China to Sudan to the United States or Britain, the local Red Cross or Red Crescent societies will almost invariably be the first to respond and have the fastest feedback from the ground. Their local volunteers will be the first people to set up rest centres, assist with first aid or – if things are really bad – help bury the dead in mass graves. In war, their work is normally coordinated by the International Committee of the Red Cross (ICRC) and in peace-time disasters by the International Federation of Red Cross and Red Crescent Societies (IFRC). Both deploy international staff on the ground to assist and coordinate, and their headquarters in Geneva can usually provide good contacts and material. If local officials are overwhelmed, they may well be the first source of credible death estimates – as in the case of the 2007 Bangladesh cyclone.

United Nations agencies may also be good for estimates such as the number of displaced, food aid requirements or death tolls. The United Nations Office for Coordination of Humanitarian Affairs (OCHA) may produce situation reports – although they may not always be on the ground in the early days and hours of a crisis. The other large UN agencies, particularly the WFP, United Nations Children's Fund (UNICEF) and the UN High Commissioner for Refugees (UNHCR), will also usually send out press releases and briefing material and deploy press officers to the field.

Other aid agencies such as Oxfam, Save the Children or CARE International usually have smaller geographical footprints than the Red Cross/Crescent or UN agencies. They may be running one refugee camp or supplying one particular need such as water and sanitation. They may be helping UN agencies to distribute food – although they may be understandably keen to pass this off as entirely their own work.

They may also be more outspoken than those in the Red Cross/ Crescent or UN system. But while aid groups have got increasingly involved in advocacy in recent years, their main priority usually remains their operations on the ground – and this may limit what they are willing to say, at least on the record. For example, in Sudan's Darfur region aid groups say they are reluctant to speak out about rape or violence for fear of alienating the authorities and losing access.

On the other hand, if you can build up personal rapport with aid workers they may still be willing to give you good material off the record – or simply quotable to 'aid workers'. Obviously, like other unnamed quotes these must be handled with caution but they can provide a valuable insight into what is going on. Aid workers may also be able to access areas that journalists are denied permits for. They may be able to provide photos and video from areas journalists and media crews cannot.

CARE International head of executive communications and former Africa press officer Lynn Heinisch says that when disaster strikes, aid workers and journalists effectively rely on one another to get the story out.

It's a highly stressed situation. The communications and logistics are often a challenge. There is typically a tiny window to capture the world's attention with stories that help generate support for immediate and longer-term responses. Valuing this relationship, aid agencies dispatch press officers – usually former reporters. It's important to learn from each other and work better together. A few observations …

Place a crisis in the longer term context. Natural disasters such as floods are often related to environmental degradation. Civil conflict can be oversimplified if not well understood. Aid workers can be a good source of information on context and culture.

The poor – particularly women – are always the most affected. They've survived a traumatic event and still have to hold their families together. Most have never seen a video camera. Journalists will soon leave but survivors and aid workers remain to deal with any negative repercussions from their visit. For example, a rape victim with a compelling story might be stigmatised afterwards by her community. Be sensitive about guarding identities in such cases.

Keep in mind that media requests can involve sacrifice by survivors and aid agencies of which you are not aware. When survivors take time out for an interview, they may be forgoing a place in a queue for assistance or missing a work opportunity. When aid workers let a journalist use a satellite phone or Internet connection, they may be delaying something they need to do.

Once again, there are limits to what aid groups are usually willing to say. For example, while ICRC delegates often cross frontlines and visit prisoners and hostages, you will almost never be able to extract any useful information from them – their silence is the price of access.

Instead of aid agencies, you may be able to get more critical comment from advocacy groups such as Amnesty International, Human Rights Watch or more emergency-specific groups such as Save Darfur – although some of the latter have distinct political agendas and may sometimes be seen as supporting specific rebel groups. For example, in Sri Lanka the aid group the Tamils Rehabilitation Organization (TRO) was banned for its reported links with Tamil Tiger rebels. The International Crisis Group (ICG) is an international think tank specifically aiming to provide information on emergencies without endangering or compromising aid efforts on the ground.

Aid agencies are often a good way of getting access to hard-to-reach areas and getting access to communities. They are often willing to offer journalists rides in their four-wheel-drive vehicles and trips to the field. They may be able to provide translators and accommodation.

This can inevitably bring with it the charge that journalists and aid agencies are simply too close. Reuters has very strict rules about what hospitality and support we accept from organizations. But – just as sometimes embedding with a national military is the only and the best way to cover a story – sometimes joining an aid agency in the field is simply the best option, though it should never alter or impact on the reporting.

That means aid agencies should be held to account just as governments and private companies should be, particularly when it comes to wastage. It also means not falling into the trap of concentrating on aid groups and ignoring efforts by local governments. For example, during floods in India, China, Bangladesh and numerous other countries, the heavy lifting of the relief effort is often done by the nation's own military – who may get understandably irritated if Western aid agencies are seen as taking the credit.

As well as providing crucial access and information in times of crisis, aid agencies are also keen for journalists to cover underlying issues around poverty – and their attempts to deal with them. While few editors will take a straight story on what an agency is doing – particularly as it is often far from clear if it is actually working – it can be a good route into looking at issues in the country or region which may have wider political, economic or human interest angles.

Bear in mind that aid agencies invariably have to negotiate access with local officials, and this can be as delicate a diplomatic dance as anything in broader international affairs. Everything in Bridget Kendall's chapter above on high-level diplomacy is equally applicable to dealing with this – and bear in mind that both sides may try to use the media to gain the upper hand. Know that it is going on and act – and write – accordingly. Bear in mind that either aid agencies or officials may start quietly briefing against you if they feel you have got it wrong. Sometimes, even a dispute over refugee numbers can lead to death threats – so it helps if everything you write, particularly numbers, is properly sourced. Then, your critics are more likely to go after the source and less likely to go after you … which may make you very unpopular with the source.

Working with aid agencies can get good results – for both sides. But as ex-aid agency press officer Mark Snelling found, there is a risk of over-simplification.

The international response to the food crisis in Niger in August 2005 was, in some ways, a textbook definition of how media organisations and aid agencies can and should work together. Aid worker warnings of devastating food shortages had fallen on deaf ears until BBC images of starving children galvanised the necessary funding and political will for a large-scale humanitarian intervention. The aid agencies got the publicity and funding they needed, the journalists got a good story.

Yet I was left with the uncomfortable impression that we were in danger of buying into a version of events not entirely in line with the realities on the ground. That many people were in desperate need of food was not in doubt. But by the standards of the region, this was not a catastrophically bad year. The Famine Early Warning Systems Network (FEWS Net) found national cereal production was only 11% lower than the five-year average. A few aid workers with years of experience in West Africa told me in private the situation – while horrendous for many people – was not unusual. But somewhere along the line, Niger had crept up the news agenda as Africa's latest 'biblical crisis'.

A few reporters teased out the complex, nuanced back story. There was, in fact, rather a lot of food knocking around. The problem was no one could afford it due to chronic poverty and failed free-market reforms. But again and again, the crisis was cast in the same mould as Ethiopia's Band Aid moment in 1984. Camera crews queued up outside feeding centres for the severely malnourished, jostling for precious skinny baby shots. Even a cursory tour of the much larger operation aimed at the moderately underfed would have told a less dramatic – but more accurate – story.

Fantastic work was done by all sides in 2005, and many lives were saved. But Niger's structural difficulties remain unaddressed, the vulnerability to future shocks as stark and bare as ever. I wonder if the aid workers and journalists became so embroiled in catering to each other's agendas that we all missed the one that actually mattered – that of the people who actually live there.

Getting On the Ground

It may not always be possible for financial, logistic or security reasons, but there are few substitutes for getting on the ground and talking to real people. It allows you to see the scale of the damage, get first-hand accounts from real people, and potentially circumvent aid agencies and officials to get a much rawer vision of what is going on.

Accommodation may be difficult – it may have been destroyed, or more likely blocked up by descending hordes of aid workers. Transport may be equally difficult – not only may essential infrastructure have been destroyed, but commercial traffic may be avoiding the area – for example, as with outbreaks of Ebola or similar viruses or due to fighting. Again, it may have been bought up by aid agencies or desperate refugees. Communications may be overstretched or simply out of action – which can make satellite phones invaluable, despite the expense.

Sometimes, you may be part of a vast press pack. Sometimes, particularly with the slow-onset disasters such as food crises or even a less than high-profile war, it may just be you.

Sometimes, the story may be obvious. Sometimes, as Alistair Thomson writes below, pinning it down may be more difficult.

While the reality of what is happening around you may be somewhat overwhelming, it is crucial that you bear in mind your own health, safety and security – and your own mental health. If there are aid agencies or other journalists around, see what precautions they are taking. Bear in mind that they are probably seeing, experiencing and feeling the same things – which makes them an effective peer support group, even if what that means in reality is simply sharing a beer or three in the evening.

Covering Conflict

Sometimes, the humanitarian consequences of a conflict can be the main story – for example, in Darfur or the vast exodus from Rwanda at the end of the 1994 genocide. But sometimes, it can almost be overlooked.

Reuters AlertNet uses an automated computer program called the World Press Tracker to monitor coverage of humanitarian crises in English-language newspapers. Unsurprisingly, in 2006–7 Iraq and Afghanistan dominated – but in reality few of the stories more than touched on the humanitarian impact which, in the case of Iraq, produced the world's fastest-growing refugee crisis.

Competing agendas will always try to influence and restrict reporting even in a disaster in a peaceful democracy, but in conflict areas such issues become much more serious. Governments and rebel groups may try to restrict aid shipments and redirect aid to military purposes, and aid workers can find themselves targets.

Even apparently innocent, suffering refugees may be trying to put across their own political agenda – or maybe pushing a line they have been intimidated into parroting by rebels or military. Be sceptical of what you are told, ideally without appearing insulting ...

Reuters West Africa deputy chief correspondent Alistair Thomson found just that problem in the Central African Republic in 2007.

The silver-haired German pilot brought the light plane down into the heat haze of the dirt airstrip with ear-numbing speed, and I trusted the yellow-turbaned soldiers pointing their anti-aircraft gun in our direction had been warned of our arrival. We were in Birao, Central African Republic, one of the remotest towns in one of the remotest countries in Africa, where armed attacks from across the border in Darfur made a tough life even harder for local people. Offered a short trip with Hollywood star Mia Farrow to draw attention to the war spreading from Darfur, we had just a few hours.

The town was desperately poor and still bore the signs of a rebel attack a few months earlier. It quickly became clear that without Arabic I was hamstrung. As I asked around for people who spoke French, I came across one civil servant after another eager to give me the government official view, complete with demands for international military and humanitarian aid. Through these ad hoc interpreters, old men told me how the rebels attacked before dawn, raped women and girls and carried off livestock and grain stores. But as my questions probed for more details, the old men fell silent and drifted away under the watchful eyes of policemen and the yellow-turbaned warriors who an aid worker told me quietly had come from neighbouring Chad. Not for the first time, I was unsure who I could trust for a balanced account.

One man showed me the town's only water pump, 16 years old and breaking down. Moments later, other people assured me there were several working pumps across town. Climbing back on board the plane, the website address of a German skydiving club emblazoned on the wing struck me as starkly incongruous. We took off into the sunset with more questions spinning in my head than when we arrived.

Money Counts

Particularly for a financial news agency like Reuters, but also for general output, it is always worth looking at financial issues – both for the country, people and communities affected and for the wider world. When news of an earthquake or hurricane reaches Reuters, one of the first priorities – alongside counting the dead – is to look for broader financial impact. Has an earthquake in Peru – the world's largest copper producer – hit mining? Has it impacted the London or New York metals markets? Are oil refineries continuing production? What infrastructure has been destroyed? Will the country still be able to make its debt repayments? How are local companies coping?

Even food aid can move markets, as Reuters sugar correspondent David Brough writes.

> When I was posted to Rome, I had a brief to cover the United Nations food agencies with a view to getting hard news on commodity deals. The UN WFP buys food staples such as maize and rice on world markets and ships them to the needy around the world. One of my tasks was to develop contacts in the WFP procurement and shipping divisions and break stories. Some of my exclusive stories triggered a burst of trade in the electronic futures markets such as wheat. News of heavy demand by a major buyer such as WFP – such as the purchase of a large tonnage of US and Argentine wheat for Iraq – could have a big impact on global commodity markets. If a Reuters story moved a market, Reuters clients were getting good value for their money.

The Bigger Picture

But what to do when there isn't that sudden, shocking drama question? Never have I seen more slowly dying children and adults than in southern Africa's grinding AIDS crisis, yet, as I said earlier, finding new angles to interest the world is difficult.

Aid agencies complain that interesting journalists in issues of chronic poverty and development can prove almost impossible. And yet lack of food and easily preventable disease – or complications in childbirth – kill many more than disasters or wars. So do road traffic accidents, particularly in rapidly growing countries with new infrastructure but little driver training.

Micro-credit schemes – making small loans to the poorest to allow them to grow businesses – have been hugely successful. But they lack the glamour of a famine or war, and are often under-covered. Few are interested in African economics, even in the aid agency sphere.

The human stories are still there – and, if well enough written, may still win over editors and readers. But it is harder.

Particularly in Africa, some businessmen and officials complain that through focusing on poverty, conflict and disaster the media and aid agencies make developing countries look less appealing to invest in – starving them of economic growth they need to get out of poverty.

Too often, humanitarian, conflict and disaster stories are too short-term in their approach. They don't look at whether a country is learning to adapt better. They don't look at the long-term impact or the underlying causes. They may not question received wisdom enough. They do not necessarily look at how the event fits into the greater world picture, be it political or economic.

Covering humanitarian stories can be physically uncomfortable and mentally harrowing. It can be logistically difficult and financially expensive. And it can be singularly maddening and distressing to watch the suffering and feel that somehow you are failing to communicate it to the world.

I've heard several veteran foreign correspondents talk movingly about how helpless they felt at the scene of various disasters. I can understand the feeling – but to be honest I could not disagree more.

Reporting these sorts of stories is rarely, if ever, going to change the world. Aid may occasionally flow, political pressure be exerted or abuses stop as a result of media coverage – and it can be a great feeling when it happens – but generally the bad things continue almost regardless.

But ultimately, being there and having the ability to shine that spotlight on otherwise unseen troubles so the world finds it that bit harder to ignore does not feel like complete helplessness.

Note

1 All quotations in this chapter were written and contributed by the correspondents or press officers involved specially for this chapter and edited by Peter Apps.

Useful Links

The charitable Reuters Foundation website AlertNet (www.alertnet.org) brings together news from both Reuters and aid agencies on humanitarian disasters around the world, together with background information. AlertNet for Journalists (http://www.alertnet.org/mediabridge/index.htm) brings together that background, interactive maps, aid agency contacts and press releases as well as an early warning email service covering emerging disasters, designed to help media around the world cover crises more easily. Setup costs for AlertNet for Journalists were partly funded by Britain's Department for International Development.

United Nations-run website Relief Web (www.reliefweb.org) also contains regular reports and maps from crisis areas.

Red Cross and Red Crescent societies in conflict areas are coordinated by the ICRC, and their website (www.icrc.org) contains regular updates. In non-conflict-related disasters, the coordinating body is the IFRC, and their website is www.ifrc.org.

Questions for students

1 Discuss the issue of how much journalists should rely on the information provided by humanitarian and relief organizations. How do journalists guard against misleading or hyped representations of the crises?

2 What can be done to encourage more first-hand reporting of disasters? Do governments have a role?

3 Discuss ways of telling stories that break the mould of what appears to be formulaic coverage of on-going humanitarian crises such as famine and HIV stories. For example, evaluate the impact of the approach taken by African documentary producer and correspondent Sorious Samura in his series on 'Living with …' the victims of famine and AIDS and refugees (http://www.insightnewstv.com/store).

Index

274

Index

Index

Printed in the USA/Agawam, MA
December 10, 2013

582672.009